Wieder was zu lesen!

J. Holts 6/6/91

Trotzdem viel Spaß!

THE JOINT
PRESS CONFERENCE

Recent Titles in
Contributions to the Study of Mass Media and Communications

EFE: Spain's World News Agency
Soon Jin Kim

Media Freedom and Accountability
Everette E. Dennis, Donald M. Gillmor, and Theordore L. Glasser, editors

Choosing the News: The Profit Factor in News Selection
Philip Gaunt

Muckraking and Objectivity: Journalism's Colliding Traditions
Robert Miraldi

The News as Myth: Fact and Context in Journalism
Tom Koch

Cold War Rhetoric: Strategy, Metaphor, and Ideology
Martin J. Medhurst, Robert L. Ivie, Philip Wander, and Robert L. Scott

Foreign Policy and the Press: An Analysis of *The New York Times*' Coverage of U.S. Foreign Policy
Nicholas O. Berry

Sob Sister Journalism
Phyllis Leslie Abramson

The Course of Tolerance: Freedom of the Press in Nineteenth-Century America
Donna Lee Dickerson

The American Trojan Horse: U.S. Television Confronts Canadian Economic and Cultural Nationalism
Barry Berlin

Science as Symbol: Media Images in a Technological Age
Lee Wilkins and Philip Patterson, editors

The Rhetoric of Terrorism and Counterterrorism
Richard W. Leeman

Media Messages in American Presidential Elections
Diana Owen

THE JOINT PRESS CONFERENCE
The History, Impact, and Prospects of American Presidential Debates

DAVID J. LANOUE and
PETER R. SCHROTT

Contributions to the Study of Mass Media and Communications, Number 26
BERNARD K. JOHNPOLL, *Series Editor*

GREENWOOD PRESS
New York • Westport, Connecticut • London

Library of Congress Cataloging-in-Publication Data

Lanoue, David J.
　　The joint press conference : the history, impact, and prospects of American presidential debates / David J. Lanoue and Peter R. Schrott.
　　　　p. cm.—(Contributions to the study of mass media and communications, ISSN 0732–4456 ; no. 26)
　　Includes bibliographical references and index.
　　ISBN 0–313–27248–4
　　1. Presidents—United States—Election. 2. Campaign debates—United States. 3. United States—Politics and government—1945– 4. Public opinion—United States. I. Schrott, Peter Richard. II. Title. III. Series.
JK524.L36   1991
324.7–dc20   90–45322

British Library Cataloguing in Publication Data is available.

Copyright © 1991 by David J. Lanoue and Peter R. Schrott

All rights reserved. No portion of this book may be reproduced, by any process or technique, without the express written consent of the publisher.

Library of Congress Catalog Card Number: 90–45322
ISBN: 0–313–27248–4
ISSN: 0732–4456

First published in 1991

Greenwood Press, 88 Post Road West, Westport, CT 06881
An imprint of Greenwood Publishing Group, Inc.

Printed in the United States of America

The paper used in this book complies with the Permanent Paper Standard issued by the National Information Standards Organization (Z39.48–1984).

10 9 8 7 6 5 4 3 2 1

To Suzanne and Marketa,
and to the memory of Richard John Frizzell
(1957–1976)

Contents

Tables and Figures	ix
Acknowledgments	xi
1. Introduction	1
2. Presidential Debates: Developing the Conventional Wisdom	11
3. Debate Content: Do Voters Hear What the Candidates Say?	55
4. The Impact of Presidential Debates on Viewers	87
5. Putting It All Together: Debates, Politicians, and Voters	131
Bibliography	161
Index	169

TABLES AND FIGURES

TABLES

Table 3.1	Content Analyses of the 1960 Kennedy–Nixon Debates	77
Table 3.2	Content Analyses of the 1976 Carter–Ford Debates	78
Table 3.3	Content Analyses of the 1980 Reagan–Carter Debate	79

FIGURES

Figure 4.1	Social Learning Theory	88
Figure 4.2	Cognitive Dissonance Theory	90
Figure 4.3	Uses and Gratifications Theory	93
Figure 5.1	A Model of Debate Effects	134

ACKNOWLEDGMENTS

We are grateful to a number of people whose contributions, large and small, have helped us to produce this book. In its earliest stages, our work benefited from the comments and criticism of Steven Finkel, Ruth Hamill, and Helmut Norpoth. As our research agenda progressed, a number of colleagues at our home institutions and at conferences made available their ideas, insights, and, in our occasional quest for experimental subjects, their students. At the risk of leaving anyone out, we would like to acknowledge the help of Ryan Barilleaux, Stephen Bennett, Brian Borlas, Bob Bradley, Charles Franklin, Ed Fuchs, George Gordon, Gary Klass, Alan Monroe, Carol Neff, John Scholz, and Tom Wilson. Intramural grants from the State University of New York at Stony Brook, Illinois State University, the Free University of Berlin, and the University of California, Riverside, helped to fund the execution and presentation of some of the research reported herein.

In terms of the present manuscript, we are indebted to still more friends, family, and colleagues. Shaun Bowler, Rosalys Lanoue, and Suzanne Lanoue read large portions of this manuscript and provided valuable criticism on both substance and style. Gerd Orfey and Joseph Snipp contributed first-rate research assistance. Any errors, of course, are ours alone.

Finally, but most importantly, our wives, Suzanne and Marketa, remained patient and supportive throughout the entire ordeal. We gratefully dedicate this book to them.

THE JOINT
PRESS CONFERENCE

1
INTRODUCTION

Consider the following description, as it might appear in a television viewers' guide: "Two politicians will take turns answering journalists' questions about campaign issues for an hour and a half." Few would imagine that such a program would cause even a blip in the Nielsen's ratings radar. Surely, it would not captivate over half the viewing public. The description, after all, sounds very much like that of the typical Sunday morning news interview show. These programs are not known for their massive audiences.

We are, of course, describing American presidential debates as they are currently conducted. And, perhaps surprisingly, these "joint press conferences" do indeed generate enormous interest among the electorate. It has been estimated that nearly 90 percent of American adults saw at least one of the Kennedy–Nixon debates in 1960.[1] Subsequent encounters have also been witnessed by large numbers of voters. To be sure, debates are not exactly like the Sunday talk shows. Debates feature both presidential candidates standing side by side, "forced" to address identical questions, and given the opportunity for rebuttal.

Nevertheless, presidential debates do, in some sense, bring to mind the modern TV programmer's nightmare—ninety minutes of talking heads discussing politics. Rarely are the proceedings dramatic or heated. While occasional flashes of anger may occur during candidate exchanges, viewers are far more likely to see two self-consciously polite, upbeat contenders, satisfied to take turns discussing economic policy, foreign affairs, and social issues. That these typically staid events receive the sort of attention they do from voters, scholars, and journalists ought to tell us something. There is, however, no consensus as to just *what* it should tell us.

This book is, in a way, our attempt to come to grips with this question. The conventional wisdom about presidential debates is oddly bifurcated. The media, by and large, continue to regard debates as events of significant magnitude. For all their complaining about the limits of the format and the overly rehearsed candidate presentations, journalists expend large amounts of ink and airtime on the debate story. Beginning with the assumption that each debate is consequential, reporters set themselves to the task of determining who was helped and who was hurt, and what effect the event should have on the outcome of the election. Turn to the editorial pages of most newspapers after any debate and you will find political columnists writing extensively about the importance and impact of these confrontations.

Social scientists, on the other hand, are far less convinced about the power of presidential debates. They look to empirical studies (particularly those conducted in 1960 and 1976) and conclude that such events have little effect on voting behavior. At best, they "merely" reinforce the biases already held by viewers. But they do not affect electoral outcomes in any substantial way. One of the authors of this book once wrote a paper in which he recommended that political scientists continue to study debates in order to build a larger sample of voters' attitudes under various conditions.[2] An anonymous journal reviewer wrote back suggesting that the passage be deleted. It was, he or she said, a fairly settled matter that debates do not make much of a difference. Further research, the referee concluded, was certainly not needed.

In spite of this view, some scholars have continued to study these events. A small amount of research emerged after the 1980, 1984, and 1988 debates, as did at least one study of the effects of debates during primary election campaigns. Interestingly, some of this research started to question the assumption of non-effects. Under some conditions, these papers argued, debates *do* matter, and their impact may be substantial.

In addition, some researchers have begun to reconsider not only the direct effects of debates on voting behavior, but also the importance of these events in changing and reinforcing viewers' candidate images and issue positions. In the literature on presidential debates, such effects are not usually linked with the question of vote choice. Nevertheless, they may be seen as part of a larger picture in which debates contribute to the factors that ultimately determine how viewers vote. If these effects are not direct, that does not necessarily imply that they are trivial.

Introduction

Our joint work on presidential debates started in 1984, and consisted of a small, quasi-experimental study, using a student sample, of the first debate between Ronald Reagan and Walter Mondale.[3] The debate was not, of course, a turning point in the election; in retrospect, the 1984 race had no real turning points. However, even when judged against the other fourteen general election debates held since 1960, the first Reagan–Mondale debate was a particularly interesting study in the power and limits of debating.

The first 1984 debate is recalled today as Mondale's one brief moment of triumph, the night he took the measure of the "Great Communicator" and trounced him at his own game. Our student sample recognized this without prodding from the media. Mondale's post-debate "thermometer score"—a 100-point scale measuring general affect toward each candidate—shot up by an average of 8 points. Moreover, Reagan's lead over his opponent on the "horse race" question (asking about expected vote choice) dropped by 7 percent. Given the weaknesses of our sample, this change was not statistically significant. It did, however, mirror post-debate changes measured by some of the major public opinion polls, and suggested that the event had the potential to be consequential.[4]

At the same time, of course, the Louisville debate was simply one event in a much longer campaign. Reagan's lead was such that it could easily withstand the erosion and, shortly thereafter, Reagan recovered even the amount he had lost. It is possible that George Bush's solid performance in the vice presidential debate helped Reagan out, and that the president himself aided his own recovery with a more polished and confident showing in his rematch with Mondale in Kansas City. Unfortunately, we may only speculate about these possibilities since almost nobody was there to study these events. In any case, after Reagan's forty-nine-state win over Mondale, few were talking about that evening in Kentucky four weeks earlier. A presidential debate, however significant, may only be evaluated in the context of the entire campaign.

Still, to us, the emerging lesson was that presidential debates are potentially important, a conviction that has been strengthened by subsequent work on primary and general election debates in 1980 and 1988,[5] and is consistent with other work we have done on debates in Canada and West Germany.[6] In the following pages, we will attempt to tie together the research of social scientists in order to find common threads and common themes in their work. We will try to deal with a number of questions: Under what conditions do debates have direct effects on voting behavior? Under what conditions are these effects indirect? What debating strategies are most and least successful? And, finally, are there any reforms that would cause debates to have a greater (or lesser) effect on voters?

We will argue that many scholars have understated the ability of presidential debates to influence voters and elections. In part, the evidence in favor of this assertion rests with many of the same books and articles used by others to support a finding of limited effects. We maintain that a strong case can be made, simply by reading the studies from 1960 and 1976, that debates are often quite influential. Perhaps some earlier researchers were expecting strong, immediate, and overnight effects, and came away unimpressed by what they found. Nevertheless, in many of these studies, scholars find that debates exert substantial effects—if not on voting behavior, at least on candidates' images and respondents' issue preferences. If images and issues are important short-term factors affecting the vote, then any campaign event that influences them must, by definition, have the capacity to affect the outcome of the election.

Both authors are practiced "behavioral" political scientists, which is to say that we are sympathetic to the quantitative study of political phenomena. Our own debate studies have been quantitatively oriented. We are convinced, however, that not all questions can be answered through statistical analysis of data and that important insights can be found by looking beyond social science and academia. Thus, we have also paid close attention to the analyses and interpretations of journalists and political professionals in mounting our arguments.

We are, of course, sensitive to the limitations of media observation. As we suggest above, journalists are paid to report a story and, if assigned to the debate "beat," they will invariably find something to say. There is little doubt that they exaggerate the impact of many of the events they cover, and presidential debates are no exception. On the other hand, journalists, unlike political scientists, are intimately familiar with each campaign and candidate. Among other things, they may be able to uncover the intangible (or at least unmeasurable) effects of these events, including their impact on campaign "momentum," candidates' and supporters' enthusiasm, and voters' doubts and suspicions.

This book will also attempt to bring a theoretical focus to the study of presidential debates. Too many debate studies have reported effects in a nontheoretical manner (we, too, have been somewhat guilty of this on occasion). Many others have considered just one theoretical outlook in a relatively uncritical way. Any study of the effects of political communication should be informed by the dominant theoretical models of attitude development and attitude change.

Social science, of course, is often trendy, and theories fall into and out of favor from time to time. We will, therefore, sometimes refer to theoretical outlooks that are no longer in vogue among scholars. We believe, however, that whatever their weaknesses, each perspective has something to offer. Rather than trying to fit the study of debates neatly into one theoretical pigeonhole, we will consider what each theory can tell us about the expected and actual effects of debates on public opinion. If, for example, a theory (say, cognitive consistency theory) would predict only limited effects, we consider the conditions under which these effects *should* occur and analyze them appropriately. In the end, we will propose a model of direct and indirect debate effects that, we believe, can help us explain the power and limitations of debates, as well as why different debates often have very different effects on the public.

While we will cover a number of topics in some detail, our primary focus will be on the impact of presidential debates on voters. Thus, when we consider candidate strategies, we will be concerned with how they help to influence and convert viewers. When we take up the issue of information gain, we will be most interested in how citizens use information to help them make their final choice at the polls. When we deal with the controversial issue of debate formats, our objective will be to analyze linkages between the structure of presidential debates and voters' responses to the candidates. At times, we will take up some of the normative questions surrounding these topics, but that will not be our primary objective.

Indeed, there are a number of things this book is not intended to do. First, it will not provide an elaborate description or much critical analysis of how debates are produced, how formats are negotiated between the opposing camps, and how the networks and sponsors prepare for these events. Further, we will not be very much concerned with the legal issues surrounding the "fairness doctrine" or other equal-time requirements. A number of other studies of American presidential debates have written extensively about Section 315 of the Communications Act and its effects on the scheduling and conduct of these events. For election-specific discussions, we recommend the two volumes edited by Sidney Kraus after the 1960 and 1976 elections.[7] In addition, a comprehensive and well-researched discussion of these issues is available in Kraus's more recent book, *Televised Presidential Debates and Public Policy*.[8]

In addition, we will briefly discuss the role of debates in satisfying certain expectations of democratic theory, particularly the requirement that voters have useful, reliable information about the candidates and their stands on the issues. In particular, we will argue that content analysis is one of the best—and most neglected—ways to test whether or not presidential debates are successfully performing that function. Once again, however, our immediate focus is not on the normative issues of what role debates play in helping to create "better" voters and otherwise furthering democratic goals. Rather, for those interested in these issues, we recommend another book, *Presidential Debates: The Challenge of Creating an Informed Electorate.*[9] Its authors, Kathleen Hall Jamieson and David Birdsell, devote much of their attention to normative questions about enhancing the role and quality of debates as a primary source of voter information.

Finally, this book is not a campaign primer. While some information contained herein may be useful to campaign consultants and their clients, this is not a how-to guide to successful debating. We are, first and foremost, interested in debates as campaign events that help to explain fluctuations in public opinion and election outcomes. There are a number of ways to approach this topic; we approach it as researchers schooled in political science, voting behavior, and political psychology. For the best campaign insider's guide to the use of political debates to convert voters and win elections, we suggest Myles Martel's *Political Campaign Debates: Images, Strategies, and Tactics.*[10] Martel served as part of the team that prepared Ronald Reagan for his successful effort against Jimmy Carter in Cleveland in 1980. His book is a fascinating blend of perspectives between the dispassionate analysis of an academic observer and the firsthand knowledge of a one-time campaign consultant.

Having now recommended a number of other books, let us say a few additional words about this one. We have, to our knowledge, completed the first comprehensive analysis of the issue of debate effects. We have attempted to bring order and coherence to the wide range of studies conducted from a number of disciplinary perspectives over the course of three decades. We have also tried to ground much of this work theoretically, and develop a model of debate effects that ties together the major findings of this thirty-year-old enterprise. At the same time, we raise a number of questions that still require answers. We consider this book to be, in part, a progress report on thirty years of scholarship on debate effects, as well as a plea for renewed interest and work—especially by political scientists—in this field.

Our organization is very straightforward. In chapter 2 we present an analytical and, in some cases, critical history of presidential debates since 1960. A large part of our focus in this chapter is on the evolution of the conventional wisdom on presidential debates as collected, separately and together, by academic researchers and media professionals. We argue that a number of consistencies may be found between journalistic accounts and academic research on the debates. Further, we suggest that much of the conventional wisdom, some of it nearly unchanged since 1960, has not been supported by subsequent developments.

Chapter 3 deals with the content of presidential debates. This is an area that has been largely ignored by students of debating. We contend that to understand fully the effects of debates on their audience, it is necessary to become familiar with the actual statements made by the candidates in response to panelists' questions. Even if we agree that debates do have the capacity to alter voters' opinions about candidates and issues, that information is incomplete if we remain ignorant about what features of the debates motivated these changes. West German scholars, for example, have found that West German debate watchers evaluate candidates far more favorably when the politicians maintain a positive, upbeat approach. Unfortunately, no comparable studies exist in the American case.

Nevertheless, some researchers in the United States have begun to consider debate content as an important source of information about candidates' statements and viewers' reactions. In chapter 3, we recount the findings of some of these studies in detail. We also present a brief history of the use and evolution of content analysis in the study of political communication, and how earlier findings relate to the specific needs and goals of debate researchers. Finally, we consider the much larger body of work content-analyzing leadership debates in West Germany, arguing that the German approach represents one profitable direction in which American researchers might move. In addition, we consider a number of interesting and unusual findings from West German studies and how they might help us to learn more about presidential debates in the United States.

Chapter 4 is concerned with organizing and tying together the findings of empirical social scientists since 1960. First, we place our discussion of attitude development and change in theoretical perspective. Next, we reconsider the findings that debates affect viewers' images of the candidates as well as their understanding and retention of political information. If issue positions and candidate images are two of the most important predictors of vote choice, then any event that influences these factors must clearly be considered important. Therefore, we discuss both images and issue positions in detail.

In addition, we assert that the absence of direct effects does not necessarily render debates meaningless. In fact, social and cognitive psychologists (and quite a few political scientists) have written extensively about the indirect and mediated paths to opinion change. Most voters possess well-developed cognitive filters that influence the ways in which they attend to and process political information. Many researchers, of course, have found that these filters are so strong that the main effect of debates on viewers is reinforcement of prior predilections. We agree that reinforcement effects are common, but also argue that reinforcement is an electorally significant phenomenon. It often solidifies voters' allegiance to a candidate and can turn ill-informed and not-quite-certain supporters into committed loyalists.

Finally, we consider the direct effects of debates on viewers' voting behavior. To be sure, this is a heavily studied area in which limited findings and nonfindings have been the general rule. Within many of these studies, however, we find some evidence that significant direct effects can, under some circumstances, occur and that they are not always trivial. We argue that presidential debates do have the capacity to change some votes and that these effects—in, for example, the case of primary election debates—may actually be quite profound.

Chapter 5 ties together all of the matters discussed above. In this chapter, we propose our model of debate effects, taking into consideration the direct and indirect paths between debate watching and attitude change, and including the crucial role of the media in interpreting and highlighting certain aspects of the candidates' presentations. This model suggests new ways of interpreting and understanding debate effects and indicates that early reports of the electoral triviality of debates were, to say the least, premature.

In chapter 5 we also take up the issue of debate formats. While we are sympathetic to many of the doubts expressed about the typical "press conference" format, we also question the likelihood that format changes would address many of the major criticisms leveled against presidential debates since 1960. We also express skepticism that such changes would improve the level or quality of information presented to the viewers.

Clearly, we do not expect all readers to agree with and accept each of our analyses of presidential debates. We do, however, hope that by joining many of the debates about debates, we have contributed to, extended, and refueled some of the arguments. Journalists, consultants, and "ordinary" citizens may exaggerate the impact of presidential debates on the course of election campaigns. Nevertheless, they are important events, and their consequences are worth considering.

NOTES

1. Frank Stanton, "A CBS View," in Sidney Kraus, ed., *The Great Debates: Background, Perspective, Effects* (Bloomington: Indiana University Press, 1962), pp. 65–72.

2. David J. Lanoue, "The 'Turning Point': Viewers' Reactions to the Second 1988 Presidential Debate," *American Politics Quarterly* 19(1991): 80–95.

3. David J. Lanoue and Peter R. Schrott, "Voters' Reactions to Televised Presidential Debates: Measurement of the Source and Magnitude of Opinion Change," *Political Psychology* 10 (1989): 275–85.

4. *New York Times*, October 11, 1984, p. B11.

5. David J. Lanoue, "One That Made a Difference: Cognitive Consistency, Political Knowledge, and the 1980 Presidential Debate" (Paper presented at the 1990 meeting of the Midwest Political Science Association, Chicago); David J. Lanoue and Peter R. Schrott, "The Effects of Primary Season Debates on Public Opinion," *Political Behavior* 11 (1989): 289–306; and Lanoue, "Turning Point."

6. David J. Lanoue, "Debates That Mattered: Viewers' Reactions to the 1984 Canadian Leadership Debates," *Canadian Journal of Political Science* (forthcoming 1991); and Peter R. Schrott, "The West German Television Debates: Candidate's Strategies and Voters' Reactions" (Ph.D. dissertation, State University of New York, Stony Brook, 1986).

7. Kraus, *The Great Debates*; and Sidney Kraus, ed., *The Great Debates: Carter vs. Ford, 1976* (Bloomington: Indiana University Press, 1979).

8. Sidney Kraus, *Televised Presidential Debates and Public Policy* (Hillsdale, NJ: Lawrence Erlbaum and Associates, 1988).

9. Kathleen Hall Jamieson and David S. Birdsell, *Presidential Debates: The Challenge of Creating an Informed Electorate* (New York: Oxford University Press, 1988).

10. Myles Martel, *Political Campaign Debates: Images, Strategies, and Tactics* (New York: Longman, 1983).

2

PRESIDENTIAL DEBATES: DEVELOPING THE CONVENTIONAL WISDOM

When social scientists engage in superstitious learning, we often refer to it as "generalization." In the case of presidential debates, the same holds true for political journalists. What we "know" about presidential debates and their influence on voters is the product of a very small number of observations. From 1960, we "learned" that candidates must wear proper makeup and dress conservatively. From 1976, we "learned" that the gaffe—that verbal miscue that dominates post-debate news coverage—can destroy one candidate and rescue his opponent. As it happens, both elections were closely contested and narrowly decided. In both cases the media (and the winning nominee) determined that victory at the polls resulted, at least in part, from victory in the debates.

Are these generalizations valid? Imagine, for example, that Richard Nixon had won the 1960 election or that Gerald Ford had triumphed in 1976. What lessons might we then draw about televised debating? Polsby and Widavsky point out the dangers in such facile generalization. If Nixon "had won the [1960] election, rather than losing it by a wafer-thin margin," they note, "he would hardly have been reminded of any error on his part, and there would probably have been discussions of what a brilliant move it was for him to go on TV."[1] Indeed, had Nixon captured the 1960 race, we would probably still be talking about the critical role of foreign policy toughness and the importance of two small Chinese islands named Quemoy and Matsu.

In order to understand the role, if any, of presidential debates in affecting election outcomes, we must first examine the lessons learned (properly or not) from the five instances of televised debating. To be sure, we are disadvantaged by the relative inactivity of scholars in studying later debates. While the 1960 and 1976 encounters generated literally volumes of research, recent debates have been largely ignored. Fortunately, academicians are not the only acute observers of political affairs. The following section will evaluate the lessons of presidential debates as drawn by scholars and journalists alike. Particular attention will be paid to determining which findings have stood the test of time (and replication), and which have been thrown into question, or even disproven, by subsequent analysis.

1960—KENNEDY VS. NIXON: THE TRIUMPH OF STYLE

We remember 1960 as the first television election, although the medium certainly covered the races of the 1950s, and both the Eisenhower and Stevenson campaigns produced television advertisements. To a large extent, this characterization of 1960 owes itself to the substantial publicity generated by the Kennedy–Nixon debates. Indeed, the debates commanded attention as no previous televised news event had ever done. Approximately 90 percent of the potential viewing audience saw at least one of the encounters.[2]

The first Kennedy–Nixon debate occurred on September 26, 1960, in Chicago. It was regarded as a victory for the telegenic Senator Kennedy, or, perhaps more correctly, as a defeat for Vice President Nixon. In his 1960 campaign diary, Theodore H. White noted that "everything that could have gone wrong that night [for Nixon] went wrong."[3] The first debate, White said, "had been a disaster" for the GOP nominee.[4] The debates, and especially the first one, turned Nixon from frontrunner to underdog, and Kennedy from likely loser to ultimate winner.[5]

Interestingly, Nixon did not lose on the substance of the debate, the so-called "debating points." In fact, said the *New York Times* in its post-debate coverage, "on sound points of argument, Nixon probably took most of the honors."[6] Instead, it was the physical appearance of the two candidates that seemed to make the greatest difference. John Kennedy had been coached in television performance—what to wear (dark suits), how to sit (legs crossed), and where to look when not speaking (at his opponent).[7]

Nixon, on the other hand, was less wise to the ways of television. His light suit faded in against the background of the stage. His legs were sometimes crossed, sometimes not; his eyes darted nervously between Kennedy, the moderator, and the camera. In addition, a poor makeup job and an untimely case of the flu combined to make the vice president look sweaty, poorly shaven, and pasty-faced. So stark was the contrast between the televised images of the nominees that those who only heard the debate on the radio rated it a draw, while television viewers gave Kennedy a solid victory.[8]

Lost in the discussion of image was the substance of the debate.[9] Much of the early discussion in Chicago centered on issues of experience in government, an area that was thought to favor the vice president. Kennedy was able to counter effectively with a discussion of his congressional experience (he entered the House in the same year—1946—as Nixon). Moreover, during the course of the questioning, Nixon was reminded of a recent quote from President Eisenhower suggesting that Nixon's role in his administration had been minimal.[10]

In response to questions about the role of the federal government in national life, Kennedy was able to make the case for his New Frontier programs, especially federal aid for agriculture, medical care, and education. While Nixon complained about the cost and intrusiveness of the Democrat's plans, he often found himself agreeing with the basic goals of the Massachusetts senator. "Nixon . . . ," reported *Time* magazine after the debate, "had an unexpected 'me-too' sound."[11]

By the time of the second debate (primarily on foreign policy), Richard Nixon had learned the lessons of Chicago. His suit was dark, his legs were crossed, and his makeup was properly administered. While John Kennedy was still a more attractive television performer, questions of candidate image no longer dominated the news. Apparently gaining confidence from his strength in foreign affairs, Nixon found his voice in the Washington debate. Journalists cautiously declared the Republican the winner of the second encounter (largely because of an exchange discussed below).

The candidates' discussion of foreign policy ranged widely from the "loss" of Cuba to the U-2 spy plane incident and the direction of the Cold War. The candidates disagreed, predictably, on whether the responsibility for foreign policy failures rested with congress or the president. The nominees did address some domestic concerns as well, particularly the question of civil rights. Both candidates spoke forcefully (if not very specifically) about their commitment to equal rights, and Nixon criticized Kennedy for his choice of Lyndon Johnson (then considered a civil rights opponent) as vice presidential nominee.

The most dramatic confrontation of the evening involved the defense of two small islands off the coast of the Chinese mainland, Quemoy and Matsu. After the Chinese Nationalists had been driven to Taiwan by the Communist forces of Mao Zedong, a number of islands in the China Strait were claimed by both nations. The government of the People's Republic had threatened to move against the islands and put them under Communist control. Both candidates were asked how the United States should respond if Quemoy and Matsu were invaded by Chinese forces.

Kennedy argued that the strategic importance of the two islands was minimal, and that the United States should not be dragged into war over their defense. Nixon countered pointedly that the issue was not the size or strategic importance of the islands. Rather, he argued, freedom was at stake here, and any lack of resolve on the part of the United States could send a dangerous signal of weakness to America's adversaries, particularly those in Beijing. This, Nixon suggested, could set off a chain reaction of Communist aggression and expansionism. Nixon accused Kennedy of "woolly thinking" on the issue and said that he hoped the Massachusetts senator would change his mind on the subject if elected president. In the post-debate news coverage, journalists speculated that Nixon had shored up his strength in the foreign policy arena, and that Kennedy had made himself vulnerable to charges of Democratic weakness in confronting Communism.[12]

After the first two contests, the remaining debates appeared anticlimatic. Perhaps the most interesting aspect of the third debate was the fact that the candidates were actually appearing in different cities, Kennedy from New York and Nixon from Los Angeles. The third Kennedy–Nixon debate devoted a substantial amount of time to further discussion of the defense of Quemoy and Matsu. In addition, the encounter was marked by some heated personal exchanges over whether Nixon was "trigger happy," whether President Eisenhower had restored "dignity" to his office compared to his earthy predecessor (Democrat Harry Truman), and which party's platform would cost taxpayers the most money. Despite the occasional broadsides, some substantive issues were also aired: The nominees debated their views on tax policy, agriculture policy, and the oil depletion allowance.

The final debate, held in New York City, centered again around foreign affairs. And once more, the issue of Quemoy and Matsu found its way into the proceedings. The name-calling of the third debate also continued: Nixon called Kennedy's position on Cuba "irresponsible" and Kennedy replied that Nixon was "misinformed." Otherwise, the final debate was characterized by the nominees trading charges over their proposed conduct of the Cold War and the question of U.S. prestige abroad.

By one of the narrowest popular vote margins in history, John F. Kennedy defeated Richard Nixon in 1960 to become the 35th president of the United States. In such a close race, of course, any number of factors might have been critical to the final outcome. As political scientist Herbert Asher notes, the debates may have had little effect on overall voting behavior, but "that impact may have been sufficient to swing an election as close as the one in 1960."[13] As suggested above, the closeness of the 1960 election magnified all the conclusions drawn from the "great debates."

It should be noted that pollsters and scholars alike were nearly unanimous in detecting little or no change in voting behavior associated with the debates. This may have come as a surprise to many in light of the anticipation that attended the encounters. "Pollsters," *Time* magazine reported, " . . . found that hardly a vote had been changed by the long-awaited debates."[14] Echoed the *New York Times*, "it was apparent that the encounters had not had any decisive effect on the electorate."[15] Systematic research from the academic community, reported in the months and years following the election, confirmed these overall findings.[16]

Nevertheless, a strong perception remained, particularly among pundits and politicians, that the debates had been, if not decisive, a major boost to Kennedy in his defeat of Nixon. Even the Democratic nominee himself was quoted as suggesting that he would have lost the election except for his performance in the debates.[17] The *New York Times*, which only two months before had spoken of the debates as electorally inconsequential, noted them among the four major factors contributing to Kennedy's success.[18]

Social scientists were more skeptical of the decisive role attributed to the debates by the media, but even they reported some effects that may have worked in Kennedy's favor. For example, Lang and Lang found that the debates helped to bring wavering Democrats back into the party fold, perhaps helping Kennedy to some narrow but critical victories in such states as Illinois and Texas.[19] Further, the Langs suggest, the debates may have produced some "sleeper" effects that might not have registered immediately in public opinion polls. Specifically, the enthusiasm generated by Kennedy's perceived victory in the first debate may have emboldened the candidate and energized his supporters, thus creating useful momentum.

The lessons of the 1960 presidential debates make up much of today's conventional wisdom. Debates, according to students of the Kennedy-

Nixon encounters, are more important for their ability to reinforce candidate and party preferences than to alter them.[20] So long as they remain the majority party (at least in terms of party identification), that should be expected to help the Democrats. In addition, it was determined that debates aid challengers and hurt incumbents. The mere presence of the senator from Massachusetts on the same stage as the vice president of the United States elevated John F. Kennedy in public esteem.[21] If he could hold his own against a man who had represented his country around the world, that would certainly reduce much of the anxiety and apprehension over Kennedy's relative youth and inexperience. Finally, researchers found a "primacy" effect over the course of the four debates. The first debate (which Kennedy "won") had a more lasting impact on viewers than any of the subsequent encounters.[22]

The analyses of the 1960 debates also introduced some issues that would receive much greater attention in the future. Tannenbaum et al. saw evidence of the power of post-debate news coverage, finding that Nixon's image suffered not only among those who actually watched the first debate, but also among those who did not view the live broadcast but did see the subsequent news coverage.[23] In addition, some complaints began to emerge about the format of the debates, in which candidates answered queries from panelists but did not directly confront one another. These events were "counterfeit debates," said some, and were inadequately revealing of the men or their issue positions.[24] And last, at least one scholar suggested that voter interest and attention diminished over the course of the four debates[25] (although another researcher found that the audience enjoyed the heated personal clashes of the later debates more than the calmer, issue-oriented exchanges in the first and second encounters).[26]

1976—CARTER VS. FORD: THE YEAR OF THE GAFFE

During the final Kennedy–Nixon debate in 1960, moderator Quincy Howe praised the candidates for their courage in debating the issues before a live television audience. "Surely," he said, "they have set a new precedent." Nevertheless, despite the optimism of 1960, sixteen years would pass before the next televised presidential debates.

Frontrunners and incumbents had taken to heart one "lesson" of the Kennedy–Nixon debates: debates elevated the underdog, providing a national platform that was otherwise unobtainable. In 1964, Lyndon

Johnson, with a huge lead in the polls over Republican Barry Goldwater, declined to debate his opponent and went on to a landslide victory. Four years later, Richard Nixon, holding a substantial edge over then-Vice President Hubert Humphrey and mindful of his unhappy earlier experience, refused to enter into an encounter with his opponent. He held to that decision in 1972, when public opinion polls predicted, correctly, that he would be overwhelmingly reelected over Democratic Senator George McGovern.

In 1976, a number of unusual circumstances combined to convince both presidential nominees that debating would be in their best interests. Gerald Ford, of course, was elevated from congress to the vice presidency after the resignation of Spiro T. Agnew over bribery charges in Maryland. He succeeded to the presidency when Richard Nixon resigned in the wake of the Watergate scandal, making Ford the first unelected vice president or president in American history. His public standing, although beginning quite high, was severely damaged by his very unpopular pardon of former President Nixon for any crimes the latter may have committed while in office. Further, Ford suffered from an image as a bumbler, an accidental president whose most memorable moments on television included tumbles on the ski slopes and near falls on airplane steps.

With President Ford trailing badly in preelection polls, his advisers urged him to take the bold step of challenging his opponent to a series of debates. They were convinced that Ford could redeem himself during these encounters simply by appearing articulate and "presidential." Ford, they felt, could defend a record of economic recovery and national healing; he could offer stability and success compared to his relatively unknown opponent. In any case, by the summer of 1976 his election appeared to be such a longshot that nearly any risk seemed worth taking.

Jimmy Carter's problems were less apparent that summer, but they were also quite real. The Democratic nominee had started the year as the practically unknown former governor of Georgia, built momentum after a series of strong showings in the early presidential primaries, and virtually coasted to his party's nomination. While early polls suggested that his election was a near certainty, his advisers noticed some hints of apprehension among voters, a questioning of who this man was and what qualified him to be president. As the election season progressed, they expected the Ford campaign to emphasize the issues of experience and competence. The public, they determined, should be given a chance to know Jimmy Carter. They decided to accept Ford's challenge, hoping that

Carter's performance on television would alleviate some of the anxieties about him.

The first Carter–Ford debate was held on September 23 in Philadelphia, and dealt with domestic policy and economic issues. From the post-debate reaction, it appeared that the Ford campaign strategy might succeed. The president was the clear winner in public opinion polls over his Democratic opponent. One observer described the outcome in the language of boxing as "a presidential TKO."[27] Carter had "started slowly" in the debate and had been " 'too reticent' about attacking the president."[28] Mindful of the supposed importance of images, Ford's advisers dressed their champion in a vested suit in an effort to make him look more commanding and presidential.[29] Post-debate news coverage only served to enhance the perception that Ford had defeated Carter.

One odd but telling incident during the debate occurred shortly before its conclusion. Because of a malfunctioning capacitor, the sound went dead on stage for twenty-seven minutes.[30] While technicians worked frantically to restore the sound, each candidate remained fixed at his podium, eyes forward, unwilling to move. For almost half an hour, the nation watched the two presidential contenders paralyzed by this technical failure. Observers have speculated that both nominees had learned, perhaps too well, the "lessons" of the first Kennedy–Nixon debate: afraid the camera would catch them in an awkward stare or an unflattering pose, they simply stood silently and waited for their next cue.[31]

The debate itself was largely concerned with economic issues, as Ford attempted to paint Carter as a big spender and Carter accused Ford of insensitivity to the needy. The candidates differed noticeably on their approaches to tax policy, energy conservation, and the question of whether or not to pardon Vietnam War draft resisters.

In addition, President Ford, in keeping with his "game plan," made numerous efforts to describe his opponent as inexperienced and superficial. The major issue in the election, he argued, "is whether you should vote for his [Carter's] promises or my performance in two years in the White House." Responding to Carter's opening discussion of what he would do as president, Ford attacked his opponent: "I don't believe Mr. Carter's been any more specific in this case than he has been on many other instances." Commenting on the Democrat's discussion of the energy issue, Ford complained that "Governor Carter skims over a very serious and a very broad subject." If post-debate news accounts can be believed, Ford's attacking style (along with Carter's rather timid defense) was quite effective.

The second presidential debate of 1976 took place almost two weeks later in San Francisco. This time the topic was foreign policy. Both candidates were very much on the attack in the second debate. President Ford accused Carter of being unprepared and inexperienced, and of speaking in "broad generalities." For his part, Carter accused the incumbent of surrendering his leadership in foreign affairs to his controversial secretary of state, Henry Kissinger. The candidates clashed on relations with the Soviet Union and China, as well as human rights policy. Carter charged that under Ford's leadership, the United States was "no longer respected" by other nations. Ford answered that "America is at peace, with freedom."

Clearly, observers noted, Carter had acquitted himself better in the second presidential debate. Journalists described his performance as "tough, relaxed, assured, and confident."[32] Carter's new vigor, however, was not the story of the San Francisco debate. The exchanges between Ford and Carter during the second debate may have been pointed, but the debate was to become best known for the following exchange between Ford and one of the panelists, Max Frankel of the *New York Times*:

Ford: There is no Soviet domination of Eastern Europe, and there never will be under a Ford administration.

Frankel: I'm sorry, . . . did I understand you to say, sir, that the Soviets are not using Eastern Europe as their own sphere of influence in occupying most of the countries there and making sure with their troops that it's a Communist zone . . .

Ford: I don't believe, Mr. Frankel, that the Yugoslavians consider themselves dominated by the Soviet Union. I don't believe that the Rumanians consider themselves dominated by the Soviet Union. I don't believe that the Poles consider themselves dominated by the Soviet Union. Each of these countries is independent, autonomous, it has its own territorial integrity, and the United States does not concede that those countries are under the domination of the Soviet Union.

In that single response, said one observer, Ford "dropped a bomb on his own campaign."[33] Ford, said the *New York Times*, "seemed to ignore the long-standing Soviet control of most countries in Eastern Europe."[34] For days afterward, the media centered their discussions of the debate around the issue of Ford's gaffe. *Time* magazine called Ford's pronouncement "the blooper heard 'round the world."[35] Ford did not help himself, either, in his post-debate statements. In what "should have been a quick fluff-it-and-fix-it situation," the president chose to adhere stubbornly to his counterintuitive position.[36] In his battle to woo white ethnic Democrats, observed journalist Tom Wicker, "the president slipped in front of just the wrong audience."[37]

Ford's problems, however, were not limited to Americans of Eastern European descent. As news coverage of the gaffe continued, even those who hadn't paid much attention to Ford's statements while viewing the debate suddenly "recalled" it during later interviews. In early post-debate polls, only about 10 percent mentioned the Ford–Frankel exchange as a turning point in the debate; in later interviews, the gaffe was mentioned by 60 percent of respondents.[38] According to another study of the San Francisco debate, the influence of the media was nothing less than profound: between noon and midnight on the day following the event, the percentage of viewers naming Ford as the winner of the debate dropped from 31 percent to 19 percent; the corresponding proportions naming Carter the winner rose from 44 percent to 61 percent. The author of that study, Frederick Steeper, suggests that the effect of the gaffe may have been to "halt a two month trend toward [Ford], a trend that he never was able to start again at a rate sufficient to win."[39]

By the time of the third and final presidential debate in Williamsburg, Virginia, both candidates had become quite wary of the dreaded gaffe. To be sure, presidential debates were never carefree, spontaneous events, but observers began to note something of a paranoia creeping into the opposing camps. Noted *Time*, "both Ford and Carter did their best to avoid a gaffe, but the result was something less than inspiring."[40]

Nevertheless, with the candidates being more cautious in their charges and countercharges, some journalists suggested that the nominees had finally, if belatedly, begun to address the issues of the campaign. James Reston of the *New York Times* argued that the third debate "clarified the issues for decision on election day."[41] William Greider of the *Washington Post* agreed, saying that the Williamsburg debate "did exactly what it was supposed to do—provide a sharp portrait of the choice."[42] Indeed, a reading of the transcript of the final debate discloses sharp and substantive contrasts in the nominees' views on the environment, urban renewal, abortion, gun control, and civil rights. Unfortunately, the law of diminishing returns was at work here: the Williamsburg debate drew the smallest audience of any of the three encounters.[43]

Finally, it should be remembered that the 1976 debates included one new feature—a face-off between the two candidates for vice president, Republican Senator Robert Dole of Kansas and Democratic Senator Walter Mondale of Minnesota. While conventional wisdom generally dictates that vice presidential nominees are of little importance outside their home states, some observers saw the Mondale–Dole debate as influencing the 1976 election.

The main contrast was in the personal styles of the senators. "Mondale," noted Bitzer and Rueter, "debated ably and with dignity," while Dole relied on "ridicule and personal abuse."[44] Most controversial was Dole's claim that all the wars of the twentieth century, including World War II, were "Democrat wars," and that somehow the Democratic Party was responsible for the deaths than ensued. Mondale responded indignantly that the fight against Nazi Germany and Imperial Japan was hardly partisan and that Dole had "really earned his reputation as a hatchet man" during the evening. That exchange, not surprisingly, dominated the post-debate news coverage.

No authoritative evidence exists as to what real effect the Mondale–Dole debate had on its audience. Many observers shared the view that it was beneficial to the Carter campaign and a liability to the Ford effort. Even twelve years later, *Newsweek* referred to the Kansas senator as a man "blamed by some for having blown the 1976 election with one bitter aside about the dead in 'Democrat wars' from Verdun to Vietnam."[45] Nevertheless, while Dole's comments were hardly the sort of publicity the Ford campaign wanted just nine days after the Eastern Europe gaffe, there is no evidence that they actually contributed to Ford's loss.

Jimmy Carter's early lead in the polls dwindled steadily over the course of the campaign and, in the end, he won with very few votes (popular or electoral) to spare. And, like John Kennedy in 1960, Carter was convinced that his performance in the debates helped carry him to his defeat of Gerald Ford.[46] "The debates," said Carter adviser Gerald Rafshoon, "were . . . a great leveler."[47] The analogies to 1960 seemed compelling: the poorly known Democratic challenger went toe-to-toe against a national leader and in the process won over the electorate and proved his presidential mettle. Moreover, the Republican opponent in both instances supposedly hurt himself during the debates—Nixon by his physical appearance, Ford because of verbal mistakes. Indeed, one study found Ford overmatched by Carter, calling the Republican incumbent limited in his powers of expression and especially prone to error.[48] The study suggests that even without the celebrated Eastern Europe gaffe Ford would still have caused himself problems.

The conventional wisdom of 1960 seemed, at first glance, to survive the 1976 debates intact. Scholarly studies of the Carter–Ford debates found that the encounters served more to reinforce candidate and party allegiances than to change them.[49] And, once more, that effect benefited the Democratic candidate. In addition, the debates seemed, as in 1960, to aid the challenger and hurt the incumbent. President Ford, after all, was better known than Carter and had a record to defend. Carter, many felt, gained ground simply by sharing equal billing with the president and being given a national platform from which to attack Ford's record in office.

More questionable was whether the findings of 1976 supported the supposed "primacy effect" (i.e., that the first debate in a series should have the most impact on voters). If that effect was true in general, Gerald Ford, the consensus winner of the first Carter–Ford debate, should have been the net beneficiary. In 1976, however, the most memorable debate was clearly the second one, in which Ford committed his famous gaffe. Was the primacy effect unique to the 1960 election? Was it simply dwarfed by the magnitude of Ford's misstatement? Or, could it be that despite the Eastern Europe comments, Gerald Ford still came out the overall winner of the 1976 debates?

As noted above, most scholarship from 1976 found little change in voting behavior associated with any of the Carter–Ford debates. Nevertheless, 1976 was another close election and scholars and journalists worked hard to discern any small advantage the debates may have provided. Unfortunately, the analysis was mixed. By and large, most observers supported the prevailing view that the edge, if any, went to Carter.[50] If nothing else, he was able to appear as Ford's equal, rally the numerically superior Democrats, and attack the Republican administrations of the previous eight years. When he couldn't do the job himself, Ford helped him out with his momentum-crushing gaffe.

While this view may represent the opinion of a majority of the analysts, it was not held unanimously. In the most comprehensive analysis of the debate studies of 1976, Sears and Chaffee concluded that the first debate (which Ford won) had the only net impact on the vote.[51] Despite his gaffe, they argued, Ford gained the most from the debates (although, of course, this effect was slight). This view is shared by Ford's advisers, who credit the debates with having helped to turn a thirty-point Carter lead in the polls to a "photo-finish" ending.[52] Richard Cheney, who served as Ford's White House chief of staff, argued that the full airing of the issues hurt Carter because it forced him to discuss some of his more controversial stands (such as his support for pardoning Vietnam War draft resisters). Cheney further claimed that the Eastern Europe comments were "not as decisive as some have suggested."[53] Even with the Eastern Europe gaffe, however, Ford's advisers felt that their man had looked and acted presidential and had gone a long way toward erasing his image as a bumbler.

As we noted at the outset of this chapter, conventional wisdom is as often the product of superstitious learning as it is the result of systematic empirical analysis. And in this sense, the new lesson of the 1976 presidential debates was that the gaffe was deadly and must be avoided at all costs. Certainly, the media began increasingly to focus attention on such verbal miscues. From 1976 on, one feature of post-debate commentary would be to speculate on whether any gaffes had been committed. Further, the debates after 1976 were marked by more extensive coaching and well-packaged answers, motivated by a real fear of spontaneity.

Perhaps a more justifiable addition to the conventional wisdom drawn from the Carter–Ford debates was the conviction that the media had a critical role in framing and interpreting these events. Two separate studies (of two different debates) concluded that viewers were strongly influenced by post-debate media accounts of who won each encounter and which exchanges during the evening were most significant.[54] As noted above, most viewers of the second debate had virtually ignored the president's discussion of Eastern Europe; they recognized it as critical only after the media had presented it as such.

In later years, two products of this realization began to emerge. First, candidates, aware of the power of the media, began to dispatch spokespersons to the press briefing room after each debate in order to put the best face on their side's performance (in 1988, these propagandists became known as "spin doctors"). Second, the media appeared to become somewhat reluctant to discuss winners and losers in the debate unless reporting results of a public opinion poll (although even that practice took on a questionable coloring in 1980).

Finally, complaints about the format of the debates, muted by the novelty of the 1960 encounters, received a great deal more attention in 1976. The format, critics said, gave candidates too little time to develop clear positions on the issues. The medium (television) elevated image over substance. Perhaps worst of all, the media panelists got in the way of real candidate confrontation and sometimes even changed the tone of the evening.[55] Consider, for example, the adversarial tone of this question, asked during the third Carter–Ford debate by syndicated columnist Joseph Kraft:

Mr. President, the country is now in something that your advisers call an economic pause. But I think to most Americans that sounds like an antiseptic term for low growth, unemployment, standstill at a high, high level of decline in take-home pay, lower factory earnings, more layoffs. Isn't that really a rotten record, and doesn't your administration bear most of the blame for it?

Despite these concerns, however, most observers regarded the debates as beneficial to the viewing audience and were supportive of their continuation. Said Kraft, "So imperfect as they undoubtedly are, the debates still seem to me to be the best way the public can develop insight into the character of the men who would be president."[56]

1980—REAGAN VS. CARTER (AND ANDERSON): "THERE YOU GO AGAIN"

Four years after his defeat of Gerald Ford, Jimmy Carter was himself in serious electoral trouble. The chronic inflationary woes of the 1970s came to a head during Carter's term, spurred on in 1979 by the second major nationwide oil shortage in seven years. In his hapless effort to deal with double-digit inflation, Carter moved to slow down the growth of the economy. Unfortunately for the president, the result of this move was to leave him, during his reelection campaign, having to answer for both high inflation and rising unemployment.

Many observers felt Carter would be denied the Democratic Party's nomination to seek a second term in office. He was challenged by Edward M. (Ted) Kennedy, youngest brother of the slain president. While Kennedy faced his own image problems, early polls showed him with a comfortable lead over the incumbent. Carter's fortunes did not improve until militants in Iran stormed the U.S. embassy in Tehran and held fifty-three Americans hostage. As it typically does in times of crisis, public opinion lined up behind the embattled president and by April 1980, Jimmy Carter was virtually assured of renomination.[57]

By the summer of that year, however, Carter's fortunes were once again on the decline. The Republican Party nominated Ronald Reagan, the conservative former governor of California, and Reagan soon led Carter by a wide margin in the polls. The continuing economic difficulties, along with public frustration over the president's inability to win release of the hostages, had sapped voters' confidence in their leader. In addition, Carter was faced with the "third-party" challenge of independent candidate John Anderson, a former GOP contender who decided to continue his bid for the White House past the convention. Since Anderson's views were considered moderate-to-liberal (i.e., closer to Carter's than to Reagan's), most analysts felt that a serious Anderson candidacy would take votes away from the president and aid his Republican challenger.

In the end, John Anderson's greatest impact on the 1980 campaign probably took place in the planning and scheduling of that year's presidential debates. Jimmy Carter, who was both incumbent and underdog, wanted to debate Reagan "head-to-head." His advisers felt that Reagan had a penchant for misstatement and exaggeration that could lead him to commit a major gaffe.[58] For his part, Reagan would agree to debate only if John Anderson were included. The Republican campaign was anxious to legitimize and publicize Anderson's effort, hoping that it would do damage to Carter.[59] The issue was a stalemate during September of 1980: Reagan wouldn't agree to debate unless Anderson could participate, and Carter wouldn't debate unless the Illinois congressman was excluded.

The League of Women Voters organized a presidential debate to be held in Baltimore on September 21, 1980. In addition to Carter and Reagan, the League invited John Anderson to participate in the encounter, reasoning that his standing in the polls (at the time he had the support of about 15 percent of the electorate) legitimized him as a serious contender.[60] Reagan quickly accepted the League's offer, but Carter continued to insist on a confrontation limited to the Democratic and Republican nominees. The League of Women Voters decided to hold the debate with or without Jimmy Carter and, after the League dismissed a suggestion to have an empty chair on stage, the first debate of the 1980 general election campaign was held.

"The Reagan–Anderson confrontation," said the *New York Times*, "had all the trappings of a full-fledged presidential debate, except for the president."[61] Without Carter, noted one observer, "the debate was dismissed as second-string stuff."[62] Indeed, the viewing audience for the Baltimore debate was lower than usual for such an event. Nevertheless, one could argue that both participants received some of what they wanted from the affair. Anderson got the chance to be treated as a serious presidential contender. Reagan got a national audience and used the opportunity to speak to the issues in a situation of fairly low pressure. Said political scientist John Kessell, "the former California governor emerged from the Baltimore debate as a plausible presidential candidate."[63]

The debate between what were, until that summer, two Republican politicians, was marked by substantial disagreement on a number of issues, including how to deal with inflation, energy shortages, and urban decay. The two candidates also engaged in a very telling discussion of the role of religion in American government. Anderson's positions (such as using higher gasoline taxes to encourage conservation) were probably bolder and more innovative, but such is clearly the luxury of a candidate with little to lose. Reagan, however, did what he needed to do. He was, noted Germond and Witcover, "unfailingly good humored, articulate, and . . . knowledgable enough."[64]

Analysts spent much of the period after the Reagan–Anderson debate evaluating President Carter's decision to stay home. Joseph Kraft was convinced that "the loser in Baltimore was Jimmy Carter."[65] When the two debating candidates attacked him, he was unable to reply. He gave Ronald Reagan a chance to go on national television, relatively unchecked, and make his case to the American people. If the Carter campaign had been hoping for a gaffe from the Republican, it was not forthcoming. Rather, said his critics, the president acted as a man under siege, hiding in the White House while the campaign continued in his absence.

Some, however, saw merit in Carter's strategy. *Newsweek*, in contrast to many observers, speculated that the "real winner may well have been the man who wasn't there, Jimmy Carter."[66] His absence kept the audience for the debate much lower than it might have been. To some extent, it also may have delegitimized the proceedings. Most important, it deprived John Anderson of equal billing with the president of the United States. It is probably no coincidence that Anderson's standing in the polls declined steadily in the last two months of the campaign. In the heady days of September, the Anderson campaign, at least publicly, harbored hopes of putting together a winning coalition in the electoral college. By November, however, the challenger and his allies were reduced to hoping for the 5 percent vote share necessary to receive federal matching funds.

After early October, few observers were speaking about a three-way race. As Anderson's support faded, Jimmy Carter began to rise in the polls, and another close election appeared on the horizon. Reagan's managers continued to insist that Anderson should be included in any debate, but that position was becoming increasingly less tenable. The League of Women Voters, noting Anderson's dismal prospects, announced that they would now be willing to sponsor a two-way Reagan–Carter debate.[67] Finally, the candidates agreed to meet in Cleveland, Ohio, on October 29, exactly one week before election day.

Carter's advisers were much less desperate for a debate, with their man essentially tied with Reagan in the polls. But after months of lobbying for the head-to-head encounter, they could hardly back down now. In any case, they still hoped Reagan could be goaded into a gaffe, reinforcing his image (in the eyes of some) as a bumbler and an extremist. On the other side, the Reagan team was alarmed by the erosion in their man's lead. They felt he had to put to rest the "mad bomber" issue—the fear of many voters that Reagan's policies and temperament could lead to war. In addition, Republicans feared an "October surprise," a last-minute release of the hostages in Iran that would sweep Carter to victory in its euphoric wake.[68] If such a surprise should occur, they wanted a final platform from which to attack Carter on economic issues.

The candidates prepared in very different ways for the Cleveland debate. "Reagan," wrote one analyst, "approached the event as a *performance* . . . [while] Carter prepared . . . mostly on substance."[69] The difference was apparent in the candidates' presentations. "The president," said *Time* magazine, "tightly wound and always on the offensive scored the most points on substance; Reagan, with a relaxed, reassuring demeanor . . . came out ahead on style."[70] Both candidates, of course, stuck with their original plans: Carter to attack his opponent as inexperienced and untested on military issues, and Reagan to present himself as a seasoned and reasonable man.

Myles Martel, who helped to prepare Reagan's debate strategy, suggested what amounted to a two-pronged strategy for the former California governor.[71] First, Reagan should reassure the audience, showing himself to be a compassionate leader. He should use humor and self-confidence to disarm his opponent, but occasionally show righteous indignation at Carter's expected attacks.

Reagan began early in the debate to accomplish this goal. "I'm here," said the Republican nominee, "to tell you that I believe with all my heart that first priority must be world peace, and that the use of force is always, and only, a last resort when everything else has failed." When Carter attacked him as a heartless man, prepared to slash medicare benefits for the elderly, Reagan smilingly rebuked the president with the now-famous phrase, "There you go again." He protested that Carter was unfairly characterizing his comments on a specific piece of legislation, not on the overall issue of old-age benefits. His strategy of warmth and firmness impressed many analysts. Observed the *New York Times*, "Reagan used his calm demeanor to offset Jimmy Carter's contention that he was 'dangerous.' "[72]

According to Martel, the other major Republican strategy was to keep the focus of the debate on Carter's record, suggesting that Carter had failed as president and that Reagan offered hope. Reagan took a number of opportunities to remind the audience of the president's economic record, and spoke of the "misery index" (a statistic, combining the inflation and unemployment rates, created by Carter in 1976 to attack Gerald

Ford). Reagan noted that Carter's "index" exceeded that of his predecessor.

He saved his most effective shot, however, for his closing remarks. The most important issue in the election, he said, boiled down to a single question, which he urged voters to ask themselves: "Are you better off than you were four years ago?" It was, columnist Flora Lewis said, "his moment of assault."[73] Another observer noted simply, "It was a devastating point."[74] Reagan, his advisers felt, had succeeded in both of his major objectives, appearing cool and confident while skewering his opponent's record.

What Martel does not mention in his book (presumably because he was unaware of it) was that the Reagan team had gained one further advantage in their preparations. The Republicans had, somehow, received a copy of the briefing book used by the Carter campaign to ready their man for the confrontation.[75] It is unclear just how helpful this information was to the challenger (Ronald Reagan, for the record, claims ignorance of the briefing book caper). What is clear, though, is that Reagan was consistently prepared for Carter's attacks and often was able to repel them with well-chosen phrases and rebuttals. Whether this is a tribute to his campaign's foresight or its inside knowledge (or both) we will apparently never know for sure.

Jimmy Carter's strategy in the debate was hardly a mystery. As the incumbent president, perceived by many voters as presiding over economic disaster and foreign policy humiliation, he had little to offer except his experience and expertise. He attempted to combine this emphasis with an attack on Reagan's supposed "trigger-happiness." The Carter team agreed with columnist Anthony Lewis that "the result [of the debate] may turn on whether undecided viewers worry more about peace or economics."[76]

Even at the risk of appearing argumentative, Carter emphasized the peace issue and attacked Reagan's judgment and compassion. "There is," he said at one point, "a disturbing pattern in the attitude of Governor Reagan" on various arms control agreements. Attempting to personalize the nuclear issue, he told the audience that his daughter Amy had counseled him that arms control was the most important issue of the time.

That remark became the target of disapproval and ridicule. Political scientist John Kessel noted that the comment was seen by many as "trivializing the war and peace issue that had been one of his few real advantages."[77] Football commentator Roger Staubach, whose daughter shared the same name as Carter's, angered many viewers when he joked, during a telecast, "I was talking to my daughter Amy about [the game]. She says St. Louis' biggest problem is the bomb."[78]

Despite Reagan's hard-hitting performance and Carter's mini-gaffe, most commentators immediately after the debate had trouble choosing a winner. "The presidential debate," wrote Flora Lewis, "produced no knockout blow, no disastrous gaffe, and no immediate undisputed winner."[79] Germond and Witcover, echoing Lewis's thoughts, commented that "the consensus of most commentators was that [the debate] . . . had been a wash."[80] They did add, however, that given Carter's perceived failures, perhaps Reagan "needed only to prove he could hold his own." Immediate post-debate polls showed the public choosing Reagan as the winner, but only by a narrow margin.

The most publicized "poll" of the evening, though, was also the most controversial, and it gave Reagan a substantial edge over Carter. The poll was conducted by ABC News in conjunction with its late-night news analysis program, *Nightline*. Two 900-number telephone lines were set up for viewers to call at a charge of fifty cents per connection. One number would count those who thought Carter had won, and the other would tally viewers who thought that Reagan had emerged victorious. While ABC conceded that the poll was unscientific, it did little to explain all the flaws and biases inherent in the system.[81]

First, there was no attempt to sample a random cross-section of the U.S. population; indeed, there was no prohibition against calling either number multiple times. The fifty-cent fee for each call might seem nominal to some, but it might well have discouraged poorer people (typically Democrats) from participating in the poll. In addition, by the time the debate ended and phone lines were opened, the hour was quite late in the Democratic eastern United States and in Carter's native south. On the other hand, most people were still wide awake in the Republican strongholds of the western and Rocky Mountain states.

Polls, of course, are meant to reflect public opinion and not to shape it. It remains a very controversial question whether polls create momentum for candidates, and thus do more than simply monitor the public "pulse." Thus, it is impossible to say whether or not the ABC News poll added fuel to the impending Reagan landslide. In any event, in the week between the Reagan–Carter debate and the general election, a narrow race turned into a solid Reagan victory in the popular vote and an electoral college blowout. Reagan's coattails carried the GOP to control of the U.S. Senate for the first time in nearly thirty years, and to substantial gains in the House of

Representatives. It was, perhaps, inevitable that analysts would credit the debate with at least helping the Reagan bandwagon to gain momentum in that final, critical week.

Every member of the Reagan team saw the debate as crucial to the Republican victory. "The debate with President Carter," said Ronald Reagan, "was, in my view, a critical element in our success in the election."[82] Added Reagan's campaign manager, Jim Baker, the debate "put a lock on it for us."[83] Even Republican pollster Richard Wirthlin, who had opposed the idea of debating, found that Reagan's closing remarks were important in focusing public attention squarely on the economic failures of the Carter years.[84]

Impartial analysts agreed with these views. Robert McClure argued that "the second debate, coming late in the campaign, set the tone and the agenda for the final week before the election." Further, "Reagan was able to dampen the impact of the 'mad bomber' issue."[85] According to Abramson, Aldrich, and Rohde, "Six percent [of sampled voters] said they had changed their vote because of the second debate." Of that group, Reagan won their ballots by a two to one margin.[86]

Not all observers, however, agreed that the Cleveland debate was the turning point in the 1980 election. Jimmy Carter's pollster, Patrick Caddell, points to another factor that coincided, unluckily for Carter, with the election. The one-year anniversary of the seizure of the hostages in Iran happened to fall right around election day, 1980. Caddell believes that the hostage issue, and the supposed American weakness it symbolized, were much more damaging to Carter's prospects than the president's loss to Reagan in their debate.[87]

As noted above, little empirical research has been done on the post-1976 presidential debates. This is especially true of the Reagan–Carter confrontation in 1980. Because the candidates could not agree on whether or not to debate until shortly before election day, few researchers were able (even if inclined) to commit their time to a systematic study of the event. Perhaps because of Carter's absence, the Reagan–Anderson debate was similarly ignored.

Nevertheless, lessons were learned (or relearned) from the Cleveland debate. Probably most important, many observers considered the timing of the debate to be critical. Had the debate not taken place so close to election day, many felt, Carter might have had time to recover from its effects.[88] The risks of debating were only magnified by the proximity of the event to the election; any mistakes would still be fresh on the minds of voters as they cast their ballots. After 1980, candidates (particularly those ahead in the polls) would take care to schedule debates well in advance of election day.

Earlier studies of presidential debates found that such events reinforced party loyalties and helped lend status to candidates challenging an incumbent national leader. In 1980, both candidates could take heart from these findings. The Carter campaign apparently hoped that the reinforcement effect would "call home" undecided Democrats. In the debate, the president emphasized his ties to the Democratic Party while castigating the Republican Party as a servant of the economic elites.

Ronald Reagan, on the other hand, was clearly anxious to share the stage, as an equal, with the incumbent president. He concentrated his debating efforts on appearing presidential, intending to blunt the effectiveness of Carter's appeals on the issue of experience and stability. The Reagan team hoped that debating would do for the former California governor what many observers believed it had done for challengers Kennedy in 1960 and Carter in 1976.

The 1980 election, of course, was assumed to be another vindication of the conventional wisdom that debates help challengers and hurt incumbents. The evidence, in fact, appeared so compelling that few analysts expected that any incumbent, however desperate, would ever again risk sharing the stage with an opponent. Even the supposed penalties of refusing to debate (i.e., public perceptions of cowardice, insecurity, etc.) seemed to pale in comparison with the disadvantages of meeting a challenger head-on. After all, while Jimmy Carter was being criticized for refusing to debate Reagan and Anderson, his electoral prospects were steadily improving. After he met Reagan in Cleveland, however, his campaign fell apart. Many observers were more than willing to make the causal link between the debate and the Reagan landslide.

One disturbing report from the Reagan–Carter debate seemed to echo a finding buried in the analysis of the Kennedy–Nixon encounters twenty years before. In both cases, analysts were convinced that style had won out over substance. Richard Nixon's appearance in the first 1960 debate overshadowed his message; radio audiences gave Nixon high marks while television viewers considered him the clear loser. William Safire, the conservative political columnist, found a clear analogy between 1960 and 1980. Safire said that "like Nixon, in edging his opponent in the debating points battle, President Carter lost the television war."[89] The implications of this finding for democratic theory and voter "rationality" were, to say the least, troubling.

With social scientists largely ignoring the 1980 debates, we are left with the reactions of journalists and political professionals. As we have already seen, such analysts are not at all shy in drawing conclusions about the effects of the debates on public opinion. Unfortunately, those conclusions are rarely supported by any evidence other than fluctuations in opinion polls. Nevertheless, these analysts have spent their lives honing their political "instincts" and evaluative skills, and their observations are worth noting. We should, however, bear in mind that such observers have a clear stake in finding meaning in the events they cover. This point was made nicely by the *Washington Post* after the Reagan–Anderson debate: "The idea that this debate won't have much impact on the course of the campaign got no ink or air time at all. Instead the question was, which way would the impact run?"[90]

1984—REAGAN VS. MONDALE: THE FRONTRUNNER DEBATES

If the 1960, 1976, and 1980 debates had one feature in common, it was that in all three years debates were held between candidates who were, according to the polls, nearly even in public support. Such was not the case, however, in 1984. After seeing his popularity drop sharply during the economic recession of 1982–83, Ronald Reagan entered his reelection campaign riding the crest of economic and political recovery. By the late summer of 1984, many analysts treated the election as already decided.

The Democrats nominated the capable but uncharismatic Walter Mondale for president. Mondale had been Jimmy Carter's vice president, and the connection with the failed Carter administration was yet another hurdle faced by the Minnesotan. In a move variously regarded as bold and desperate, the Democrats nominated New York representative Geraldine Ferraro for vice president, the first woman to run on a major party ticket. If the party expected its historic choice to change voters' minds, it was to be disappointed. As the traditional Labor Day campaign "kick-off" approached, the Reagan–Bush ticket led the Mondale–Ferraro ticket by over twenty percentage points in some polls.

With control of the White House and a big lead in opinion polls, few observers expected Ronald Reagan to agree to debate his opponent. Many were surprised, therefore, when Reagan acceded to three debates, two between the presidential candidates and one between the vice presidential nominees. The president's decision to debate, wrote one observer, "had more to do with ego than with election savvy."[91] Ever the performer, the former actor apparently felt his speaking skills were superior to Mondale's (a judgment with which few would disagree) and that he could defeat the Democrat, thus fulfilling public expectations while losing nothing in the process.

When Ronald Reagan and Walter Mondale met for the first time in Louisville, Kentucky, on October 7, most saw the event as Mondale's last, best hope for mounting a serious challenge. "The debates," said the *New York Times*, "may be Mr. Mondale's best opportunity to crash through the political psychology that presumes Mr. Reagan has already won re-election."[92] By the time the Louisville debate was over, few were willing to call the election close, but the Democrat had clearly improved his position. Mondale debated with the vigor and confidence of a man whose campaign had nowhere to go but up. Reagan, on the other hand, looked and sounded tired, even at times confused, and his performance was, at best, lackluster.

According to agreement, the debate centered on domestic issues, and economic concerns quickly took center stage. Mondale, fighting the perception that his opponent's policies had produced a strong and growing economy, emphasized the increasing budget deficits. He tried to persuade viewers that the Reagan recovery was illusory, and that massive government overspending would eventually prove damaging. Reagan defended his record and attacked Mondale's proposal for increasing taxes to lower the deficit. When the candidates were not arguing over economic policy, they were disagreeing about the morality of abortion, the role of religion in society, and the state of the environment.

Most observers, however, did not concentrate on these issues in their post-debate analyses. Rather, there appeared to be a nearly unanimous sense of surprise that Ronald Reagan, the popular actor-turned-politician, had been outperformed by a staid representative of the unsuccessful Carter presidency. Complained pro-Reagan columnist William Safire, "Incredibly, the man who helped bring us inflation whipped the man who brought us prosperity."[93] On the opposite end of the political spectrum, Mondale supporters gleefully assailed the now-vulnerable chief executive. The debate, wrote liberal pundit Anthony Lewis, "stripped away the illusion that Ronald Reagan is governing."[94] If nothing else, there seemed a sense that the election was, if not yet close, no longer a settled issue. The results of the Louisville confrontation, said one observer, "will probably produce a more alert electorate in the last month of the campaign."[95]

It was so bad for Reagan that even his most memorable line of 1980 was turned against him in the first debate. After Mondale suggested that the president had a secret plan to raise taxes after the election (in order to lower the budget deficit), Reagan could not resist. He was not planning to repeat the line, he said, but Mondale had almost forced him to say it: "There you go again." Mondale's response, clearly prepared, was the most dramatic of the evening, and was repeated on news programs throughout the next day. Turning toward his opponent, the former vice president chastised the incumbent:

Mondale: Now, Mr. President, you said, "There you go again." Right? Remember the last time you said that?

Reagan: Um hmm

Mondale: You said it when President Carter said you were going to cut medicare. And you said, "Oh no, there you go again, Mr. President." And what did you do right after the election? You went out and tried to cut $20 billion out of medicare. And so, when you say, "There you go again," people remember this, you know.

The post-debate media coverage, highlighted by that exchange, reinforced the consensus that Mondale had defeated Reagan in the debate. According to one national poll, viewers immediately after the event chose Mondale as the winner by a margin of 43 percent to 34 percent. Two days later, respondents gave the debate to the Democrat by a whopping 67-17 edge.[96] More important, the polls were showing some movement toward Mondale on the all-important "horse race" question (the question asking voters to reveal their intended vote choice).

As the days passed, the story of the Louisville debate increasingly became Ronald Reagan's health and vigor. "Reagan," observed one reporter, appeared "visibly tired in the last half of the hour-and-a-half debate."[97] While "Reagan did not appear to do himself any serious damage," said *Time* magazine, he did seem "somewhat hesitant and occasionally became tangled up in facts and figures."[98] Reagan's age had been a largely unspoken issue during his presidency; he was, in fact, already the oldest president in U.S. history, and, if reelected, would end his second term at nearly eighty years of age. With his problems in the first debate, the age issue suddenly came "out of the closet." Reporters overtly speculated about the effects of aging on the president, and his fitness to govern for four more years. More than anything else, because of the age controversy, "the stakes on the next presidential debate had risen sharply."[99]

The next Reagan–Mondale debate would not be held for two more weeks, but the Mondale campaign hoped its momentum would be enhanced by the vice presidential debate scheduled for October 11 in Philadelphia. Since Mondale selected Geraldine Ferraro at the Democrats' San Francisco convention, a controversy had arisen over her family's private finances. The Democrats hoped that a strong performance by the New York representative would keep the pressure on the GOP and divert attention from Ferraro's financial difficulties. For their part, the Republicans no doubt hoped that a solid showing by Vice President George Bush would convince voters concerned about Reagan's age that the president was backed up by a talented, competent leader who could, if need be, become an effective president in his own right.

In the end, the Bush–Ferraro debate probably accomplished very little for either camp. Said one observer after the event, "nothing terribly important seems to have happened, or to have registered on the voters."[100] If there was any beneficiary of the Philadelphia debate, it was probably the Reagan campaign, which at least saw the Bush–Ferraro story temporarily move the age issue off the front pages of most newspapers. The candidates did disagree on the economy, civil rights programs, and arms control, but few of the exchanges were notable.

Perhaps the most significant aspect of this debate was that it included the first woman candidate running on a major party's ticket. Indeed, the most memorable (and most widely reported) confrontation of the evening directly involved the question of gender. In a discussion about international terrorism, Ferraro compared the failures of the Carter administration in Iran with the problems of Reagan's policy in Lebanon (where over 200 U.S. Marines were killed in their barracks by a truck bomb). Bush offered to "help" his opponent with the differences between the two situations. Geraldine Ferraro replied that she resented the vice president's patronizing tone and that she could discuss foreign policy without his help. While Ferraro's response was probably developed in advance, her anger appeared quite sincere. In a related development, Bush, exulting over his performance in the debate, told a longshoreman in Baltimore, "We kicked a little ass last night."[101] Bush denied that his comment was sexist, but many observers interpreted it as such.

The interest in the Bush–Ferraro debate (and the vice president's ill-conceived remarks) died out fairly quickly, and polls began, once again, to show the Reagan–Bush team holding a commanding lead. The final Reagan–Mondale debate, scheduled for October 21 in Kansas City, would deal with issues of defense strategy and foreign policy. Most observers, however, had only a secondary interest in the nominees' worldviews. Instead, attention focused on whether Ronald Reagan could deliver a confident performance and put the age issue to rest. Likewise, many analysts were anxious to see whether Walter Mondale could, by decisively winning both presidential debates, mount the greatest electoral comeback since at least 1948. The two questions, of course, were closely linked—for a "miracle" finish to occur Mondale would likely need to better his strong showing in Louisville, and Reagan would have to appear as tired and confused as he had before.

In Kansas City, the nominees discussed their policies toward Communism in Central America, the proper use of military force, and the ways they might deal with terrorism. Finally, panelist Henry Trewitt asked the question that was on the minds of most Americans: How would the president answer those critics concerned about his age and fitness to hold office? Reagan's reply was clearly practiced. It was also the highlight of the evening. The president answered, "I will not make age an issue of this campaign. I am not going to exploit, for political purposes, my opponent's youth and inexperience."

With that confident, humorous response, Ronald Reagan seemingly put to rest the one remaining doubt in the minds of most voters. "At that moment," some observers concluded, "for all intents and purposes, the presidential election of 1984 was over."[102] Indeed, that exchange set the tone for the rest of the debate. Reagan appeared to draw strength from his success and Mondale seemed to be a beaten man. "On television," wrote Abramson, Aldrich, and Rohde, "Mondale looked tired and drawn and Reagan appeared rested and fit."[103]

Afterward, the issue was not whether the president had actually defeated Mondale in Kansas City. Rather, reporters noted that he had done nothing to endanger his huge lead in the polls, and had left Mondale without much hope of a comeback. Fittingly, *Newsweek* titled its coverage of the event, "Reagan Wins a Draw."[104] In his closing remarks, Reagan slipped slightly with a rambling, disjointed story about a letter he was once asked to write (for a time capsule) to the people of the future. But by that time, it seemingly didn't matter. Gloated conservative pundit William Safire, "Mr. Mondale was flat and the president was fine."[105]

Those viewers who paid attention to the debate after the age issue was settled heard a fairly substantive airing of some of the major foreign policy themes of the 1984 campaign. Both candidates struggled with the thorny issue of immigration. Reagan chided Mondale for his one-time support of the nuclear freeze movement. Mondale took the president to task on U.S. support for Third World dictators (particularly in the Philippines), and

Reagan defended his administration's support of Philippine strongman Ferdinand Marcos. Nevertheless, foreign policy issues did not dominate the post-debate news coverage; candidate images did. One reporter, summing up most analyses of the Kansas City debate, said "Mondale didn't do well enough, and Reagan didn't do badly enough."[106]

On the surface, the debates appeared to make little difference in the 1984 presidential election. Reagan went into the debates with a massive lead in the polls and came out of the campaign with a historic landslide victory. The president won every state except Mondale's native Minnesota. His popular vote margin was similarly stunning.

If debating hurt this incumbent (or helped his challenger), it would be hard to discern such effects from the election tallies. Indeed, even after Mondale scored one of the most one-sided debate victories ever in Louisville, his gains in the polls were short-lived. To be sure, this one example is insufficient to nullify the conventional wisdom about presidential debates (the challengers *had*, after all, apparently gained in 1960, 1976, and 1980). Nevertheless, in 1984 the "experts" had been wrong: Ronald Reagan lost nothing by accepting Walter Mondale's challenge to debate.

In our own study of the first Reagan–Mondale debate, we find that the event had a significant, positive effect on viewers' evaluations of Walter Mondale, although their opinions of Ronald Reagan did not decline perceptibly, despite the Republican's poor performance. We could not, however, find a significant change in viewers' voting intentions after the debate.[107] This finding, of course, is not important for its novelty—the literature, by 1976, had persuasively established that debates do not evoke widespread changes in vote choice. Still, viewers overwhelmingly felt that Mondale had won his first debate with President Reagan, and it is notable that not even this debate could significantly alter voting patterns.

Another interesting finding from this study deals with the question of issues and images in presidential debates. Most studies prior to 1984 revealed that candidates' images were far more important than their issue positions in influencing voters' evaluations of the debates. We discover, like most other studies, that candidate images had a significant impact on voters' assessments, and that this effect favored Mondale.

Issue pronouncements, however, also influenced viewers' evaluations, this time to the benefit of Ronald Reagan, the supposed loser. We find that Reagan's pledge not to raise taxes—and his attacks on Mondale for taking the opposite stand—appealed to many of the subjects in the study.

The effectiveness of Reagan's arguments, we contend, may have partially offset the effects of the president's overall loss to Mondale.[108]

1988—BUSH VS. DUKAKIS: "THE ICE MAN AND THE NICE MAN"

The 1988 election marked the first time in twenty years that no incumbent was in the race for president. The Republican Party nominated the sitting vice president, George Bush, for the top job; the Democrats chose Massachusetts governor Michael Dukakis to run for the White House. The electorate seemed especially volatile that year. In July, Dukakis led Bush in the polls by as many as 17 percentage points. By September, however, Bush had erased that lead with a flurry of negative television advertisements accusing the Democrat of being "soft" on crime and national defense. Many observers looked for a closely fought election in 1988.

While both candidates may have had mixed emotions about debating, neither was confident enough to refuse. The autumn of 1988 was marked by a number of debate-related controversies, including the question of sponsorship. The League of Women Voters, angry with the candidates' insistence on control over the format and panelists for the debate, ultimately refused to sponsor the confrontations. The league was replaced as sponsor by a bipartisan commission. In the end, the debates of 1988 were similar in format to those of 1984: two presidential debates were scheduled, with a vice presidential match sandwiched in between.

On September 25, George Bush and Michael Dukakis met for the first time in Winston-Salem, North Carolina. The debate was surprisingly substantive; the *New York Times* subtitled its post-debate report, "Televised Contest Offers a Clear View of Where Nominees Divide."[109] The candidates disagreed on President Reagan's satellite weapons program (SDI), the role of government in providing health insurance, the morality of abortion and the death penalty, and the need for various nuclear weapons systems. Dukakis also attacked Bush for making an issue of the governor's decade-old veto of a bill requiring Massachusetts schoolchildren to recite the Pledge of Allegiance. In one of the most heated moments of the evening, Dukakis accused the Republican nominee of smearing his Americanism. "Of course the vice president is questioning my patriotism," charged Dukakis, " . . . and I resent it."

Before he was governor of Massachusetts, Michael Dukakis had been a minor television personality, the host of a legal issues program on public television. His experience with the medium appeared to aid him in his confrontation with Bush. Post-debate polls showed that viewers, by a narrow margin, had chosen Dukakis as the winner of the Winston-Salem debate.[110] As the challenger, many felt, he already held an advantage, and his polished performance was even more of a plus. "Michael Dukakis," wrote William Safire, "more than held his own with his better known opponent, and to that extent gained from the debate."[111]

Debates, however, are not always about issues, and the first Bush–Dukakis confrontation included one telling line of questioning about the candidates' personalities. One question in particular asked Dukakis about his supposed lack of passion, the sense among some observers that he was a "technocrat" with no vision or, to use one panelist's words, "the smartest clerk in the world." His aides did not feel he handled the question well. "He had," they felt, "simply declared passion and walked away."[112]

George Bush, for all his difficulties in speaking, seemed more appealing and "human." The race had been framed, in the words of *Newsweek*, as "the ice man vs. the nice man."[113] Even the day after the debate, as most pundits were cautiously declaring a Dukakis victory, *New York Times* columnist Tom Wicker noticed the clouds on the Democrats' horizon. "Mr. Bush," he wrote, "seemed to . . . have an edge in warmth, humor, and Reaganesque bumbling."[114] In any event, Dukakis' slight post-debate improvement in the polls quickly faded, and attention soon turned to the vice presidential debate scheduled for October 5 in Omaha, Nebraska.

Perhaps more than any time since Richard Nixon chose Spiro Agnew to run with him twenty years before, the vice presidential position generated a good deal of controversy in 1988. Michael Dukakis had chosen Lloyd Bentsen, veteran senator from Texas, as his running mate, employing the fairly typical strategy of "balancing" the ticket (matching the liberal New Englander with the moderate-to-conservative Southwesterner). George Bush, on the other hand, chose the young (41) conservative Senator Dan Quayle of Indiana as his vice presidential nominee. The choice struck many as odd since Quayle did little to balance the ticket ideologically, and solidly Republican Indiana—unlike Texas—was not going to be a battleground state in November. More damaging, however, were suggestions that Quayle was ill-equipped, by intellect or experience, to assume the presidency in the event of tragedy. The senator did not help his standing with a string of campaign trail gaffes and misstatements.

Democrats looked upon the Omaha debate as a shining opportunity to attack George Bush's judgment by attacking his chosen successor.

Indeed, the debate itself seemed almost entirely devoted to Quayle's fitness to lead the nation. Moderator Judy Woodruff, in her opening remarks, commented that "based on history since World War II, there is almost a 50–50 chance that one of the two men here tonight will become president." In the context of the 1988 campaign, noted one scholar, Woodruff's lead-in amounted "to a campaign commercial for Dukakis/Bentsen."[115]

In keeping with this theme, Dan Quayle was asked early in the debate what he would do if, by some unhappy circumstance, he were to become president. He responded that while he would consult advisers and pray for guidance, his background would qualify him for the job. Apparently, Quayle's response was inadequately specific for the panelists, and he was asked the same question twice more. On his third attempt to reply, he mentioned that his congressional experience was equal—in years—to that of John F. Kennedy when he ran for president. At that point, Lloyd Bentsen was ready with a memorable put-down: "Senator, I served with Jack Kennedy. I knew Jack Kennedy. Jack Kennedy was a friend of mine. Senator, you're no Jack Kennedy."

It is probably unfair to argue, as one observer did, that the panelists "sided with Bentsen against Quayle."[116] Bentsen was also asked some potentially embarrassing questions about his ideological disagreements with Dukakis and his cozy relationship with capitol lobbyists. Nevertheless, it was clear that the debate had damaged Quayle's political credibility. Bush's managers, perhaps recalling the harm supposedly done by Bob Dole to Gerald Ford's 1976 campaign, nervously awaited the public verdict.

The verdict, of course, was overwhelmingly in favor of the Democrat Bentsen. So thorough was his victory that some Dukakis staffers privately joked about changing the order of the ticket.[117] Immediately, the Dukakis campaign aired commercials warning voters of the possibility of "President Quayle." Commentators spoke of the likelihood of a profound impact of the debate on the course of the campaign.

In the end, however, the impact was much less than profound. The polls temporarily changed, in Dukakis' favor, but the movement was insignificant and left Bush with a still-sizable lead. The focus, it seemed, would remain where it had always been—at the top of the tickets. Michael Dukakis' final opportunity to face George Bush head-on would occur only a week later in Los Angeles. Many observers felt that the Massachusetts governor "needed at the very least to de-ice his image."[118] His mastery of substance in the first debate had not earned him a breakthrough in the polls. In the overly personal politics of 1988, it seemed, he needed to make himself warm and likable.

The second Bush–Dukakis debate was much less enlightening than the first, and covered much of the same substantive ground (including the issues of taxation, abortion, and capital punishment). Instead, the theme seemed primarily to be the candidates' personalities and, particularly, Dukakis' passion. One panelist even prefaced a question to the Democratic nominee by saying, "You won the first debate on intellect and yet you lost it on heart." Indeed, even issue-oriented questions were often loaded emotionally, as when Bernard Shaw of the Cable News Network asked Dukakis how he would feel about the death penalty if his own wife were raped and murdered. At another point, the nominees were asked to name their personal heroes. Still later, they were challenged to say something nice about one another.

In the passion and humor sweepstakes, Dukakis appeared to be at a distinct disadvantage. He responded to Shaw's question about capital punishment without reference to its "unbelievably tasteless" premise.[119] "Perhaps," wrote one observer, "Dukakis felt that the proper response to a sensationalist and, in some eyes, offensive question was to ignore its deliberately personal character."[120] If so, he erred, at least in the opinion of most pundits. The question, after all, was not really about the candidate's stand on the death penalty: that issue had already been covered in Winston-Salem. Rather, the question was intended to evoke some emotion from the Democratic nominee. Dukakis also had trouble with another query intended to personalize the candidates. When asked to name his heroes, he could do no better than list a few worthy professions (teachers, astronauts, etc.) and mention Dr. Jonas Salk. Bush, by contrast, had a number of names close at hand.

Defined as it was as Dukakis' last chance to undo George Bush's lead in the polls, the Los Angeles debate was a failure for the Democratic campaign. In the battle of personalities, the "nice man" led the "ice man" 2-0. "Bush," said *Time* magazine, "won the debate largely because he triumphed in the congeniality competition."[121] Dukakis, complained the *New York Times*, responded to the panelists' probing and personal questions with "passionless laundry lists."[122] According to columnist David Broder, the vice president "topped his performance in the first debate and saw his rival . . . miss one opportunity after another to turn the course of the debate—and more importantly, his flagging campaign."[123]

Like their predecessors, the victorious Bush debate team credited the debates (particularly the last one) with ensuring Republican success in the election.[124] What might have been a close race turned into a substantial victory for the vice president. While his popular vote margin was only about 6 percent, George Bush won forty out of fifty states for an overwhelming electoral college advantage. It is unclear whether or not the debates were decisive in the Bush victory. Clearly, though, they did not hurt his effort.

Analyses are still being written about the 1988 presidential election. It may be a year or two before we have a meaningful perspective on the Bush–Dukakis debates. It is still possible, however, to examine the conventional wisdom developed during the previous years. In particular, for the second straight election year, the 1988 debates challenged the notion that such confrontations help lesser-known challengers against their opponents. George Bush, of course, was not running as the incumbent president in 1988. He was, like Richard Nixon in 1960, the sitting vice president. Nevertheless, as a former presidential candidate (in 1980) and a fairly visible number-two man in a popular administration, it is clear that any "stature gap" between the nominees favored the Republicans. Unlike 1960, though, the vice president seemed to get the best of the challenger from Massachusetts. At the very least, it can no longer be argued with certainty that presidential debates invariably help the unknown quantity.

The 1988 debates also seemed the strongest confirmation to date of the contention that such events are won and lost on style, and that a candidate can actually lose on substance but win on image. "Although voters judged Dukakis the 'better debater,' " said *Time*, "they found Bush 'more presidential' and 'more likable'—qualities far more likely to guide them in the voting booth."[125] One can certainly make the argument that voters are entitled to desire a president with whom they feel comfortable. Nevertheless, it may be cause for some concern when, in at least three different years, the perceived winner of the debates was the candidate whose issue presentations were judged inferior.

In terms of viewer response, there is, once again, little evidence that either of the presidential debates was decisive. One study of the second Bush–Dukakis debate (supposedly the most critical one) indicates that little significant opinion change occurred with respect to the candidates or issues, despite claims to the contrary by politicos and journalists.[126] Moreover, even those few effects uncovered during the evening faded away within two weeks of viewing. This study not only supports the general consensus that presidential debates do not affect voting behavior in any big way, but it is also far more pessimistic about the importance of such events in general.

Finally, if nothing else, the 1988 presidential debates appeared to demonstrate the relative unimportance of vice presidential confrontations. If post-debate analyses can be believed, Dan Quayle's performance in Omaha was probably the worst in the entire history of televised debating. Indeed, the best that one observer could say was that Quayle had not "been reduced to stammering incoherence."[127] Despite the lopsided nature of the event, it had virtually no effect on the electorate. Even post-debate Democratic commercials about "President Quayle" were insufficient to scare voters away from the Republican ticket. *Newsweek*, in a tongue-in-cheek election analysis, wrote a new commandment for presidential candidates in the wake of the 1988 results: "Pick anyone you want for VP . . . If Quayle can't sink a ticket, nobody can."[128]

THE SPECIAL CASE OF PRIMARY SEASON DEBATES

The first broadcast debates between candidates for president did not take place during a general election campaign—they occurred during 1948, as the Republican Party was deciding whether to give its nomination to Thomas Dewey, the governor of New York, or Harold Stassen, the young chief executive of Minnesota. Despite the fact that primary debates predate general election debates by twelve years, they have received relatively little attention from scholars or journalists. This is, of course, not totally unreasonable—most observers correctly suppose that public interest in general election debates is greater, and that the stakes of such confrontations are much higher. In addition, it is also possible that analysts simply assume that the lessons drawn from general election debates also apply to similar events held before the nominating conventions.

There are, however, a number of important differences between these two types of debates. First and foremost, primary election debates involve only members of a single political party. For the debate watcher, this means that the candidates must be evaluated without regard to party labels. Research on general election debates has conclusively demonstrated that pre-existing partisan biases color viewers' assessments of the debaters and their arguments—Republican and Democratic identifiers most often see "their" candidate as the debate winner. This "partisan anchor" helps to limit the amount of opinion change that can take place.

In a primary season debate, however, the party label is shared equally by all participants; it provides no built-in bias to influence the viewer. While some debate watchers may lean toward a certain candidate on racial, ethnic, or geographical grounds, most viewers will have few "anchors" for their attitudes. Thus, it is possible that primary debates, unlike their general election counterparts, may generate substantial opinion change. Candidates who perform particularly well (or poorly) in such a debate may improve (or damage) their standing significantly.

For the candidates themselves, the primary season debate provides a very different set of challenges. Unlike a general election debate, there are likely to be few ideological differences between the contestants. Hubert Humphrey and John Kennedy, for example, favored a similar liberal agenda in 1960, as did Humphrey and George McGovern in 1972. It was sometimes difficult to find substantial differences between the liberal views of the Democratic candidates in 1984 and 1988, or between the conservative positions of the Republican debaters during the latter year. Because of these ideological similarities, as well as the larger number of debate participants, candidates must approach primary season debates differently than they do general election debates.

Martel cites a number of strategies available to candidates in primary season debates.[129] One possible strategy, for example, might be for the candidates trailing in the polls to "gang up" on the frontrunner(s). Similarly, candidates may attack the contender just ahead of them in the polls, in order to move up a notch. But most importantly, the candidates (especially those who are not well known) must distinguish themselves from the field. This can take the form of gimmickry (as when Bruce Babbitt physically "stood up" for higher taxes in 1988), or of choosing one unique, identifying issue (as when Richard Gephardt embraced protectionist trade policy during the same year).

According to the reports of journalists and scholars, primary season debates have had profound effects on various campaigns. In 1948, for instance, Republicans Dewey and Stassen debated on radio from Oregon, where a primary election was about to occur. They argued over a single proposition: whether or not the American Communist Party should be outlawed. According to accounts of the event, Dewey made an articulate appeal against banning the Communists on civil libertarian grounds, while Stassen presented an inferior argument that internal security demanded the regulation of subversive groups.[130] "Dewey," write Jamieson and Birdsell, "won on issue and image, and with that the [Oregon] primary and his party's nomination."[131]

In 1972, Senators George McGovern and Hubert Humphrey debated prior to the critical California primary. Humphrey, whose congressional voting record was very similar to that of his opponent, attacked McGovern as a dangerous radical. Humphrey assailed McGovern's welfare policy, his views on Israel, and especially his proposal to cut the military budget. "I think," said Humphrey, "that [McGovern's proposals] will cut into the muscle, into the very fiber of our national security."[132] Theodore White observed that Humphrey's attack was most effective in appealing to undecided and blue-collar voters.[133] He suggests that the debates contributed to a Humphrey comeback that almost cost McGovern the California primary (and thus, possibly, the nomination).

During the 1976 election year, the Democrats had a large field of generally distinguished but little-known candidates. Former Georgia governor Jimmy Carter entered the primary season virtually unknown to most Americans; he left it as the Democratic nominee for president. Many observers saw his performance in the primary election debates as critical to his surprising achievement. Carter developed a reputation as a moderate in a field of liberals, and a candidate who radiated honesty and self-confidence. "It is doubtful," Martel argues, "that Jimmy Carter could have risen from a 2% recognition factor nationwide to win the Democratic nomination without his performance in the 1976 candidate forums."[134]

The interesting primary debates were on the Republican side in 1980, and gimmickry supposedly played an important role in their outcome. Ronald Reagan, the consensus frontrunner, had been upset by George Bush in the Iowa caucuses, and he desperately needed a victory in the New Hampshire primary to sustain his candidacy. While the Republican field was fairly crowded, only Reagan and Bush were considered likely nominees, and they were invited to debate in Nashua, New Hampshire, shortly before the primary (the Reagan campaign helped to finance the event).

Unbeknownst to Bush (or the debate organizers), Reagan had invited the other GOP contenders to join in the proceedings. When they appeared on stage, Reagan demanded their inclusion. The moderator, angered by Reagan's initiative, ordered the Californian's microphone silenced. Reagan stood, took the microphone in hand, and shouted, "I paid for this microphone, Mr. Green."[135] Throughout the exchange, George Bush sat silently, unable or unwilling to contribute to the decision.

Many observers credited Reagan's performance in the Nashua debate with rescuing his candidacy. "The old man in the campaign," wrote Stacks, "had shown himself again to be capable of anger and full of life. It was all that was really necessary to rouse his conservative constituency."[136] Likewise, some felt that Bush's silence had hurt his image. He was painted as somehow unfair in his desire to exclude his opponents from the debate. "Bush's efforts to keep several of his rivals out of the debate," observed

Bartels, "was widely viewed as an embarrassing blunder."[137] In addition, Bartels notes that the "blunder" received a good deal of attention from the media. In any event, Ronald Reagan went on to win the primary, the nomination, and the presidency. To some, that brief exchange in New Hampshire was the turning point.

Since 1980, other debating incidents have been recognized as important in different campaigns, but usually because they dealt with issues that were already receiving attention in the media and on television advertisements. In 1984, Gary Hart, a virtual unknown who had vaulted to prominence in Iowa and New Hampshire, was starting to draw criticism in the press as a superficial candidate. Reports circulated that he had changed his age, his signature, and his surname in order to enhance his public image.[138] It was suggested that the candidate whose slogan boasted of "new ideas" was really a creature of hype and packaging rather than substance. Along those lines, Hart's chief rival, Walter Mondale, attacked Hart during a debate in Atlanta, appropriating the popular advertising slogan of a fast food outlet. Mondale said that Hart's claims of new ideas reminded him of the line from the commercials: "Where's the beef?"[139] Shortly after the exchange, Hart's fortunes plummeted, and Mondale went on to win the nomination easily.

Four years later, Republican Robert Dole had upset George Bush in the Iowa caucuses and challenged the vice president in the New Hampshire primary, threatening to embarrass Bush in his native New England. In television commercials, Bush attacked Dole over the latter's unwillingness to rule out raising taxes. During one pre-primary debate, little-known challenger Pierre DuPont, the former governor of Delaware, handed Dole a piece of paper, daring him to sign a pledge not to raise taxes. The gimmick embarrassed Dole, who returned the paper, unsigned, to DuPont.[140] It was broadcast extensively by the television network news shows. Whether or not the gimmick hurt Dole, he was defeated by Bush in the New Hampshire primary and, within a month, was no longer a serious candidate. It should be noted, however, that the gimmick did not apparently help DuPont, whose obscurity was preserved, and whose candidacy ended shortly after New Hampshire.

These examples provide some evidence of the supposed effects of primary season debates on public opinion. Unfortunately, with social scientists largely ignoring such confrontations, it is impossible to say just how critical these debates actually were. Journalists, after all, have also ascribed major importance to general election debates despite empirical findings to the contrary. While there is some reason to believe that primary season debates do influence voters, better evidence is required.

One of the few empirical studies of a primary debate (conducted by the authors) occurred in 1988 and involved a single confrontation between the Democratic candidates in Dallas, Texas, shortly before the "Super Tuesday" southern primaries.[141] We found that the debate had surprisingly large effects on viewers' opinions toward the candidates. Moreover, there was some evidence that these effects extended to subjects' actual voting choices. We speculate that primary season debates, because they occur before many viewers have decided how to vote, have the potential to exert profound effects on electoral outcomes. We do note, however, that these effects are limited by the fact that so few voters actually watch such debates on television.

It is ironic, therefore, that the debates that get the largest audience (those occurring during the general election campaign) supposedly have little effect on viewers, while those with the potential to make the greatest difference (primary season debates) are largely ignored by the public. Nevertheless, the media do cover such debates, and particularly dramatic moments are shown repetitively on TV news. In that sense, primary season debates may still affect voting choices even if most Americans choose not to watch them. Given the nonfindings reported by much of the research involving presidential debates, the study of primary season debates represents one area of potential interest. They clearly deserve further investigation.

PRESIDENTIAL DEBATES, 1960–88: WHAT DO WE REALLY KNOW?

Social scientists have known for at least a decade that presidential debates do not motivate massive changes in voters' candidate preferences. Many journalists, however, remain convinced that debates have important effects. Politicians, too, continue to treat these confrontations very seriously, spending long hours preparing their presentations. Indeed, even some scholars are unwilling to abandon the possibility that debates may have some "hidden" or "sleeper" effects that might, in the long run, prove important. We will deal in chapter 4 with the scientific evidence surrounding this controversy. For now, it might be worthwhile to assess the conventional wisdom developed over the years to determine what experience, rather than empirical research, has taught us.

One clear finding, sustained over the course of the entire twenty-eight-year history of televised debating, involves the importance of the media.

It has long been established that the media act as "gatekeepers," deciding which information is truly important and which is trivial.[142] Nowhere is this better exemplified than in the case of presidential debates. Analysts pick out the "highlights" of each encounter, comment on the performance of the debaters, and report post-debate polling results. For those who do not watch the debate, this commentary serves as their only recollection of the event. But even for those who view the debate from beginning to end, the media may influence what they remember and what they think of as important.

One might, of course, ask what difference this makes. As long as journalists go about their jobs without bias, what is the harm in allowing these trained observers of politics to put one or two hours of rhetoric into perspective? Some argue that part of the problem is that the media tend to view debates, like other campaign events, through a "horserace paradigm."[143] They concentrate on winning and losing, rather than the substantive arguments made by the candidates. George Bush, during the 1988 debates, criticized the media over their preference for style and drama over substance.[144] He refused to agree to a third debate with his opponent, saying that if the candidates' messages weren't getting out, "it's not . . . because there are too few debates."[145]

There is, to be sure, some validity to that argument. Post-debate news programs often focus on the dramatic moment—the "sound bite"—rather than the issues being debated. They emphasize gaffes (e.g., Ford and Eastern Europe) and heated confrontations (such as Bentsen's put-down of Quayle: "You're no Jack Kennedy"). One question, however, remains unanswered in all this media bashing: are journalists depriving citizens of needed information, or merely responding to viewers' wishes?

Clearly, a majority of those watching any given presidential debate have already decided how they are going to vote in November. It is quite possible, therefore, that they tune in to political debates for the drama of the live confrontation between celebrities rather than for education or guidance (weekend political interview shows, after all, receive comparatively low ratings). Sidney Kraus rightly notes that "Americans are *fans* who want to be *entertained*."[146] Is it any wonder, then, that most post-debate news analysis seems better suited to the sports page than to the front page?

Aside from the impact of the media, few other debate effects have been consistently established. In particular, three lessons drawn from earlier presidential debates are of questionable value. First, while it has become almost axiomatic that debates help challengers and hurt incumbents, recent history has cast doubt on this proposition. Ronald Reagan did not suffer noticeably from debating Walter Mondale in 1984, and George Bush, if anything, helped himself by debating his relatively unknown challenger in 1988. Second, the "primacy effect" noted in 1960 has been called into question by every series of debates since. No longer is it automatically assumed that the first debate between candidates will be the most decisive. Finally, while candidate images may dominate viewers' evaluations of debaters, there is some evidence that issue positions are not entirely ignored. Perhaps we have not yet witnessed enough presidential debates to determine which are the rules and which are the exceptions. Or, perhaps viewers' reactions to each individual encounter are more idiosyncratic than we would like to think.

Still, if debates are indeed important, there are some potentially disturbing ramifications for electoral politics. As noted previously, journalists often report that debates are won not by the candidate who makes the strongest substantive arguments, but by the candidate who can convey warmth, humor, and sincerity on television. In all likelihood, this gives the advantage to the more practiced public speaker or television performer, regardless of his or her real qualifications.

In addition, the drama of these events may magnify truly unimportant factors. Regardless of one's opinion of Gerald Ford, it should trouble most observers if his loss in 1976 was due, even in part, to his misstatements about Eastern Europe (especially since he was almost certainly fully aware of the true status of the Soviet satellite states). In the case of Richard Nixon in 1960, it should be equally troubling, if not more so, that an election could possibly have been affected by a man's makeup and dress. Clearly, more study is needed to separate fact from fiction in presidential debating. Nevertheless, what we have learned raises serious (and still unanswered) questions.

NOTES

1. Nelson W. Polsby and Aaron Wildavsky, *Presidential Elections: Strategies of American Electoral Politics* (New York: Charles Scribner's Sons, 1984), p. 185.

2. Steven J. Wayne, *The Road to the White House* (New York: St. Martin's Press, 1980), p. 209.

3. Theodore H. White, *The Making of the President 1960* (New York: Atheneum, 1962), p. 288.

4. Ibid., 296.

5. Ibid., 291.

6. *Time*, October 10, 1960, p. 20.

7. Robert L. Scott, "You Cannot Not Debate: The Debate over the 1980 Presidential Debates," *Speaker and Gavel* 18 (1981): 28–33.

8. White, *The Making of the President*, p. 290.

9. All references to and quotations from the texts of presidential debates are taken from transcripts published in various sources or from videotape recordings of the debates themselves.

10. When asked to give an example of a major contribution of his vice president to the administration President Eisenhower said, "If you give me a week I might think of one." week I might think of one."

11. *Time*, October 10, 1960, p. 20.

12. *Time*, October 17, 1960, p. 23.

13. Herbert B. Asher, *Presidential Elections and American Politics* (Chicago: Dorsey Press, 1988), p. 144.

14. *Time*, October 10, 1960, p. 20.

15. *New York Times*, October 2, 1960, p. 2E.

16. Elihu Katz and Jacob J. Feldman, "The Debates in the Light of Research: A Survey of Surveys," in Sidney Kraus, ed., *The Great Debates: Background, Perspective, Effects* (Bloomington: Indiana University Press, 1962), pp. 173–223.

17. *New York Times*, November 13, 1960, p. 1E.

18. Ibid.

19. Kurt Lang and Gladys Engel Lang, "Reactions of Viewers," in Kraus, *The Great Debates* (1962), pp. 313–30.

20. Saul Ben-Zeev and Irving S. White, "Effects and Implications," in Kraus, *The Great Debates* (1962), pp. 331–37.

21. White, *The Making of the President*, p. 288.

22. Katz and Feldman, "The Debates in the Light of Research."

23. Percy H. Tannenbaum, Bradley S. Greenberg, and Fred R. Silverman, "Candidate Images," in Kraus, *The Great Debates* (1962), pp. 271–88.

24. J. Jeffery Auer, "The Counterfeit Debates," in Kraus, *The Great Debates* (1962), pp. 142–50.

25. Charles A. Siepmann, "Were They 'Great'?" in Kraus, *The Great Debates* (1962), pp. 132–41.

26. Richard F. Carter, "Some Effects of the Debates," in Kraus, *The Great Debates* (1962).

27. Kandy Stroud, *How Jimmy Won: The Victory Campaign from Plains to the White House* (New York: Morrow, 1977), p. 360.

28. *New York Times*, September 26, 1976, p. 8.

29. Stroud, *How Jimmy Won*, p. 360.

30. Actually, sound in the auditorium was not cut off. However, no sound was getting out to the television trucks parked outside the hall. This distinction proved embarrassing to the networks, who had claimed that they were only

covering a news event and thus were not bound by the "equal time" rule. Of course, if they were truly covering an event, the event shouldn't have stopped just because television sound was lost. For further information, see Sidney Kraus, *Televised Presidential Debates and Public Policy* (Hillsdale, NJ: Lawrence Erlbaum and Associates, 1988).

31. Jules Witcover, *Marathon: The Pursuit of the Presidency, 1972–1976* (New York: Viking, 1977), p. 578–79.

32. *New York Times*, October 7, 1976, p. 47; *Washington Post*, October 7, 1976, p. 1.

33. Martin Schram, *Running for President 1976: The Carter Campaign* (New York: Stein and Day, 1977), p. 317.

34. *New York Times*, October 7, 1976, p. 1.

35. *Time*, October 18, 1976, p. 13.

36. Schram, *Running for President*, p. 323.

37. *New York Times*, October 24, 1976, p. E15.

38. Thomas E. Patterson, *The Mass Media Election* (New York: Praeger Publishers, 1980), p. 125.

39. Frederick T. Steeper, "Public Response to Gerald Ford's Statements on Eastern Europe in the Second Debate," in George F. Bishop, Robert G. Meadow, and Marilyn Jackson-Beeck, eds., *The Presidential Debates: Media, Electoral, and Policy Perspectives* (New York: Praeger, 1978), p. 101.

40. *Time*, November 1, 1976, p. 12.

41. *New York Times*, October 24, 1976, p. E15.

42. *Washington Post*, October 22, 1976, p. 1.

43. David O. Sears and Steven H. Chaffee, "Uses and Effects of the 1976 Debates: An Overview of Empirical Studies," in Sidney Kraus, ed., *The Great Debates: Carter vs. Ford, 1976* (Bloomington: Indiana University Press, 1979), p. 230.

44. Lloyd Bitzer and Theodore Rueter, *Carter vs. Ford: The Counterfeit Debates of 1976* (Madison: University of Wisconsin Press, 1980), p. 35.

45. *Newsweek*, November 21, 1988, p. 88.

46. Newton N. Minow and Clifford M. Sloan, *For Great Debates* (New York: Priority Press, 1987), p. 20.

47. Austin Ranney, ed., *The Past and Future of Presidential Debates* (Washington, D.C.: American Enterprise Institute, 1979), p. 140

48. Bitzer and Rueter, *Carter vs. Ford*.

49. See, for example, Paul R. Hagner and Leroy N. Rieselbach, "The Impact of the 1976 Presidential Debates: Conversion or Reinforcement?" in Bishop, Meadow, and Jackson-Beeck, *The Presidential Debates*, pp. 157–78.

50. Dennis K. Davis, "Influence on Vote Decisions," in Kraus, *The Great Debates* (1979), pp. 331–47.

51. Sears and Chaffee, "Uses and Effects of the 1976 Debates."

52. Minow and Sloan, *For Great Debates*, p. 20.

53. Richard B. Cheney, "The 1976 Presidential Debates: A Republican's Perspective," in Ranney, *The Past and Future*, p. 125.

54. Gladys Engel Lang and Kurt Lang, "The Formation of Public Opinion: Direct and Mediated Effects of the First Debate," in Bishop, Meadow, and Jackson-Beeck, *The Presidential Debates*; Steeper, "Public Response."

55. Bitzer and Rueter, *Carter vs. Ford*, p. 67.

56. *Washington Post*, October 24, 1976, p. 1.

57. T. R. Reid, "Kennedy," in Richard Harwood, ed., *The Pursuit of the Presidency 1980* (New York: G. P. Putnam's Sons, 1980), p. 70.

58. See, for example, Hamilton Jordan, *Crisis: The Last Year of the Carter Presidency* (New York: G. P. Putnam's Sons, 1982), p. 353.

59. Myles Martel, "Debate Preparations in the Reagan Camp: An Insider's View," *Speaker and Gavel* 18 (1981): 34–46.

60. Scott, "You Cannot Not Debate," p. 30.

61. *New York Times*, September 22, 1980, p. 1.

62. John F. Stacks, *Watershed: The Campaign for the Presidency 1980* (New York: Times Books, 1981), p. 223.

63. John H. Kessel, *Presidential Campaign Politics*, 3d ed. (Chicago: Dorsey Press, 1988), p. 189.

64. Jack W. Germond and Jules Witcover, *Blue Smoke and Mirrors: How Reagan Won and Why Carter Lost the Election of 1980* (New York: Viking Press, 1981), p. 227.

65. *Washington Post*, September 23, 1980, p. A15.

66. *Newsweek*, October 6, 1980, p. 40.

67. Martel, "Debate Preparations," p. 40.

68. Paul A. Smith, *Electing a President: Information and Control* (New York: Praeger, 1982), p. 200.

69. Ibid., 177.

70. *Time*, November 10, 1980, p. 18.

71. Myles Martel, *Political Campaign Debates: Images, Strategies, and Tactics* (New York: Longman, 1983).

72. *New York Times*, October 29, 1980, p. 1.

73. Ibid., A29.

74. Stacks, *Watershed*, p. 244.

75. *Time*, July 11, 1983, pp. 10–12.

76. *New York Times*, October 30, 1980, p. A27.

77. Kessel, *Presidential Campaign Politics*, p. 192.

78. Germond and Witcover, *Blue Smoke and Mirrors*, p. 285.

79. *New York Times*, October 29, 1980, p. 1.

80. Germond and Witcover, *Blue Smoke and Mirrors*, p. 282.

81. Elizabeth Drew, *Portrait of an Election: The 1980 Presidential Campaign* (New York: Simon and Schuster, 1981), p. 326.

82. Martel, *Political Campaign Debates*, p. 29.

83. Ibid., 28.
84. Ibid.
85. Robert D. McClure, "Media Influence in Presidential Politics," in Paul T. David and David H. Everson, eds., *The Presidential Election and Transition, 1980–1981* (Carbondale: Southern Illinois University Press, 1983), p. 155.
86. Paul R. Abramson, John H. Aldrich, and David W. Rohde, *Change and Continuity in the 1980 Elections* (Washington, D.C.: Congressional Quarterly Press, 1982), p. 45.
87. Martel, *Political Campaign Debates*, p. 28.
88. *Time*, November 17, 1980, p. 31.
89. *New York Times*, October 30, 1980, p. A27.
90. *Washington Post*, October 23, 1980, p. A2.
91. Kraus, *Televised Presidential Debates*.
92. *New York Times*, October 7, 1984, p. E1.
93. Ibid., October 11, 1984, p. A27.
94. Ibid.
95. Ibid., October 10, 1984, p. A27.
96. Ibid., October 14, 1984.
97. Elizabeth Drew, *Campaign Journal: The Political Events of 1983–1984* (New York: Macmillan, 1985), p. 691.
98. *Time*, October 15, 1984, p. 22.
99. *Newsweek*, October 22, 1984, p. 26.
100. Drew, *Campaign Journal*, p. 697.
101. Ibid., 700.
102. Paul R. Abramson, John H. Aldrich, and David W. Rohde, *Change and Continuity in the 1984 Election* (Washington, D.C.: Congressional Quarterly Press, 1986), p. 60. 1986), p. 60.
103. Ibid., 59.
104. *Newsweek*, October 29, 1984, p. 26.
105. *New York Times*, October 22, 1984, p. A21.
106. Drew, *Campaign Journal*, p. 705.
107. David J. Lanoue and Peter R. Schrott, "Voters' Reactions to Televised Presidential Debates: Measurement of the Source and Magnitude of Opinion Change," *Political Psychology* 10 (1989): 275–85.
108. Lanoue and Schrott, "Voters' Reactions," p. 282.
109. *New York Times*, September 26, 1988, p. 1.
110. *Newsweek*, November 21, 1988, p. 124.
111. *New York Times*, September 26, 1988, p. A23.
112. *Newsweek*, November 21, 1988, p. 124.
113. Ibid., 123.
114. *New York Times*, September 27, 1988, p. A35.
115. Michael Weiler, "The 1988 Electoral Debates and Debate Theory," *Argumentation and Advocacy* 25 (1989): 215.

116. Ibid.
117. *Newsweek*, November 21, 1988, p. 138.
118. Ibid., 139.
119. J. Michael Hogan, "Media Nihilism and the Presidential Debates," *Argumentation and Advocacy* 25 (1989): 223.
120. Weiler, "The 1988 Electoral Debates," p. 218.
121. *Time*, October 24, 1988, p. 18.
122. *New York Times*, October 15, 1988, p. 30.
123. *Washington Post*, October 14, 1988, p. 1.
124. *Newsweek*, November 21, 1988, p. 140.
125. *Time*, October 10, 1988, p. 27.
126. David J. Lanoue, "The 'Turning Point': Viewers' Reactions to the Second 1988 Presidential Debate," *American Politics Quarterly* 19 (1991): 80–95.
127. *New York Times*, October 7, 1988, p. A35.
128. *Newsweek*, November 21, 1988, p. 18.
129. Martel, *Political Campaign Debates*.
130. Kathleen Hall Jamieson and David S. Birdsell, *Presidential Debates: The Challenge of Creating an Informed Electorate* (New York: Oxford University Press, 1988), p. 92.
131. Ibid.
132. Theodore H. White, *The Making of the President 1972* (New York: Atheneum, 1973), p. 127.
133. Ibid., 128.
134. Martel, *Political Campaign Debates*, p. 52.
135. Germond and Witcover, *Blue Smoke and Mirrors*, p. 128. Actually, even in his moment of triumph, Reagan was in error—the moderator's name was not Green, but Breen.
136. Stacks, *Watershed*, pp. 120–21.
137. Larry M. Bartels, *Presidential Primaries and the Dynamics of Public Choice* (Princeton, NJ: Princeton University Press, 1988), p. 39.
138. Ibid., p. 140.
139. Drew, *Campaign Journal*, p. 387.
140. *New York Times*, February 15, 1988, p. A12.
141. David J. Lanoue and Peter R. Schrott, "The Effects of Primary Season Debates on Public Opinion," *Political Behavior* 11 (1989): 289–306.
142. D. M. White, "The Gate-Keeper: A Case Study in the Selection of News," *Journalism Quarterly* 27 (1950): 383–90.
143. C. Anthony Broh, "Horse-Race Journalism: Reporting the Polls in the 1976 Election," *Public Opinion Quarterly* 44 (1980): 514–29.
144. Weiler, "The 1988 Electoral Debates," p. 219.
145. Ibid.
146. Kraus, *Televised Presidential Debates*, p. 77.

3

DEBATE CONTENT: DO VOTERS HEAR WHAT THE CANDIDATES SAY?

While scholars, journalists, and political professionals often write about the effects of debates on the public, very few have taken the time to analyze the *content* of these confrontations. Nevertheless, given our assumptions about the functions of debates in electoral democracies, the value of content analysis seems self-evident. For debate organizers (e.g., the League of Women Voters and the televised networks), the purpose of a televised debate is to provide the audience with new and relevant information, allowing viewers to cast a more "rational" vote.[1] Debate supporters regularly emphasize the provision of information in lauding debates as a truly democratic tool and, by now, an indispensable event in American presidential elections.

Therefore, one important task of debate researchers should be to find out whether or not this function is being fulfilled. The most obvious research tool to achieve this goal, it would seem, is the method of content analysis. Only through a detailed analysis of the questions asked by the panelists and the statements made by the candidates can we determine whether "real" and "important" information has been imparted.

It is, of course, possible that such analysis would render these arguments lacking. The ideal of presidential debates may not match up with the reality. One reality, after all, is that candidates' approaches to debates are inherently self-serving. Myles Martel, a campaign adviser to Ronald Reagan in 1980, cites a memo to Reagan's campaign staff that read, "If the Governor succeeds Tuesday in making Jimmy Carter's record the major issue of the debate and the campaign, we will succeed in the debate and win the general election. If, however, Carter makes Ronald Reagan the issue of the debate and the campaign, we will lose both."[2] Notice that nothing is said about information, candidates' policy stands, or party platforms. Instead, the memo suggests that by winning the debate (primarily through "personality issues"), the election may also be won.

One may argue, of course, that Reagan intended to win the debate by providing information about better substantive alternatives or by presenting a more convincing political program than that offered by Carter. In reading Martel's book, however, it is rather striking that only a few pages are devoted to substantive strategies (i.e., the issues to be discussed during the debates). Instead, more emphasis is put on tactics, the reasons for choosing certain subjects and ignoring others, and the best way to communicate information (whether to keep it vague or specific, and whether to use it to attack Carter).[3]

Clearly, then, a basic tenet of the pro-debate argument remains unresolved. Indeed, it is an argument that rages both in the United States and abroad. In addition to the American findings, a West German research team, studying candidate confrontations in that country, argues that such events amount to little more than free political advertisements for the participating politicians and their respective parties.[4] The German analysis is based on a qualitative (linguistic) study of the interactions between politicians and journalists, but neglects the actual substance of the conversations. That is, researchers consider the relative levels of agreement and disagreement between the participants, but not what was actually said in terms of issues and policies. Nevertheless, their conclusion is a rather stark claim and argues against the hypothesis that debates serve an important function in democratic theory.

If the main interest of politicians worldwide is to sell their personalities and their images as much as—or more than—their policies, then one major justification for debates (that they provide information on substantive policy programs) is in danger. That is, of course, not to say that debates are therefore worthless or even bad for American politics. Rather, it acknowledges the obvious, that the primary function of presidential debates is to help candidates appeal for votes. Since that is indeed the case, then the strongest argument in favor of televised debates must be based on the presumption that these events, regardless of the candidates' motives and strategies, still provide at least "enough" information to help the audience make a more rational vote choice (the definition of "enough," of course, is in itself problematic).

This research agenda dovetails nicely with the content-analytical approach. The primary goal of content analysis is to account as precisely as possible for the actual content—verbal and nonverbal—of a debate. The aim is to gather extensive information on what was said (and sometimes also on *how* it was said).[5] Scholars can then relate this information to a number of research concerns: Do candidates provide the audience with information? Are substantive issues discussed or are debates used as a vehicle for more personalized attacks? Do debates offer data to assist rational decisionmaking, as desired by democratic theorists? And finally, do candidates offer clear alternatives on the most important issues facing the nation?

Content analysis may also help us learn more about the effects of debates on viewers. Since the first televised debates in 1960, most researchers have simply taken a sample of the audience and asked them about the issues addressed during the debates, as well as their evaluations of the debaters. In addition, social scientists have often investigated what, if anything, each spectator learned about the candidates as a result of viewing the debates.

To be sure, no content analysis is required for this typical research approach (many, including the authors, have conducted such studies without recourse to the method). Nevertheless, if scholars wish to learn about the relationship between what is said in debates and how viewers react to them, then content analysis may be the best way to achieve this goal. Similarly, content analysis may provide valuable information about media coverage of debates, as well as the evolution of issues across debates and over time.[6]

Content analysis, of course, can serve the agenda of politicians as well as scholars. For the candidates, a content analysis of presidential debates provides important information for present and future campaigns.[7] First, political professionals can use the technique to identify, classify, and evaluate the success of various debating strategies. In addition, candidates' substantive statements can be checked by the campaign staff for completeness and for possible slips, as well as the dreaded gaffe. Simultaneously, the opponent's arguments can be scrutinized for flaws or gaffes that might then be exploited on the campaign trail.

Finally, in addition to these concerns, content analysis may also be useful for providing data with which to settle serious legal and political questions. In 1976, for example, debates were legally permissible only because they were not considered to be free political advertising for the Democratic and Republican presidential nominees (as many third-party candidates and some political pundits claimed they were). Rather, the networks argued, debates were legitimate and newsworthy campaign events that served as a means of providing valuable information to the electorate.[8]

As a result of this argument, debates were freed from the constraints of the "fairness doctrine" (which required equal broadcast time to all parties and candidates); thus, broadcasters could legally cover the events, even though they excluded all but the major parties' nominees. In recent years, some observers have even gone so far as to suggest institutionalizing—that is, requiring—televised debates as an obligatory part of the presidential campaign.[9] In both cases, these arguments are based on the assumption that debates *do* provide the audience with more than just vague platitudes and rhetoric. Instead, they must give viewers important insights that are unavailable (or at least not easily found) elsewhere. Analysis of actual debate content could certainly help to settle such issues.

This chapter will attempt to grapple with some of the questions presented above. In particular, we will be concerned with three critical matters. First, how useful are debates for providing voters with important information about the issues and candidates? Is the information that is provided vague or specific? Is it generally unavailable in campaign advertisements and overall media coverage of the candidates? In short, are debates providing a valuable and/or unique service to voters?

Second, if useful information is provided, how is it used and interpreted by voters and the media? Are viewers sensitive to the issue-oriented discussions of the candidates, or are they more concerned with personalities and dramatic confrontations? Do the media report the substantive content of these meetings, or do they reduce debates to "sporting events" in which the key issues are who won and lost and how the confrontation altered the standings in the political race?

Finally, what can content analysis tell us about the politicians themselves? What kinds of debating strategies do they employ and how successful are they? What insights can we gain about the nominees' personalities and political "styles" by analyzing their words and nonverbal cues? Do debates, in effect, reveal the "real" person, and do voters react to these revelations?

These are, to say the least, vital issues in understanding American politics and electoral outcomes. We will take up these matters shortly. We will begin, however, with a brief review of historical developments in content analysis to provide for a better understanding of the problems involved with the various content-analytical approaches to debate research.

HISTORICAL DEVELOPMENTS IN CONTENT ANALYSIS

In his seminal survey on content analysis, Bernard Berelson reviewed a number of studies, their approaches, and the general state of the art in the field of communication research during the 1940s and 1950s.[10] He outlined the uses and implications of this specific (and, for students of political communication, ideally suited) research technique. Among the questions Berelson considered are how the method is used to describe the characteristics of content (i.e., the substance and form); how to measure accurately the "readability" of printed materials; how to discover stylistic features of political communication; how to identify the intentions of a communicator through his or her statements; and how to determine the psychological state of communicators as individuals or within groups.

Berelson further describes the use of content analysis to study the *audience* of a persuasive message: its attitudes, interests, and values. In addition, he considers the effects of content on viewers' and listeners' beliefs and opinions. In conclusion, he defines content analysis as a research technique designed to achieve the "objective, systematic and quantitative description of the manifest [as opposed to latent] content of communication."[11] Berelson's emphasis, then, is set on overt content and represents the research tradition coming out of the prewar (and wartime) social science interest in topics such as propaganda research.[12]

This specific focus on the manifest content of persuasive messages has been challenged by Siegfried Kracauer.[13] He claims that most political communication reverberates with so many latent meanings that to isolate its manifest content and describe it in a "straightforward" manner is "not only almost impossible, but can hardly be expected to yield significant results."[14] He specifically challenges the possibility of a systematic and objective exploration of content by way of counting frequencies of utterances and emphasizes the "need for theoretical reorientation."[15] Kracauer describes the future of communication research as rooted in a necessary shift from quantitative to qualitative procedures.

In 1959, Ithiel de Sola Pool edited the results of a group of scholars who assembled at what became known as the Allerton Conference (after its meeting place, the Allerton House of the University of Illinois).[16] In contrast to what was prevalent in the field until then (and in keeping with contemporary criticism), these researchers turned away from mere quantitative descriptions of communication materials in favor or more sophisticated analyses. They emphasized hypothesis testing and were more concerned with inferences drawn from content analysis than with its description.

Specifically, their research focused on the social and psychological sources of verbal material, the use of symbols in political communication, and interdisciplinary links between linguistics and more traditional content-analytical techniques. The conference also raised the problem of how to analyze "instrumental" communication (attempting to understand not only what the message says on the face of it, but also what it conveys, given its context and circumstances).

Ten years later, George Gerbner and his associates published the results of the Annenberg School conference on content analysis.[17] This conference, held in November, 1967, brought scholars together once again to assess progress in the field. Between 1959 and 1967, the use of content analysis techniques in the social sciences had increased exponentially, leaving researchers with many new issues to consider. These changes motivated the participation of "more than 400 scholars from about 85 educational and scientific institutions."[18]

The Gerbner volume consists of four parts. The first deals with the theories and analytical constructs of content analysis. Klaus Krippendorff, emphasizing "scientific" reliability, defined content analysis as "the use of replicable and valid methods for making specific inferences from text to other states or properties of its source."[19] In the second part, Ole R. Holsti argued that content analysis had become a multipurpose research method suited specifically to investigating a broad spectrum of problems.[20] The only necessary link between the problems, he argued, is that in each case communication serves as the basis for theoretical inference. Part III deals with advances in the recording and notation of data. One study discusses how developments in computer technology are utilized to develop tools and methods for the automated analysis of visual records.[21]

Advances in technology also play a crucial role in the final section of the conference report. Detailed computer techniques are presented, dealing with content analysis and computational linguistics. By this time, Philip Stone and his associates had already developed the "General Inquirer," a computer approach to content analysis.[22] The focus of discussion in Stone's chapter is on the use of the General Inquirer in various projects, its shortcomings and development, and the creation of further programs. Through this extensive presentation, it becomes evident how much the interest in computer-aided content analysis had increased, and how much technological advancement had occurred in this field of social scientific inquiry.

Since then, the developments in content analysis have been in more and better computer programs, more precise manual coding techniques, and more sophisticated designs. These advances have also led to the necessity of dealing more directly with content analysis as a scientific methodology. Krippendorff, in his elaborate introduction to the technique, points out important developments in the aims and methods of modern content analysis: its fundamentally empirical orientation, the linkage of content to more recent conceptualizations of social phenomena, and the development of a unique methodology of its own.[23]

Krippendorff vehemently criticizes the notion that simply reading a newspaper and describing what the different articles say is already some sort of content analysis. As noted above, he argues for a more rigorous scientific approach that includes making explicit how the analysis is done, trying to avoid biases, and sharing results with the possibility of replication. He further argues that despite the fact that different fields face different problems with content-analytical techniques, "all content analyses share a logic of composition, a form of reasoning and certain criteria of validity. It is in these common procedures that we find the subject matter of content analysis methodology."[24]

A more recent introduction into the methodology deals specifically with newer computer-aided approaches.[25] The technological development of faster and more sophisticated computers has accelerated and further influenced the field of content analysis. Robert Weber describes the improvement of existing programs such as the General Inquirer as well as developments in "computational hermeneutics," developed in Artificial Intelligence research. He argues that these programs "may provide the bridge (or link between) so-called qualitative and quantitative approaches to social science inquiry."[26]

Despite these advances, the problems of content-analytical techniques have remained largely the same. For example, can researchers derive reliable data from communication content? And, how can they measure these data and compare them to other findings? Interestingly (especially for our topic of presidential debates), recent researchers seem to be less inclined toward fixing standardized content-analytical categories. Instead, the emphasis is more on attempting to measure specific content precisely, rather than developing a measurement that can be used to compare various data sources on similar grounds. The question remains, of course, whether it is possible to find standardized categories or, indeed, whether it is even desirable.

As most content analysts agree, it is always in the interest of the researcher that the theoretical problem under study determine, at least to some extent, the categories to be used and the unit of analysis to be defined. Nevertheless, within a fairly narrow research interest (such as televised debates), we would argue in favor of the development of standardized categories. Since one major goal is to study the impact of debates on the electorate, and to generalize these results across many years, it is clearly necessary to standardize the measures of content if one wishes to study the effects of a specific debate in any generalizable way.

In sum, the use of content analysis in social science research has not only increased over time but has also changed its goals. Mere quantification and frequency counts are no longer the state of the art; rather, researchers are increasingly concerned with the *impact* of content on social phenomena. Great effort has also been put into developing techniques to further efficiency and reliability and, to a lesser extent, to set standards by which different analyses may be compared. Again, this seems to be of particular importance in debate research if scholars intend to compare potential debate effects over time. Such research, done well, may be the key by which we unlock numerous debating secrets. In the following sections we will discuss in greater detail the relatively few content analyses in debate research, their findings, and their implications.

CONTENT ANALYSIS IN DEBATE RESEARCH

Students of debate effects have rarely been daunted by the fact that they are often unfamiliar with the actual text of each debate. Instead, they proceed as if viewers' reactions are entirely separable from debate content.[27] Similarly, journalists lauding the positive values of debates and proposing their institutionalization have rarely sought reliable data in support of their assertions.

And yet, the actual effects of debates on voters (described in chapter 4) presumably result from one or both of two sources. First, the content of the candidates' statements may lead to some sort of information gain on the part of the audience and, perhaps as a result, to a changed evaluation of the nominees themselves. Second, the *way* in which one candidate presents a certain issue may lead to a modified evaluation of that issue and, therefore, to a more positive (or negative) assessment of the candidate. While the first effect would be a product of viewers' own cognitive processes, the second would be a measure of the success of candidate strategies.[28] In either case, to determine which effects are stimulated, we have to know the strategies applied by the debaters and the various issues raised during each debate.

In the following analysis, we will consider in greater detail the research on debate content in terms of our two major topics of interest. First, we will review the content-analytical studies dealing with the question of what information is provided by debates and what sorts of issues are most commonly discussed. As noted above, this analysis will tackle the assumption that debates serve the democratic process by providing "rational" voters with better data with which to decide between the candidates. Our second concern deals with the communication theoretical perspective: how does content analysis of debates help us to understand the possible influence of these events on their audience's attitudes and behavior? Clearly, both perspectives are fundamental to understanding the function and power of televised presidential debates.

CONTENT ANALYSIS AND POLITICAL ISSUES

John W. Ellsworth was one of the first scholars to test the proposition that television debates increase voters' rationality.[29] He conducted a content analysis of selected materials from the 1960 presidential campaign to test whether "the protagonists made clearer statements of their positions and offered more reasoning and evidence to support their positions [during debates], than they did in other campaign situations."[30]

Ellsworth developed a content coding scheme with three major categories: analysis (statements in which a candidate discusses issues in depth, concentrating on problem-solving proposals); evidence (statements in which the debater provides information in support of his or her claims); and declaration (where the candidate simply presents a point without elaboration). Since debaters are supposed to be engaged in aggressive campaigning, attacking their opponents and lauding their own achievements, these three categories are further subdivided by whether the candidates' remarks are designed to criticize the opposition or defend their own record. Thus, Ellsworth places debaters' statements into one of nine separate categories: they may be analytical, evidentiary, or declarative; and, within each of these groups, the utterance is further categorized as either critical, defensive, or neutral. Only if a political statement can fit into one of these categories is it coded as "classifiable discourse."[31]

Ellsworth found huge differences between the amount of "discourse" in the Kennedy–Nixon debates (which was high) versus the nominees' campaign speeches (in which such statements were relatively rare). In addition, over the course of the debates he found a significant jump in comments of evidence and assertion but little overall change in analytical categories. He argues that these findings support the thesis that debates are somewhat akin to television quiz shows in that more stress is put on recital of facts than on analysis of problems and their possible solutions. Nevertheless, it was apparent that the debates, whatever their failings, provided more information of substance than candidate-controlled media products such as campaign addresses.

Looking at the candidates individually, Ellsworth detected an increase over time in the use of analysis by Kennedy, and an increase in statements of evidence from Nixon. In addition, he found that little classifiable discourse could be found in the debaters' closing statements. He attributed this to what he called the effect of "imminent rebuttal": knowing that the opponent will have the opportunity for an immediate rebuttal leads a candidate to make statements of a more factual and less assailable character. By the same token, a candidate knows that his closing statements will go unchallenged, and hence, substantive appeals are not required to circumvent a possible attack. Thus, it is evident that the give and take of a presidential debate does put a premium on providing careful and well-formed arguments.

Robert G. Meadow and Marilyn Jackson-Beeck content analyzed both the 1960 and 1976 debates.[32] They were specifically interested in comparing the issues addressed in 1976 to those discussed in 1960. They argued that through content analysis, debates may be treated as communication events rather than simple political events, and may be considered in the larger framework of the electoral campaign. Since political debates are major campaign stories and are widely reported in the news media (although in a relatively non-substantive manner), the authors decided to content analyze not only the debates themselves, but also their subsequent media coverage. Finally, Meadow and Jackson-Beeck were interested in the extent to which the candidates addressed major issues of public concern as expressed by the electorate in public opinion polls. Therefore, they conducted a content analysis of viewers' responses to open-ended questions about the importance of various campaign issues during both the 1960 and 1976 campaigns.

The authors found some interesting similarities between the debates in 1960 and 1976. In general, for example, the extent of candidates' discussion of issues surrounding the conduct of government and the state of the American economy was very similar during the two years. In 1960, 53 percent of all words spoken by the candidates dealt with the nonspecific role of government in American life; in 1976 the corresponding figure was 54 percent. Twenty-six percent of the words uttered by John Kennedy and Richard Nixon referred to economic issues; for Gerald Ford and Jimmy Carter, economic concerns accounted for 31 percent of all utterances.[33]

Looking at more specific sub-issues, however, it turns out that the candidates' broad approaches to economics had changed quite substantially over the years. While in 1960 economic growth was a primary concern, it received only minor attention in 1976. The reverse held for the question of controlling federal spending (which was scarcely mentioned in 1960, but was a major topic sixteen years later).

Further, health, education, and welfare issues were also addressed from very different perspectives during the two election years. In 1960 they were discussed as part of the government's responsibility to improve the quality of life for all Americans. In 1976, on the other hand, far more was made of the need to reconsider social service spending in the context of the fiscal constraints of the inflation-plagued 1970s.

The authors also touched briefly on the question of strategic differences in the candidates' styles. They pointed out that while it might seem, after casually glancing at debate transcripts, that Gerald Ford addressed economic issues more frequently than his opponent, it was actually Carter who spoke more on the topic. The reason, they report, was that Carter spoke much faster than Ford and, overall, "squeezed . . . nearly one thousand more words" into the debate than did his opponent.[34] Moreover, Carter accomplished this feat "despite the fact that [he] was cut off by audio failure during one answer and spoke only 51 words in that turn, instead of his average 355 words."[35]

Comparing the content of post-debate press coverage to what was actually said during the debates, Meadow and Jackson-Beeck found (for 1960) that very little of the actual discussion of issues found its way into the stories presented by the print media. The only important exception, the authors note, was the *New York Times*, which devoted substantial space to the candidates' discussion of issues and also published transcripts of the debate itself. In 1976 the situation was only slightly better. While the *Times* again covered the issues and printed a transcript, most other media outlets increased their coverage of debate issues only marginally. Instead, emphasis again was on the horse-race question of who won and lost, the physical appearance of the candidates, and viewers' reactions to the evening's events. Presumably, this tendency was even more pronounced in the electronic media.

The third part of the Meadow and Jackson-Beeck analysis attempted to answer the question of whether or not the debaters addressed the issues of greatest salience to the public. In short, did the debate illuminate those issues highest on the public agenda? As it turned out, such was apparently not the case. Unfortunately, the authors did not test for the opposite possibility: rather than public opinion setting the agenda for the debates, did the debates set the agenda for subsequent public discussion? Is it possible that candidates, by emphasizing certain issues (presumably those favorable to their own campaigns), can focus viewers' attention on a new set of concerns?

One problem with this part of the analysis is that Meadow and Jackson-Beeck used open-ended questions (asking for viewers' assessments of the most important issue facing the nation) collected *prior* to the debate in 1960, but *after* the debate in 1976. Thus, we cannot tell whether the most heavily debated issues became more salient after the Kennedy–Nixon confrontation. By the same token, we do not know whether the issues considered important after the 1976 debate were more or less salient *before* the Carter–Ford encounters. In chapter 4, we will consider evidence on the agenda-setting question developed without the use of content analysis.

Arthur H. Miller and Michael MacKuen also employed content analysis to study the effects of the 1976 Carter–Ford debates.[36] They investigated political cognition and viewers' evaluations of the presidential candidates, considering whether these factors were affected directly by the televised debates, by the media coverage of these debates, or by both. Focusing on the relationship between media usage and information gathering, they used a design similar to that employed by Meadow and Jackson-Beeck, comparing the content data obtained from newspaper and television coverage of the debates to data obtained from voter surveys.

Miller and MacKuen content analyzed the first Carter–Ford debate. They compared the candidates' discussion of issues with citizens' responses to a number of open-ended questions about different campaign themes. They used the answers to these open-ended items as a measure of the salience of the various issue positions embraced by the candidates during the debate. Miller and MacKuen were interested in whether debates give viewers greater insights into the character and issue positions of the presidential candidates. They were also interested in whether or not the substance of debates is reported by the media and remembered by voters.

The authors found that viewers were able (or, perhaps, willing) to make a greater number of statements about the candidates after watching the debate than they had been prior to the event. Interestingly, this was true at all levels of political interest, information, and attentiveness. Miller and MacKuen argued that debates apparently provide the electorate with some new information about the participants or, at the very least, refresh viewers' memories about earlier perceptions.[37]

Miller and MacKuen then compared these results to the actual debate content and media coverage. They found a rough correspondence between the content of post-debate media reports and respondents' own recollections. However, neither of the two reflected the actual substance of the debate. The authors demonstrated a sharp difference between the substantive debate content (i.e., the issue-oriented pronouncements of the candidates) and the relatively nonsubstantive post-debate accounts presented in newspapers and television news programs (and recounted by survey respondents). Based on these findings, Miller and MacKuen concluded that debate issues do not generally translate into public concerns.

One interesting point in this study is that the content analyses are not outlined or described in any great detail. Actually, the authors explain their coding scheme in a footnote, and it is clear that they must have had at least one table on the content of the debate included in their original text.[38] This table, however, does not appear in the final version of the article. Clearly, the content analyses are not given a major emphasis, despite the fact that the study is largely based on these analytical instruments.

The major difference between the work of Meadow and Jackson-Beeck and that of Miller and MacKuen is rooted in their basic approaches. While Miller and MacKuen conducted a content analysis in order to obtain comparable measures of the actual content of the debate and recollections of the respondents, the Meadow/Jackson-Beeck study is specifically interested in the evolution of issues over two different campaigns. The similarity (and comparability) of these studies is that both use issues as the units of analysis in their research. However, while Meadow and Jackson-Beeck give a detailed description of their method, a similar description is almost completely absent in the study reported by Miller and MacKuen. As noted above, the authors put the description of their content analysis coding scheme in a footnote, reading: "Each paragraph of newspaper coverage was coded for up to six substantive topics. . . . National TV news transcripts were obtained from the Vanderbilt Archives and coded in the same fashion."[39] Yet no word is provided about the procedure for the analysis of the debate itself. It can only be assumed that they followed an approach similar to that of other analyses.

Richard Joslyn's work concentrates on understanding candidate communication.[40] His goal is to study various types of advertising messages utilized by the candidates during the 1960, 1976, and 1980 election campaigns. He compares these scripted and rehearsed advertising "spots" to the candidates' behavior during their televised debates. For the purpose of his analysis, Joslyn defines four types of candidate appeals: the partisan appeal, the discussion of candidate attributes, the appeal to specific demographic groups, and the discussion of substantive issues. The final category is further divided into specific and vague arguments, as well as particularly "salient" issue-related appeals (that is, appeals on especially emotional or hotly contested issues).

Through content analysis of debates and television advertisements, Joslyn—like Ellsworth—finds that presidential debates tend to be more policy-oriented than campaign "spots."[41] However, the content of advertisements and debates alike is often quite vague, and many of the candidates' appeals were actually very similar (although partisan appeals were less frequent in 1976 and 1980 than they were in 1960). Further, the discussion of specific policy issues became more prevalent in 1976 and 1980 than it had been earlier.[42] Generally, incumbents tended to defend their performance in office by referring to their specific policy proposals and "achievements," while challengers made greater use of policy "salience" appeals. In thirteen out of the eighteen debates studied, the most prevalent appeal by all candidates was the vague policy appeal (i.e., nonspecific discussion of policy goals emphasizing symbolic concepts such as efficiency, fairness, and liberty).[43]

During the first presidential debate of 1984, the authors of this book conducted a quasi-experiment using content analysis to study whether "voters hear what the candidates say."[44] We showed that Ronald Reagan and Walter Mondale talked heavily about substantial issues, while simultaneously trying to convey a favorable and positive "personal style." A change of opinion in our sample of debate watchers (in favor of Mondale) was attributed mainly to the challenger's successful selling of his personal image and incumbent President Reagan's halting performance. However, some suggestive evidence was found that Reagan, while losing the debate on style, may have scored some points with voters through his conservative statements on taxation and government spending.

The coding scheme used in this work was developed by Hans-Dieter Klingemann to analyze open-ended questions about political parties in West German election studies.[45] Since then, Klingemann's coding scheme has been successfully applied in content analyses of party platforms,[46] newspaper editorials,[47] and (while not specifically developed for this purpose) numerous televised debates in the United States[48] and the Federal Republic of Germany.[49] The use of this content analysis technique represents the only approach involving comparative research of debate content in different countries with different cultures.

In 1988, the only content analysis of the general election debates—as far as we are aware—was conducted by Marjorie Hershey.[50] She content analyzed both Bush–Dukakis debates, finding that the two candidates basically adhered to their long-standing campaign strategies during each encounter. As a result, she concluded that the debates offered little new learning to viewers. However, she found that large portions of the debates were devoted to substantive policy issues, with each candidate emphasizing his platform and proposals. Interestingly, once again the author does not explain the coding scheme or method of her content analysis. The data are used in a strictly descriptive way to distinguish between information provision and personal appeals.

Another content analysis of presidential debates in 1988 dealt with one Democratic primary debate in March of that year (once again, conducted by the authors of this book).[51] This study employed the Klingemann coding scheme described above. We found that, of the five competing candidates, the two frontrunners (Richard Gephardt and Michael Dukakis) employed defensive strategies, while the underdog candidates largely "ganged up" on the favorites. This finding is consistent with Martel's analysis of primary debate strategies.[52] In addition, the study found little disagreement between the substantive appeals of this homogenous group of liberal politicians, with most candidates concentrating on emphasizing traditional party themes (employment, social welfare, etc.) or attacking the Reagan administration.

At this point, it is clear that the whole enterprise of content analysis seems to be regarded as one of questionable significance, at least in the field of political science.[53] Often the full analysis is not published[54] or is forced into footnotes.[55] Perhaps this reflects the discipline's ambivalence toward content-analytical techniques as "soft" methodologies, despite the fact that great emphasis and care generally go into these analyses, with much attention devoted to strengthening the reliability and validity of these data.

CANDIDATE IMAGES AND STRATEGIES

Another major interest in the study of political debates is how candidates present themselves and how this presentation is interpreted by the public. Edwin S. Shneidman considered candidate images in detail, presenting a "logical" model that "provide[s] a conceptual scheme for translating the logical elements contained in verbal stimuli into their related psychological attributes" (i.e., allows us to learn about candidates' personalities from their behavior during the debate).[56] He argued that each candidate has an idiosyncratic way of thinking but also shares broader universal and cultural perspectives. Through content analysis, he says, it should be possible to analyze meaningfully those unique logical elements of candidates' thinking.

The impetus for his research was the Kennedy–Nixon debates, and his idea was to study systematically the idiosyncrasies in each politician's personal style to provide insights into his psychological makeup. The implication, Shneidman claimed, "is that the important impact of the logical aspect of the verbal stimulus is not in the logic which it portrays, but rather in the personality attributes which it implies."[57] Using the verbatim texts of the debates to conduct his analysis,[58] he found, for each candidate, rather stable traits over the two debates under consideration: Kennedy's logical style, the author says, was "meandering and loose-knit and tend[ed] to be top-heavy and impulsive";[59] Nixon's style, on the other hand, was "cohesive, balanced, and univocal."[60] These underlying traits, he argued, should affect viewers' judgments about the nominees and provide clues as to what kind of president each would become. Shneidman's study, while interesting, has not been replicated, perhaps due to its rather elaborate procedure demanding a well-trained coder crew. Coming from communication research, his study has also been largely neglected by researchers in political science.

While Meadow and Jackson-Beeck touched only briefly on candidate style in the 1960 and 1976 debates, this topic was of greater interest to Miller and MacKuen. Considering candidate images critical to vote choice, these authors were interested in viewers' perceptions of the candidates as people. Disaggregating voters' responses to the open-ended questions into subcomponents of candidate images, they found that Ford and Carter were primarily being judged—and not necessarily favorably—in terms of competence and trust. Following the first debate, references to competence (particularly about Ford) showed the most systematic increase. These references were largely positive for Ford and negative for Carter (the president's Eastern Europe gaffe, of course, would not occur until the second debate), thus possibly adding to the image of the incumbent as a competent and effective leader. According to the authors, these general shifts in the frequency of such comments (about both candidates) suggested an important debate effect.[61] We will discuss more evidence of the link between debates and candidate images in the next chapter.

Studying the candidates' communication styles, Joslyn, as discussed above, was primarily interested in the nominees' behavior and strategies. For the individual candidates, he found no particularly distinctive use of partisan appeals by any of the debaters, with the lone exception of Jimmy Carter.[62] In both years, 1976 and 1980, Carter relied more on partisan appeals than his opponent. Particularly in the latter year, this may indicate that Carter pinned his flagging hopes of reelection on the loyalty of the numerically superior Democratic electorate.

Apart from Joslyn, another study has used content analysis to probe the candidates' strategies in the 1980 debate.[63] The goal of that research was to assess specifically the various strategies applied by the participants on the basis of what was said during the encounters. The focus was on comparative analysis of debates in two industrialized Western nations, the United States and the Federal Republic of Germany. The major findings were that the styles of the participants in both countries were rather personalized (partially corroborating Joslyn's results) and dependent on whether one was the incumbent or the challenger. The similarities between the two countries are, in one sense, surprising given the differing electoral systems (a separate presidential vote in the United States and a parliamentary system in West Germany). One might have expected a personalized debate style in the United States but a more institutional approach (centering on parties and platforms) in West Germany.

This study combining content analyses of American and German political debates represents an intersection between two very different traditions of debate research. While studies of American presidential debates only rarely investigate the content of each event, such analysis is the rule in West Germany. It is possible, therefore, that we might learn something about candidates' strategies and voters' reactions in the American context by considering some of the most important work done on debates in the Federal Republic. At the very least, we may gain some insights into useful directions in which our own research might profitably follow.

CONTENT ANALYSIS IN A FOREIGN SETTING: STUDIES OF LEADERSHIP DEBATES IN WEST GERMANY

The 1972 West German general election provides a starting point for much of the debating literature in that country. Kendall L. Baker and

Helmut Norpoth, for example, content analyzed the 1972 leadership debates and reported that information gain did occur and that the debates primarily affected viewers' evaluations of the opposition (nongoverning) parties.[64] In addition, they found that the winner of the debate series received a greater net improvement of his vote share among debate viewers, whereas the losers of the debates (there were four participants representing four different parties) were found to have picked up support among nonviewers. Still, despite these findings, Baker and Norpoth admitted that they were unable to demonstrate conclusively the links between debate content and viewers' responses. Unfortunately, they could not determine, on the basis of their data, whether there would have been a shift in voting behavior among debate viewers and nonviewers independent of debate effects.

Comparing the 1972 and 1976 German debates, Baker et al. found a general lack of agreement between the political content of the debates and the recall of this content by their respondents.[65] They suggested that the politicians with the most positive personal style were most likely, all else being equal, to be viewed as the debate winner. This suggests further that some types of appeals are more readily stored and recalled by viewers and that German audiences may be "turned off" by attacking, overly critical debating techniques.

In another extensive analysis of the 1972 West German debates, Hans-Jürgen Weiss was guided by two major questions.[66] First, he was interested in whether or not debates are beneficial to German democracy. For a debate to serve the democratic process, as noted above, it must provide the audience with new and useful political information. If, on the other hand, such an event is solely utilized by the participants as a means of selling themselves and their parties, then Weiss argued that it does not benefit electoral democracy. Instead, he said, it manipulates, but does not enlighten, the voter.

Weiss corroborated Baker and Norpoth's study, finding that the 1972 debates apparently *did* provide some political information: participants did talk about specific campaign issues. At the same time, however, the participants' behavior in these events, as well as the entire organization of the debates, served to "personalize" the encounters and to provide the politicians with the opportunity to campaign for votes (and not always with appeals to substantive concerns).

With respect to the audience, Weiss' analysis of the reception, use, and effects of political debates pointed to two important discoveries. First, voters' relative attention to candidates' themes did not necessarily vary with the frequency of statements about a given issue. Second, voters were willing to listen to—and were able to understand—not only the arguments of their favorite politicians, but also those of the candidates they disliked. Despite these findings, Weiss' main conclusion was that debates result in reinforcement of partisanship and some minor opinion change, but have no significant behavioral effects (i.e., have no direct impact on the vote choice). In concluding, he argued that a systematic and conclusive link between debate content and voters' responses is still needed.

Another study employing content analysis dealt specifically with debate strategies and their impact on West German audiences.[67] Guided by Weiss' argument that a link needs to be found between debate content and survey data, Peter R. Schrott utilized content analysis to derive measures of the strategies implemented by the West German party leaders between 1972 and 1987. He then linked these data to viewers' survey responses.

Presumably, a politician's goal in a debate is to fare best and gain votes through a convincing performance. Each participant wants to improve his or her own image and, at the same time, try to damage the opponent's reputation.[68] To achieve this, party leaders follow succinct strategies that are developed and outlined by the candidate and his or her campaign staff. Following Martel, five broad strategies are defined: sell, defend, attack, ignore, and "me too . . . me better."[69]

It is assumed, for example, that politicians who "sell" themselves are doing so by making positive statements about their own candidacy, their achievements in office, their party goals, and their political views. A politician using a defensive strategy will display the same traits, but more in response to a hostile opponent. An attacking strategy means that politicians address their opponent(s) in a negative way. The "me too . . . me better" approach focuses on positive statements by politicians about themselves as well as about the opposition (making it clear, of course, that their own candidacy is superior).

Since a debate in West Germany, unlike those in the United States, is an interaction between several politicians, it may be nearly impossible to pursue a pure strategy in the German context (there are, after all, multiple opponents, one of whom might even be a potential coalition partner). Instead, mixed strategies are expected and, thus, no politician is assumed to convey a purely positive or negative image. Nevertheless, Schrott argues that the overall balance of positive and negative references should still allow the researcher to infer the general strategy of each individual participant.

Quantifying the positive and negative references yielded data for assessing overall debate performance; these were then aggregated and used to test whether it was indeed the candidates' performance that determined who won the debate. The results were rather strong, pointing once again to a "positivity" effect in debate strategies. The more positive and upbeat a politician's approach, the more likely he was to be depicted as the winner.[70]

Interestingly, in the West German setting, content analyses in debate research are usually applied for two reasons. Obviously, they are used to derive information about the communicator, in terms of his or her personality, strategy, agenda, etc., But, in addition to asking *what* was said by the candidates, German researchers also ask how and about whom it was said, thus attempting to incorporate part of Lasswell's paradigm of mass media research.[71] German researchers deal not only with the democratic perspective on debates (i.e., determining whether or not any substantive content has been provided) but also collect information on the candidates themselves—their attitudes, issue positions, and overall performance in a difficult and competitive situation. Analyses of actual debate content are then compared to what the audience remembers in order to determine what effects the debate apparently had on its viewers. Thus, German research is focused on both sides of the communication "partnership": the communicators and their audience.

CONCLUSION

We leave the important questions posed above still, to a large extent, unanswered. Nevertheless, content-analytical research in the United States and Europe has provided some valuable evidence with which to begin developing answers. Debates do provide substantive information, apparently more so than campaign advertisements and speeches. Candidates in debates do speak to the issues, often clearly and specifically. One can certainly defend the argument that debates are good for democratic self-government.

Nevertheless, before we assume that presidential debates are the ultimate solution to voter ignorance and apathy, we must come to grips with some other results. As Ellsworth noted, candidates are much better at declaring issue positions than they are at analyzing problems and presenting possible solutions to them. Moreover, much of the discussion that is recorded as substantive may actually consist of vague symbolic appeals that provide little information of value to the rational voter.

Finally, it may not be enough that debates provide substantive insights if voters' recollections are dominated by non-substantive post-debate media coverage. Clearly, the relative service of debates to electoral democracy remains an open issue that requires further study.

The same might be said of the use of content analysis to explore candidate strategies and their success in appealing to voters. Much of the current evidence, while intriguing, is limited. Apparently, for example, "ganging up" on the frontrunner may be a wise strategy in multi-candidate primary season debates—at least we find that the strategy paid dividends to Albert Gore, Jesse Jackson, and, to a lesser extent, Gary Hart during one debate in 1988. In addition, if evidence from West Germany can be generalized, a candidate may well be advised, as the song goes, to accentuate the positive. Perhaps public dissatisfaction with Jimmy Carter's shrill and attacking style in his debate with Ronald Reagan in 1980 is evidence that this phenomenon applies to American debates as well.

Finally, more use must be made of content analysis in linking candidates' statements to voters' responses. Only then can we truly tease out the relative impact of debaters' arguments, media analyses, and voters' predispositions in producing debate effects. In short, content analysis is a valuable and, if performed carefully, methodologically valid tool for the study of political communication and, more specifically, American presidential debates.

THE FUTURE OF CONTENT-ANALYTICAL DEBATE RESEARCH

From this short review of the various content analyses in debate research, the lack of cohesive and comparable studies (and thus results) becomes evident. Common to all content analyses is the demonstration that some issues were discussed, and hence, some information must have been transmitted. Nevertheless, the only study to demonstrate a direct relationship between content and audience reactions didn't make use of the candidates' issue-oriented statements, but rather the interaction between the participants.[72] Thus, we do not yet know whether and how the issues discussed actually translate into information gain. And the most important shortcoming (at least for democratic theorists) is that no study has yet attempted to measure the *amount* of information disseminated by these events. Unfortunately, content analyses of presidential debates have not yet provided all the relevant answers.

A second critical issue involves the standardization of categories in debate research. We might illustrate this point by displaying results from several different content analyses focusing on the same debates. The analyses were conducted by four research groups using separate coding schemes (and therefore different categories) to describe what was said in the presidential debates of 1960, 1976, and 1980.

Table 3.1 compares data coded by Joslyn[73] and by Meadow and Jackson-Beeck[74] from the Kennedy–Nixon debates in 1960. Even at first glance it is evident that the results differ rather substantially. To be sure, the research questions are different in each case. Joslyn is interested in how candidates frame issues and who they address in their communication efforts. Meadow and Jackson-Beeck, on the other hand, are more concerned with the evolution of issues over time. Thus, one could argue that different research questions demand different strategies and should therefore achieve different results. In that sense, the use of separate coding schemes (in one case counting the number of times an issue is mentioned, in the other recording the percentage of references as a proportion of total verbiage) seems quite reasonable.

Turning to Table 3.2 however, this argument becomes somewhat weaker. This table compares three studies of the content of the 1976 Carter–Ford debates (two conducted by the authors above, and the other presented by Miller and MacKuen).[75] While it is true that Miller and MacKuen have a different research concern than Joslyn (or Meadow and Jackson-Beeck for that matter), they employ a strategy similar to that used by Joslyn. They, too, record the percentage of references to each issue as a proportion of all discourse. Looking at this table, however, it is clear that there is little hope of assessing intercoder reliability. The authors may use the same basic strategy, but their categories are not very comparable.

Finally, in Table 3.3 we compare one of our own analyses of the 1980 Reagan–Carter presidential debate[76] to that of Joslyn and, again, do not find much resemblance. While we record 12 percent of all candidate statements as references to social groups (e.g., blacks, women, senior citizens, etc.), Joslyn places only about half that percentage in this category. Although it would seem to be a fairly self-explanatory classification, these two studies are clearly defining and coding references to social groups in very different ways.

This is by no means to say that Joslyn's analysis is "incorrect" or that ours is "right." Rather, we simply employ different analytical tools, different coding schemes, and even different categories. And that is a

Table 3.1
Content Analyses of the 1960 Kennedy–Nixon Debates

Joslyn (First Debate)

Categories	% of References
Partisan	27.1
Groups	13.8
Personal Attributes	9.8
Issues	
Salience	11.3
Vague	40.6
Specific	12.7
Unclassified	5.3
N	?

Meadow/Jackson-Beeck

Categories	# of Specific Issues	# of Words	% of Words
Domestic			
Government	20	5,702	53
Health	1	147	2
Education	5	582	5
Welfare	1	99	1
Economics	12	2,757	26
Foreign Affairs/ Defense	6	932	8
Procedure			
Debate Formalities	34	476	4
Participant Pass	1	4	–
Total	80	10,699	99

Note: Some references may be represented in multiple categories.
Sources: Joslyn (1984) and Meadow and Jackson-Beeck (1978)

Table 3.2
Content Analyses of the 1976 Carter–Ford Debates

Joslyn (First Debate)		Miller and MacKuen	
Categories	% of References	Categories	% of References
Partisan	7.4	Partisan Preferences	5.2
Groups	7.3	Group Preferences	4.1
Personal Attributes	10.9	Personality	5.1
Issues		Domestic Issues	16.5
Salience	8.0	Government Trust	11.3
Vague	31.5		
Specific	30.8	Economics	21.6
Unclassified	4.0	Foreign Issues	22.7
N	?	Competence	4.1
		Previous Record	9.3
		N	?

Meadow/Jackson-Beeck (First Debate)

Categories	# of Specific Issues	# of Words	% of Words
Domestic			
Government	39	7,500	54
Economics	25	4,292	31
Resources	5	1,210	9
Law	1	143	1
Foreign Affairs/ Defense	(Not applicable: debate on domestic issues)		
Procedure			
Debate Formalities	28	617	4
Total	98	13,762	99

Sources: Joslyn (1984), Meadow and Jackson-Beeck (1978), Miller and MacKuen (1979)

Table 3.3
Content Analyses of the 1980 Reagan–Carter Debate

Joslyn		Schrott	
Categories	% of References	Categories	% of References
Partisan	4.8	Ideology	2.0
Groups	6.1	Social Groups	12.0
Personal Attributes	12.9	Women	(4.0)
		Blacks	(2.5)
Issues		Elderly	(2.0)
Salience	12.7	Domestic Policy	38.0
Vague	33.8		
Specific	28.3	Economic Policy	(14.0)
		Jobs	(6.0)
Unclassified	6.4	Social Policy	(8.5)
		Defense Spending	(1.5)
N	?	Foreign Policy	23.0
		World Peace	(1.5)
		Nat'l Security	(6.0)
		USSR	(5.0)
		Middle East	(3.0)
		Moral Qualities	8.0
		Government/Party Management	17.5
		Unspecific	(4.5)
		Performance in Office	(5.0)
		Campaign Style	(6.0)
		N (of References)	260

Sources: Joslyn (1984) and Schrott (1984)

major problem if we wish to use previously gathered data for further empirical analysis (as is done frequently by scholars in other areas). How can such data be accepted by social scientists if no clear evidence supports its reliability or validity? Indeed, this problem may help to explain the reluctance of so many researchers to use content analysis in debate research. While we know that content analysis is a proven analytical tool for collecting data on a number of research questions, we also see analyses on the same topic producing completely different data from virtually the same source.

Moreover, even if these analyses are used only in a descriptive way, it would still be helpful to have comparable measures. For example, one study discussed above counts only three issues per paragraph while the other study counts each mention of an issue no matter how often it occurs in any given paragraph. Both ask viewers open-ended questions in order to tap their learning and evaluations of various issues.

If voters record and encode information in blocks, then the first content-analytical technique may better reveal the debate as the voter actually sees/hears it. If, on the other hand, voters are sensitive to each individual mention of an issue, regardless of how often such mentions occur, then the first technique is woefully inadequate. In that case, the second method would provide more useful information. This may be a rather simple example, but it is a serious problem that most analysts do not even employ the same unit of analysis in their research. Thus, as a first step, researchers should agree on a common unit, in addition to at least some standardized categories.

Another shortcoming is the lack of statistical analysis of content data. It seems that for many researchers a simple description of debate content is sufficient. This may be due to the questionable acceptance of content analysis as a systematic (and scientific) methodological tool. However, various rigorous quantitative approaches exist to study the amount of information in a message and to study contingencies within a text.[77] One of the first and most interesting approaches to using contingency analysis can be found in the early work of Charles E. Osgood.[78]

Finally, the focus of content-analytical debate studies should be directed on gathering data. By that, we mean that data are needed that can be linked to survey (and other) information to learn more about various communication-theoretical problems. Such data could be used in time series studies to observe developments in communication styles and in electoral campaigns in general. Compared to other campaign data (advertisements, speeches, etc.), this would enhance our understanding of the success and evolution of professional campaign strategies.

Such data could also be used to test whether or not debates serve as agenda-setting events, and whether and under what conditions they engender reinforcement of uncommitted partisans and/or conversion of the truly undecided. Only a direct link between content data and survey data can tell us conclusively about these effects. A wealth of data, much of it already collected from previous years, remains to be explored.

NOTES

1. V. O. Key, Jr., *The Responsible Electorate* (Cambridge, MA: Harvard University Press, 1966).

2. Myles Martel, *Political Campaign Debates: Images, Strategies, and Tactics* (New York: Longman, 1983), p. 19.

3. Ibid., 99–115.

4. Werner Holly, Peter Kuehn, and Ulrich Pueschel, *Politische Fernsehdiskussionen* (Tübingen: Max Niemeyer Verlag, 1986).

5. The evaluative aspect of political content is of special importance in the German "tradition" of debate research. See Kendall L. Baker, Helmut Norpoth, and Klaus Schoenbach, "Die Fernsehdiskussionen der Spitzenkandidaten vor den Bundestagswahlen 1972 und 1976," *Publizistik* 26 (1981): 530–44; Kendall L. Baker and Helmut Norpoth, "Candidates on Television: The 1972 Electoral Debates in West Germany," *Public Opinion Quarterly* 45 (1981): 329–45; Helmut Norpoth and Kendall L. Baker, "Politiker unter sich am Bildschirm: Die Konfrontation von Personen und Sachthemen in den Fernsehdiskussionen, 1972–1980," in Max Kaase and Hans-Dieter Klingemann, eds., *Wahlen und Politisches System* (Opladen, West Germany: Westdeutscher Verlag, 1983); and Peter R. Schrott, *The West German Television Debates: Candidate's Strategies and Voters' Reactions* (Ph.D. dissertation, State University of New York, Stony Brook, 1986).

6. Robert G. Meadow and Marilyn Jackson-Beeck, "A Comparative Perspective on Presidential Debates: Issue Evolution in 1960 and 1976," in George F. Bishop, Robert G. Meadow, and Marilyn Jackson-Beeck, eds., *The Presidential Debates: Media, Electoral, and Policy Perspectives* (New York: Praeger, 1978), pp. 33–58.

7. For discussion of debate strategies, see Marjorie Randon Hershey, "The Campaign and the Media," in Gerald M. Pomper, ed., *The Election of 1988: Reports and Interpretations* (Chatham, NJ: Chatham House, 1989); John H. Kessel, *Presidential Campaign Politics*, 3d ed. (Chicago: Dorsey Press, 1988), p. 189; and Martel, *Political Campaign Debates*.

8. Jack W. Germond and Jules Witcover, "Presidential Debates: An Overview," in Austin Ranney, ed., *The Past and Future of Presidential Debates* (Washington, D.C.: American Enterprise Institute, 1979), pp. 191–205.

9. Sidney Kraus, *Televised Presidential Debates and Public Policy* (Hillsdale, NJ: Lawrence Erlbaum and Associates, 1988), p. 154.

10. Bernard Berelson, *Content Analysis in Communication Research* (Glencoe, IL: Free Press, 1952).

11. Ibid., 18.

12. Among others, Berelson points to a study by Harold D. Lasswell, *Analyzing the Content of Mass Communication: A Brief Introduction* (Washington, D.C.: Library of Congress, 1942).

13. Siegfried Kracauer, "The Challenge of Qualitative Content Analysis," *Public Opinion Quarterly* 16 (1952): 631–42.

14. Ibid., 638.

15. Ibid., 631.

16. Ithiel de Sola Pool, ed., *Trends in Content Analysis* (Urbana: University of Illinois Press, 1959).

17. For an overview, see Berelson, *Content Analysis in Communication Research*; Ole R. Holsti, *Content Analysis for the Social Sciences and Humanities* (Reading, MA: Addison-Wesley, 1969); and Klaus Krippendorff, *Content Analysis: An Introduction to Its Methodology* (Beverly Hills, CA: Sage Publications, 1980).

18. George Gerbner, Ole R. Holsti, Klaus Krippendorff, William J. Paisley, and Philip Stone, eds., *The Analysis of Communication Content: Developments in Scientific Theory and Computer Technology* (New York: John Wiley and Sons, 1969), p. xiii.

19. Klaus Krippendorff, "Models of Messages: Three Prototypes," in Gerbner et al., *The Analysis of Communication Content*, p. 103.

20. Ole R. Holsti, "Introduction," in Gerbner et al., *The Analysis of Communication Content*.

21. Paul Ekman, Wallace V. Friesen, and Thomas G. Taussig, "VID-R and SCAN: Tools and Methods for the Automated Analysis of Visual Records," in Gerbner et al., *The Analysis of Communication Content*, pp. 297–312.

22. See Philip J. Stone, "Improved Quality of Content-Analysis Categories: Computerized-Disambiguation Rules for High Frequency English Words," in Gerbner et al., *The Analysis of Communication Content*, pp. 199–221.

23. Krippendorff, *Content Analysis*.

24. Ibid., 11.

25. Robert Philip Weber, *Basic Content Analysis* (Beverly Hills, CA: Sage Publications, 1985).

26. Ibid., 76.

27. See chapter 4 for a complete review of individual effects research.

28. Martel, *Political Campaign Debates*.

29. John W. Ellsworth, "Rationality and Campaigning: A Content Analysis of the 1960 Presidential Campaign Debates," *Western Political Quarterly* 18 (1965): 794–802.

30. Ibid.

31. Ibid., 795–96.

32. Meadow and Jackson-Beeck, "A Comparative Perspective on Presidential Debates."

33. The differences between the debates (in terms of content) were minor and understandable. More foreign policy references were made in 1960 than in the first 1976 encounter, which was limited—by its rules—to domestic issues. And discussion of resources got far more attention in 1976 than in 1960,

presumably because of concerns over the energy shortages of the 1970s. See Ibid., 42.

34. Ibid., 45.

35. Ibid.

36. Arthur H. Miller and Michael MacKuen, "Informing the Electorate: Effects of the 1976 Presidential Debates," in Sidney Kraus, ed., *The Great Debates: Carter vs. Ford, 1976* (Bloomington: Indiana University Press, 1979), pp. 269–97.

37. Ibid., 273.

38. Ibid., 294.

39. Ibid., 292.

40. Richard Joslyn, *Mass Media and Elections* (Reading, MA: Addison-Wesley, 1984).

41. For the coding scheme, he refers to an earlier study. See Richard Joslyn, "The Content of Political Spot Ads," *Journalism Quarterly* 57 (1980): 92–98.

42. Joslyn, *Mass Media and Elections*, p. 48.

43. Ibid., 52.

44. David J. Lanoue and Peter R. Schrott, "Voters' Reactions to Televised Presidential Debates: Measurement of the Source and Magnitude of Opinion Change," *Political Psychology* 10 (1989): 275–85.

45. Hans-Dieter Klingemann, "Standardcode zur Verschlüsselung der Einstellungen zu den politischen Parteien in der Bundesrepublik Deutschland" (Mimeo, ZUMA, Mannheim, West Germany, 1976).

46. Klaus Schoenbach, "Wahlprogramme und Wählermeinung," *Politische Vierteljahresschrift* 19 (1977): 360–407.

47. Klaus Schoenbach and Rudolf Wildenmann, "Election Themes and the Prestige Newspapers," in Karl H. Cerny, ed., *Germany at the Polls* (Washington, D.C.: American Enterprise Institute, 1978), pp. 169–93.

48. Peter R. Schrott, "The Content and Consequences of the 1980 Televised Debates in West Germany and the United States" (Unpublished manuscript, State University of New York, 1984); Lanoue and Schrott, "Voters' Reactions,"; and David J. Lanoue and Peter R. Schrott, "The Effects of Primary Season Debates on Public Opinion," *Political Behavior* 11 (1989): 289–306.

49. Baker and Norpoth, "Candidates on Television"; Baker, Norpoth, and Schoenbach, "Die Fernsehdiskussionen"; and Schrott, *The West German Television Debates*.

50. Hershey, "The Campaign and the Media."

51. David J. Lanoue and Peter R. Schrott, "The Effects of Primary Season Debates" (Paper presented at the 1988 meeting of the American Political Science Association, Washington, D.C.).

52. Martel, *Political Campaign Debates*.

53. In communication research, especially in the West German tradition, content analyses are the bases for studying the communications process. The

use of such analysis as the primary method is common to virtually every major communications journal.

54. Schrott, "The Content and Consequences."

55. Miller and MacKuen had an extensive content analysis table in a previous version of their chapter; in addition, the authors (Lanoue and Schrott, "The Effects of Primary Season Debates") had to drop their discussion of content analysis for the revised version of the paper.

56. Edwin S. Shneidman, "The Logic of Politics," in Leo Arons and Mark A. May, *Television and Human Behavior* (New York: Appleton-Century-Crofts, 1963).

57. Ibid., 178.

58. Shneidman's method to derive systematically a speaker's logical style makes use of three concepts: the "ideologic" (styles of thinking), which represents the latent stimulus in a message; the "contralogic" (method of rationalizing logical idiosyncrasies); and the "psychologic" (psychological traits relevant to styles of thinking, i.e., that part of the personality that the speaker conveys). For a more detailed description of the method, see Ibid., 183–85.

59. Ibid., 185.

60. Ibid., 188.

61. Miller and MacKuen, "Informing the Electorate," p. 279.

62. Joslyn, *Mass Media and Elections*, p. 51. This, however, is not corroborated by another (unpublished) content analysis. See Schrott, "The Content and Consequences."

63. Schrott, "The Content and Consequences."

64. Baker and Norpoth, "Candidates on Television," using the coding scheme developed by Klingemann, "Standardcode."

65. Baker, Norpoth, and Schoenbach, "Die Fernsehdiskussionen."

66. Hans-Jürgen Weiss, *Wahlkampf im Fernsehen: Untersuchung zur Rolle der grossen Fernsehdebatten im Bundestagswahlkampf 1972* (West Berlin: Volker Spiess Verlag, 1976).

67. Peter R. Schrott, "Wahlkampfdebatten im Fernsehen von 1972 bis 1987: Politikerstrategien und Wählerreaktion," in Max Kaase and Hans-Dieter Klingemann, eds., *Wahlen und politisches System: Analysen aus Anlass der Bundestagswahl* (Opladen, West Germany: Westdeutscher Verlag, 1987); see also Peter R. Schrott, "West German Televised Debates from 1972 to 1987" (Paper presented at the annual meeting of the American Political Science Association, Atlanta, 1989).

68. Steven J. Wayne, *The Road to the White House* (New York: St. Martin's Press, 1980).

69. Myles Martel, a media adviser for Ronald Reagan in 1980, names two broad classes of strategies. One is the "relational" strategy. It determines the mode of conduct in the debate. The second type of strategy concerns the substance: it defines the issues and content areas of the debate. Although the

substance is determined to a large degree by the moderator of the debates and by the questions asked by panelists, the debaters generally find enough leeway to direct the debates' subject matter toward their own specific interests. Martel, *Political Campaign Debates*.

70. The "winner" variable was then found to exert an indirect effect (through candidate evaluations), but also a direct (reinforcement) effect on the vote. See Peter R. Schrott, "Electoral Consequences of 'Winning' Televised Campaign Debates," *Public Opinion Quarterly* (forthcoming 1991).

71. Lasswell, *Analyzing the Content of Mass Communication*.

72. Schrott, *The West German Televised Debates*.

73. Joslyn, *Mass Media and Elections*, p. 49.

74. Meadow and Jackson-Beeck, "A Comparative Perspective on Presidential Debates," p. 42.

75. Miller and MacKuen, "Informing the Electorate," footnote 13.

76. Schrott, "The Content and Consequences." For another treatment, see Patricia Riley and Thomas A. Hollihan, "The 1980 Presidential Debates: A Content Analysis of the Issues and Arguments," *Speaker and Gavel* 18 (1981): 47–59.

77. See Klaus Krippendorff, *Information Theory: Structural Models for Qualitative Data* (Beverly Hills, CA: Sage, 1986).

78. Charles E. Osgood, "The Representational Model and Relevant Research Methods," in de Sola Pool, *Trends in Content Analysis*, pp. 33–88.

4

THE IMPACT OF PRESIDENTIAL DEBATES ON VIEWERS

It is impossible to talk about the impact of presidential debates without referring to the purposes of which they are intended. To the candidates, such events are designed to shore up support among the faithful, convert the undecided, and discourage the opposition. To their longtime sponsor, the nonpartisan League of Women Voters, debates are a way to educate the public and generate a larger turnout on election day. To journalists, these quadrennial confrontations are dramatic media events that must be analyzed and interpreted for an eager audience. And finally, to voters, debates may serve any number of functions, including guidance in how to vote, reassurance about choices already made, or even satisfaction of a need for drama and excitement in the clash of political superstars.[1]

Given the diversity of these objectives, it is no wonder that social scientists have considered the effects of presidential debates from so many angles. In the present chapter we will divide these effects into three separate, but related, categories: attitudinal, cognitive, and behavioral. Within these categories, however, we will investigate a number of different concerns. Attitudinal effects will include not only fluctuations in feelings toward the candidates and issues, but also reinforcement of prior preferences and the effects of debate watching on political efficacy and system support. Similarly, cognitive effects will encompass the acquisition of factual information about the political world, as well as viewers' recognition of the issue positions of the candidates. Finally, behavioral effects will include the power of presidential debates to influence actual voting choices.

Figure 4.1
Social Learning Theory

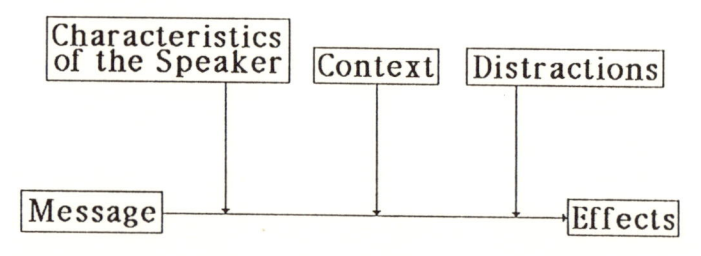

```
 Characteristics
  of the Speaker    Context    Distractions
        |              |             |
        |              |             |
  Message  ———————————————————————→  Effects
```

Central to these questions, of course, are the processes by which opinions are changed and information is gained. This chapter will attempt to deal with some of the more important of these questions. For example, does exposure to debates have a direct effect on viewers' attitudes and information levels, or is the interpretive role of the media paramount? How are the effects of debates mediated by such variables as partisanship, political interest, and socioeconomic status? And, perhaps most important, are the effects of debates short-lived, or do they persist over time?

ATTITUDINAL EFFECTS: DEBATES AND OPINION CHANGE

Presidential debates, like political advertisements and stump speeches, are a form of persuasive political communication. Above all else, each candidate is engaged in an effort to convince voters that he or she deserves their support. Therefore, if we are to understand the effects of debates on voters, we must first understand the nature, preconditions, and limits of attitude change. Armed with that knowledge, we will be better able to put the research findings of the past thirty years into perspective. Perhaps many of the "surprising" discoveries of earlier studies will then make more sense.

The pioneering work in attitude change theory was published in the early 1950s by Carl Hovland and his associates.[2] These studies were rooted in behavioralism or *social learning theory*. (See Figure 4.1.) Hovland and his colleagues determined that attitude change took place in three steps: attention to a persuasive message, comprehension of that message, and finally, acceptance of the argument itself. A person's openness to new arguments, according to this model, depends on a variety of internalized cues learned over the course of one's life.

A large body of research has focused on the factors influencing each of Hovland's three stages, particularly attention and acceptance. A number of studies, for example, have dealt with the importance of the *source* of a persuasive message. Often, it turns out, the characteristics of the speaker are as important as the substance of his or her arguments. Researchers have found that an audience will be most amenable to persuasion when the speaker appears to be free of bias, to possess expertise in the relevant subject matter, and to have a physically attractive or commanding presence.[3]

The applications of this research to presidential debates have not been lost on politicians or their handlers. Richard Nixon's unattractive appearance during the first 1960 debate supposedly blunted the effectiveness of his substantive appeal. Since then, politicians and their staffs have come to believe that even the most trivial differences in candidates' visual images might affect voters' reactions to a debate. Indeed, during at least one presidential campaign, the shorter candidate requested (and received) permission to stand on a small riser during debates in order to compensate for his disadvantage in height.[4]

Learning models of attitude change have also emphasized the characteristics of the message itself (considering, for example, the effectiveness of fear-arousing appeals), as well as the context in which the message is delivered. The latter point is one of potential interest in the study of debates, but one that has been largely ignored in the literature. Research in social psychology has found that distractions (such as audience applause, booing, or heckling) can influence the effectiveness of a persuasive message.[5] As debate hall audiences become more vocal in their reactions to the candidates, we might ask what effect their outbursts have on viewers at home. Interestingly, we find that the winners of one primary debate in 1988 were the candidates whose presentations were most often interrupted by applause and supportive laughter.[6]

Consistency theories of attitude change contend that inconsistent opinions cause uneasiness, and that most people will do whatever is necessary to alleviate this anxiety. The most widely known of these theories is Leon A. Festinger's concept of "Cognitive Dissonance."[7] According to Festinger, dissonance occurs when people are faced with information or arguments that contradict previously held attitudes. The theory predicts that people will react to such dissonance in one of three ways: first, they might decrease the importance of the dissonant element (ignoring or downplaying contradictory information); second, they might increase the importance of consonant elements (elevating and emphasizing more

Figure 4.2
Cognitive Dissonance Theory

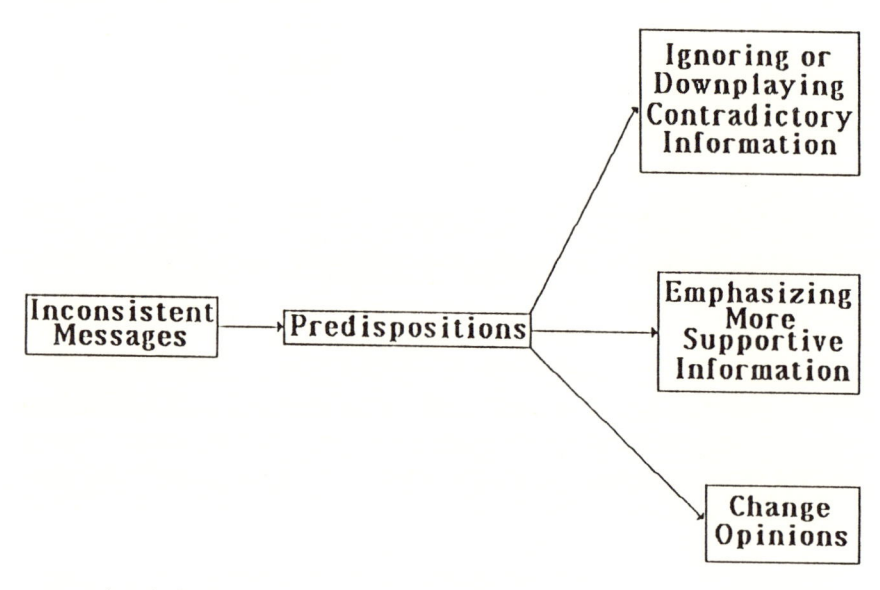

Inconsistent Messages → Predispositions →
- Ignoring or Downplaying Contradictory Information
- Emphasizing More Supportive Information
- Change Opinions

supportive information); finally, and most rarely, actual opinion change might occur in an effort to reduce the anxiety caused by dissonance-producing facts and arguments.[8] (See Figure 4.2.)

It should be apparent that consistency theory is quite relevant to the study of presidential debates. If voters prize cognitive consistency above all else, we should expect debate-induced opinion change to be fairly limited. Viewers' reactions to a debate would probably conform with their prior leanings. Supporters of a given politician should be most likely to denigrate the efforts of opposition candidates, regardless of their actual debate performance. Similarly, such voters might choose to emphasize portions of the debate in which their preferred candidate made his or her strongest showing. While opinion change is, of course, possible, it would likely be attenuated by this drive toward consistency.

Social judgment theory recognizes that attitudes have both a cognitive and emotional component.[9] It assumes that people have an underlying ordering of preferences related to any given situation (such as deciding how to vote in an election). Within this "attitude dimension," options may be placed into one of three categories: the latitude of acceptance (where attitude change is likely), the latitude of noncommitment (where it is possible), and the latitude of rejection (where it is very rare).

The size of these latitudes (and thus the amount of opinion change that is likely to occur) is influenced by a number of factors. Attitudinal "anchors," for example, are "particularly potent reference points" that influence a person's preferences.[10] In the case of presidential debates, party identification may serve as an important anchor, limiting potential attitude change by relegating all candidates and issues (other than those favored by the preferred party) to the latitude of rejection. In addition, the size of the latitude of rejection is influenced by a person's "ego involvement"—that is, how much emotional attachment he or she has to a given opinion. The greater the ego involvement, the smaller the likelihood of attitude change.[11]

Like consistency theory, social judgment theory would also predict a relatively small effect for presidential debates on public opinion. Indeed, those citizens most apt to watch debates (politically interested voters) are probably those least likely to be influenced by them. In many cases, their political attitudes are central to their self-image, and their high ego involvement with politics would probably negate the persuasive efforts of the candidates. Similarly, strong partisans are likely to reject the appeals of "opposition" candidates out of hand. Debates, it would seem, should have their greatest effect on the attitudes of those voters with low political interest and/or weak partisan ties. Further, they would probably be most effective early in a campaign, before voters begin to develop strong attachments to either of the candidates.

The *functional theory* of attitude formation and change describes attitudes in terms of the purposes they serve for the individual.[12] According to one popular version of this theory, opinions generally serve one of four functions. "Instrumental attitudes" aid a person's social adjustment. "The child," says Daniel Katz, "develops favorable attitudes toward those objects in his world which are associated with satisfaction of his needs and unfavorable attitudes toward objects which thwart him or punish him."[13] Party and candidate loyalties, for example, might reflect a person's desire to fit in with family, peer group, or co-workers.

"Ego defensive attitudes" are developed as defense mechanisms (an idea based on the works of Freud and his successors). They serve to alleviate anxiety, and allow people to avoid facing inner conflicts. One commonly cited example of this phenomenon would occur if a person developed racist attitudes in order to project his or her own self-hatred upon others.

Attitudes serve a "knowledge function" when they help someone to organize or evaluate information. Attitudes toward the political parties, for instance, help the voter to deal with the flood of political data that flows to every citizen during an election year. Voters may use long-standing attitudes about parties or candidates as informational "short cuts" to make the voting decision more manageable. For example, rather than conduct a costly and time-consuming investigation of the candidates in a given campaign, a citizen might decide to vote for the Democrat because he likes that party's traditional commitment to "the little guy."

Finally, "value expressive attitudes" have "the function of giving positive expression to a person's central values and self-concept."[14] Such attitudes help a person define who he or she is and gain satisfaction from the expression of that identity. Thus, even people whose cognitive understanding of politics is quite limited may hold and express strong attitudes toward political candidates and issues.

According to the functional perspective, attitude change depends on which purpose a certain opinion serves in a person's life. In the context of the present study, the specific persuasive appeals of debating candidates may actually influence some viewers and be ignored by others. Instrumental attitudes, for example, will be changed only if the speaker can convince his or her audience that a competing set of preferences will better serve their needs (for belonging, safety, self-esteem, etc.). Attitudes that serve a knowledge function might be changed if the speaker can persuade listeners that their old attitudes are no longer relevant for understanding current affairs. Ego defensive and value expressive attitudes, being rooted in a person's psychological makeup, are far less likely to be altered as the result of a public forum such as a debate.

To be sure, these theories are a great deal more complicated than described above, and we have no doubt done some injury to them in our summaries. Nevertheless, it should be clear that these different viewpoints are essential to the study of presidential debates, and should certainly guide our assessments of debate effects. These theoretical perspectives, of course, are not mutually exclusive—for example, the importance of emotional attachment to attitudes is emphasized in both social judgment theory and functional theory. Moreover, similar phenomena might be accurately predicted by more than one theory. As noted above, both consistency theories and social judgment theory would predict limited effects for debates on viewers. Clearly, however, each of these perspectives can make a unique contribution to helping us come to grips with the findings of previous research.

It should be evident from the preceding discussion that political attitudes are not easily changed. Any early assumptions that presidential

Figure 4.3
Uses and Gratifications Theory

User Needs → Media Offering → User Gratification

debates would serve as turning points in campaigns or that nominees could be made or broken by their performances were unrealistic. A number of factors serve to limit the effectiveness of most persuasive communication, and there is no reason why this should not apply equally to presidential debates. Indeed, studies by social psychologists have even called into question the longevity of some of the opinion change that *has* been observed by researchers (suggesting that the effects of debates, even if profound, might be short-lived).[15]

Before analyzing these effects, we will consider one more theoretical perspective, borrowed this time not from social psychologists, but from students of communication. A number of researchers have considered presidential debates in terms of the "uses and gratifications" they provide to viewers.[16] Daniel Nimmo identifies five major needs that motivate consumers of political information: guidance in how to vote, reinforcement of existing preferences, acquisition of general political information, desire for excitement and political "drama," and desire for supporting material for political discussions and arguments.[17] (See Figure 4.3.)

Candidates may see a debate as an opportunity to convert new supporters, but, as David O. Sears and Steven H. Chaffee point out, voters may watch debates for reasons that have nothing to do with their ultimate electoral decision.[18] Indeed, many will have made an irrevocable choice between the candidates weeks before. Therefore, viewers' reactions to a given debate may well depend on which "needs" motivated them to watch in the first place.

It is, of course, difficult to determine the motivations of those who choose to watch presidential debates. If we rely on respondents' own reports, our data will likely be contaminated by self-serving rationalizations. Viewers may well provide answers that place themselves in the best possible light (claiming an interest in information and issues, for example, rather than a preference for drama and excitement).

By the same token, there are dangers in trying to infer motivations from post-test survey items. Many studies, for example (cited below), have shown information gain to be the major effect of viewing presidential debates. Nevertheless, it is impossible, on that basis, to say with certainty that information gain is a primary gratification sought by debate viewers. It is, of course, possible that many viewers choose to watch the presidential debate because of the drama and excitement of the "head-to-head" battle between political celebrities, and that information gain is simply a by-product of watching. Clearly, the benefits received by viewing such events may have little to do with people's reasons for tuning in.

If we are unable to verify accurately the motivations of those who decide to watch presidential debates, it is still useful to learn the effects of that decision. Are debate watchers information-hungry, rational citizens interested in making the best possible choice between candidates? Or are they passive, star-struck "couch potatoes" whose interest in the debate has been piqued only because of the media's emphasis on the drama of the confrontation? In reality, of course, each of these views represents something of an exaggeration. Nevertheless, it should be evident that the effects of debates on voters will be strongly influenced by the "gratifications" sought by viewers, and that this theoretical framework might help us to understand why some debates seem to "matter" while others appear trivial.

Candidate Evaluations and Candidate Images

One important gratification of debate watching should be the acquisition of information with which to evaluate the candidates. We would, of course, expect candidate images to be closely linked with vote choice. After all, voters presumably cast their ballots for the candidate they find most appealing. There are, however, important differences between these two indicators. Vote choice is a sort of "zero-sum" variable—to pledge a vote to one candidate is to withhold it from the other(s). Any debate-induced vote change that helps one politician automatically hurts his or her opponent(s). In the case of candidate images, on the other hand, the choices are not nearly so clear cut. A debate might improve (or hurt) the images of *all* candidates in the minds of viewers. Similarly, it might help one candidate's standing while having no real effect on that of the other(s).

Unfortunately, the concept of an "image" is fairly elusive, especially compared with an easily measurable phenomenon such as vote choice. More has been done to operationalize the concept than to define it and, as a result, it is often difficult to know if different researchers are writing about the same thing. A number of debate studies have defined images by asking viewers to assess how well certain adjectives (honest, strong, intelligent, etc.) apply to each candidate. Other students of presidential debating have employed semantic differential measures, having subjects place the nominees on a five- or seven-point scale, with opposing descriptions at each endpoint (fair-unfair, positive-negative, passive-active, and so forth). Still other researchers have avoided defining images altogether, simply asking respondents to report "how they feel" toward the candidates, or to rank them on a "feeling thermometer" (where a score of zero suggests very "cold" feelings and a score of 100 represents "warm" thoughts).

However it is defined, the concept of candidate image has been investigated in nearly every election year during which debates have been held. Like most other areas of debate research, the findings have been mixed, with some studies reporting profound debate-induced effects, while others are unable to discern *any* post-debate fluctuations in viewers' attitudes toward the candidates. Nevertheless, it is at least possible to list some of the most interesting findings and present the consensus of current research.

Debate-induced changes in candidate images are often found, but are rarely large. Typically, researchers have found that candidates' composite images are affected, at least temporarily, by their performance in debates. Once again, however, these changes are usually not of a magnitude either to rescue or destroy a candidacy. One example of such limited findings occurred in the wake of Walter Mondale's shocking (and overwhelming) win over Ronald Reagan in their first 1984 debate. In our study of that debate, we found that Mondale's average rating on the 100-point thermometer scale improved by a significant, but hardly earth-shattering, eight points.[19] Other scholars, too, have reported similar effects, some of which are of only borderline statistical significance.[20]

Exceptions, of course, do exist. As noted above, some studies have uncovered no measurable image change. In addition, a few papers have reported rather dramatic shifts. Primary election debates, for instance, seem to have a particularly strong potential to define (or redefine) the images of previously "unknown" contenders.[21]

Post-debate image changes, like changes in candidate preferences, are influenced by media analysis. This argument should be fairly familiar by now. As a whole, voters evaluate candidates differently after having been "contaminated" by the comments of television (and, to a lesser extent, radio and newspaper) analysts. For example, just as television "created" Gerald Ford's image as a "bumbler," it apparently strengthened it through near-endless discussion of his gaffe over Eastern Europe during the second 1976 debate. It has been consistently demonstrated that viewers' impressions of who won a given debate are driven, at least partially, by post-debate reporting.[22] Candidate images, in turn, are closely linked to assessments of winning and losing. Thus, the media apparently have a great deal to say about the personal characteristics voters attribute to presidential candidates as a result of debate watching.

Candidates' images are linked to viewers' evaluations of their personalities, rather than their pronouncements. Ideally, we are told, debates create the possibility of a more rational electorate, one that can learn and evaluate the nominees' stands on the issues and vote accordingly. In reality, though, viewers are far more likely to use debates to gain insight into each candidate's personality and character. Debate-induced changes in candidate evaluations (in both primary and general election debates) have generally been based on perceptions of the politicians' personal qualities rather than their mastery of substance.[23] To be sure, the image/substance dichotomy is somewhat artificial—it is likely that debaters who excel at issue presentation will also improve their reputation for honesty, competence, sincerity, and so on. Nevertheless, as noted in chapter 2, a superior "personal" presentation appears to be more important to voters than accumulation of issue-oriented debating "points."

Winners' images are often helped by debates, but losers aren't necessarily harmed. Reporters tend to see debates in black and white terms. Debates, they believe, have winners and losers, and if winning is inherently beneficial, losing may inevitably prove damaging. Voters, however, may not see debates in the same way. Even if they judge one candidate to have given a superior performance, they may still credit his or her opponent for an intelligent, articulate presentation.

Certainly, if one candidate outshines the other(s), his or her image will likely improve, perhaps dramatically. But since images—unlike vote choices—are not a zero-sum game, there is no reason why the losing candidate must inherently suffer. Indeed, a number of studies have found that even in supposedly one-sided debates (in 1960, 1976, and 1984), the loser's post-debate image changed little, if at all.[24]

Viewers may simply be a great deal more generous with candidates than we might have thought. Once again, of course, some exceptions can be found—Tannenbaum et al., for example, reported a major loss for Richard Nixon after his first debate in 1960,[25] although Saul Ben-Zeev and Irving S. White were able to detect no net damage over the course of the campaign.[26] The consensus, however, seems to indicate that, at least in terms of candidate images, it is much easier to win a debate than it is to lose one.

By and large, general candidate images are, not surprisingly, influenced by many of the same factors that affect specific vote choices. Nevertheless, major differences may be found between the two. First, significant post-debate shifts in candidate images are commonly found, while changes in voters' actual candidate preferences are not. Second, in the case of images, one politician's gain is not necessarily another's loss (whereas changes in vote choice that help one nominee invariably hurt the other). Theories of attitude change, of course, tell us that the most difficult opinions to alter are those that are more specific and central to a person's worldview.[27] Since attitudes about candidates' images are a great deal more amorphous than candidate preferences, it makes sense that they are also somewhat more malleable.

Nevertheless, some problems do remain with research linking debates and candidate evaluations. For one thing, the longevity of debate-induced image change is rarely measured, and is thus open to question. In addition, the lack of a clear, universal definition of candidate images calls into doubt the comparability and generalizability of these findings. Finally, few debate researchers have attempted to demonstrate the links between candidate images and voting behavior, suggesting that their findings may be of questionable substantive significance. Despite these concerns, we assume that candidate images and evaluations influence not only voters' political preferences, but also the strength and persistence of these choices. Thus, it may well be meaningful that presidential debates have the capacity to build up (and possibly tear down) such images.

Reinforcement

Consistency theory argues that our need for cognitive consonance colors our processing of political information. If this is so, then debate watchers may not see the "real" debate occurring between presidential candidates; rather, they may see the debate they *want* to see, the one in which their champion triumphs over the opposition, projecting a more appealing personal style and scoring countless points on issue-oriented exchanges. There is no question that Democratic and Republican viewers are especially prone to name "their" candidate as the debate winner. On the basis of consistency theory, then, we would expect that the major effect of debates on viewers would be reinforcement, as biased assessments of each contest strengthen partisans' confidence in their choice.

One difficulty with searching for this effect is that there is little agreement as to how reinforcement should be defined. Paul R. Hagner and Leroy N. Rieselbach suggest that reinforcement occurs when "the campaign preserves and sustains previously held views" or "when preexisting dispositions seem to influence debate evaluations."[28] In that case, we would report reinforcement effects any time a majority of Democratic identifiers name the Democratic candidate as the debate winner, or whenever most Republican viewers claim victory for the GOP nominee.

We would, however, challenge this viewpoint as inadequate. "Reinforcement implies something more than the preservation of preexisting biases. To say that a debate sustained previously held views is to say that the debate itself had no effect on viewers' attitudes. Strictly speaking, a reinforced bias is a strengthened bias."[29] Reinforcement should be operationalized as a *widening* of the gap between viewers' relative candidate evaluations and/or an *increase* in post-debate agreement between candidates and their supporters on the issues.

Along these lines, other studies have defined reinforcement in terms of a "bonding" between candidates and supporters, during which candidate images move closer in line with candidate preferences. A number of studies, for example, have found that partisans, after viewing a debate, develop a more positive image of the preferred candidate and a more negative view of the opponent. Indeed, one study of presidential debating suggests that voters evaluate candidates primarily on the basis of their personal qualities, and are often unable to distinguish between their positions on the issues.[30] Thus, according to this view, reinforcement takes place not because candidates' supporters are moved by the issue pronouncements of their favored nominee; rather, it occurs because exposure to the debate bonds viewers to "their" candidates in a much more personal way. The preferred politician, fresh from his or her high-pressure, high-stakes battle, gains in the voter's esteem and takes on more favorable characteristics. The "opposition" candidate, on the other hand, may find his or her dissonance-producing arguments falling on deaf ears, and these hostile viewers may even downgrade the nominee's arguments and find fault with him or her personally.

In contrast to these findings, some students of political debating have found that candidate-supporter bonding, while certainly personality-oriented, may also be issue-oriented.[31] A rather simple reading of consistency theory would argue that people wish to maintain balance between their interpersonal relationships and their personal opinions. Either we choose agreeable friends, according to this view, or we mold our own views to match those of the people with whom we associate.[32]

It might therefore be argued that voters choose a candidate on the basis of some combination of factors (party identification, certain specific issue stands, personal style, etc.) and then attempt to set their views in "balance" with those of their champion. Research indicates that in 1976, debate watchers moved closer to their chosen candidates on several of the major issues discussed during the confrontations. Alan Abramowitz notes that such viewers are not acting in accordance with the expectations of "rational actor" theories, which would assume that voters use debates in order to gain information upon which to base their decisions.[33] Rather, their candidate preferences ended up, at least in part, influencing their stands on the issues.

It should be noted that reinforcement effects have not been uncovered in every study of presidential debates. Some research has found that viewers are no more supportive of their favorite candidate after a given debate than they were before. Likewise, some scholars have been unable to discern any issue-oriented bonding between nominees and their supporters.[34]

Moreover, some studies have even called into question the electorate's consistency in choosing debate winners. Researchers find that many candidate supporters are, under some circumstances, able to recognize and acknowledge that the opposition candidate won the debate. To be sure, Democratic and Republican identifiers react very differently to these candidate confrontations and, in a closely fought debate, most viewers will give the win to "their" nominee. Nevertheless, the presumed need for cognitive consistency, while it may bias debate evaluations, does not overwhelm them. Voters, says Mark H. Davis, despite their loyalties and predispositions, "still demonstrate some sensitivity to nuance in the debate."[35]

Since reinforcement, although common, has been found by some researchers but not others, it is useful to consider the circumstances that appear most likely to engender reinforcement effects:

Reinforcement occurs when candidates use debates to amplify their major themes. John G. Geer argues that debates may effect changes in candidate preferences when voters learn something new from them.[36] By the same token, Geer argues, reinforcement is the likely result when debates serve simply as a new forum for old material. Viewers, in that case, are hearing the same arguments to which they have become accustomed, the same ones that have presumably led them to make their choice in the first place. Seeing the candidates side by side arguing along well-established lines is unlikely to change anyone's vote, Geer says. It may, however, invigorate supporters and irritate opponents, thus resulting in some of the reinforcement effects noted above. Indeed, if the overly coached and rehearsed debates of 1988 represent the new state of the art, it is possible that reinforcement may become the *only* observable effect in future encounters.

Reinforcement occurs when candidates' debate performance corresponds with trends in public opinion. John Kennedy may have been the underdog in 1960, but he was an unusually attractive and vigorous one. As voters "met" Kennedy during the course of the campaign, he was clearly able to alleviate some of the uncertainties in voters' minds having to do with his youth, his experience, and his faith. If nothing else, he probably benefited from the tendency among long shots in American presidential campaigns to close the gap prior to election day. Indeed, some positive movement in Kennedy's favor was already occurring in the polls before his series of presidential debates with Richard Nixon.

According to Ben-Zeev and White, the Kennedy–Nixon debates, rather than creating Kennedy's winning momentum, benefited from it (and, perhaps, ultimately augmented it).[37] The favorable effect of the debates on the Democratic nominee, they write, "was due not entirely to the debates themselves as separate events, but with the fact that they fitted in with the emerging image of Kennedy as it was reflected in other events of the campaign."[38] In short, Kennedy's strong performance in the candidate forums had *reinforced* voters' increasingly positive impressions of him. Ben-Zeev and White add that if Nixon's debate performance had "been consistent with the image he was projecting outside the debate[s]," he, too, might have benefited from similar reinforcement.[39]

Reinforcement occurs when viewers discuss the debate with one another. Sears and Chaffee report that the 1976 presidential debates "stimulated a good deal of talk, even among those who rarely talk about politics."[40] These interpersonal discussions, they contend, reinforced viewers' images of the debates (and the debaters), generally to the benefit of the perceived debate winner. In large part, this was because "predebate preferences were quite strongly related to the preference of the discussion partner."[41] As consistency theory would suggest, we enjoy discussions more when our views are in consonance with those of the people with whom we speak. Thus, in the post-debate dialogue between political "soulmates," the original impressions of each are strengthened. Interestingly, this effect was by far strongest after the first debate, and much less notable after each subsequent encounter. Apparently, the novelty of the first debate caused voters to talk politics in September and October rather than other fall topics such as the World Series or college football.

What we call reinforcement may at first glance seem substantively trivial. As researchers, we sometimes expect (or even hope) to observe actual attitude change, and are often disappointed to find consistency and stability instead. Nevertheless, reinforcement is far from insignificant. Candidates certainly recognize this, and devote a great deal of time and effort to reassuring the faithful and reinforcing their faith. Strengthening of preferences may be electorally consequential, particularly in a close race.

Debates and Campaign Issues

As noted above, political scientists are often the first to criticize the media overemphasis on evaluation of presidential debates in terms of their effects on the "horse race." When left to their own devices, however, students of political debating have betrayed much the same emphasis. The majority of debate studies over the past thirty years have dealt primarily with the influence of these events on candidates' images and voters' choices, and few scholars can resist asking some questions intended to determine the debate winner. As a consequence, we have developed a substantial body of knowledge about these debate effects. Other questions, though, have received much less attention.

One such question involves the extent to which voters are swayed by the issue pronouncements of the candidates. Do presidential debates affect the way people look at the issues? Do they actually cause voters to change their minds about government spending priorities, social welfare programs, military strategy, or foreign policy? Indeed, do voters even pay attention to the substance of the nominees' arguments? While these questions have not received the attention they deserve, some evidence has been accumulated. In this section, we will concentrate on two major questions: Do debates motivate opinion change on the issues? Do debates perform an agenda-setting function (that is, do they elevate certain issues to national prominence)?

In order to answer these questions, of course, we must first determine whether or not voters pay attention to, and comprehend, the candidates' arguments. Here, reports are decidedly mixed. John E. Bowes and Herbert Strentz report that "candidates [in the 1976 debates] were distinguished on personality attributes, but blended together on issues."[42] This finding corresponds with other scholars' contentions that debaters are often evaluated in terms of the images they present rather than the views they espouse.

Not all findings, however, are so pessimistic. For example, Jacob Jacoby and his colleagues consider presidential debates as a form of political communication, investigating viewers' comprehension of the statements and arguments of the candidates.[43] They find that debate audiences show high levels of comprehension when compared to consumers of other types of political information. In addition, a number of studies (to be discussed below) find that debate watchers gain a great deal of information about candidates' ideologies and specific issue positions. On balance, then, it appears that voters, especially those with already high levels of political interest, do become more aware of the issue pronouncements of the nominees as a result of viewing the debate. Whether they make use of that information is, of course, another matter altogether.

Debates and Voters' Stands on the Issues

Our first concern is whether voters change their opinions on various issues as a result of viewing presidential debates. As noted above, comparatively little evidence is available on this question. Some previous research, however, has suggested that opinion change is related to reinforcement and may be explained by cognitive consistency theory—candidates' supporters adjust their views in accordance with the opinions expressed by their preferred candidate.[44] Thus opinion change is simply an effort on the part of voters to achieve consonance between their candidate preference and their own issue positions.

Other scholars have suggested that the effects of debates can go beyond simple reinforcement. Our own study of the first Reagan–Mondale debate in 1984 finds that while Mondale won the debate in terms of images, Reagan may have scored some points on the issues.[45] In post-debate surveys, viewers moved closer to the Republican's position on taxation (against increases) and government spending (in favor of cutting the domestic budget). Further, the study suggests that Reagan's success in framing these issues may have cut into the advantage Mondale enjoyed as a result of his superior overall debate performance.

On the other hand, our study of one 1988 Democratic primary debate reports that opinion change on the issues was fairly minor.[46] Because all debate participants were relatively liberal Democrats, the little opinion change that occurred was in a liberal direction (on issues such as government spending priorities, dealing with the Soviet Union, and evaluating the performance of outgoing President Ronald Reagan). Nevertheless, in this case significant change was the exception rather than the rule.

The findings above, while based on few studies, suggest that debate-induced opinion change on the issues is generally limited, especially when compared with debate-generated changes in voters' candidate perceptions. Perhaps this is the result of the media's emphasis on reporting debates in terms of candidates' personalities and "horse race" concerns (i.e., who did well, who did poorly, who gained the most, etc.). It might also result from the viewers' interest in the interpersonal competition of debates rather than their substance. Finally, it may simply be that the issues discussed during debates generally represent a rehash of the major issues already emphasized by the candidates and media; voters may, therefore, have already made up their minds about these matters. Whatever the explanation, given the paucity of studies dealing with these concerns, future research concentration on issue presentations is clearly indicated.

Debates as Agenda-Setters

The agenda-setting function of the media is well known. It implies "a positive relationship between what various communications media emphasize and what voters come to regard as important."[47] This process, of course, generally takes place over a much longer period of time than a single evening of viewing, suggesting that debates may have limited effects on the nation's political agenda. Nevertheless, few events dominate political news during a campaign season the way that a presidential debate does. It is possible, therefore, that the magnitude of such events, the massive audience they generate, and the attention they receive from the media may combine to thrust certain issues into the spotlight.

In their comprehensive study of the 1960 debates, Elihu Katz and Jacob J. Feldman reported that the Kennedy–Nixon encounters "made some issues salient rather than others."[48] Clearly, for example, the debate-driven tempest over the protection of Quemoy and Matsu gave those small islands a centrality in American political discourse that they would not otherwise have enjoyed. In addition, the authors noted that the debate helped to elevate issues such as U.S. prestige in the world, health insurance for the elderly, farm policy, and aid to education. Interestingly, all of these issues—with the notable exception of Quemoy and Matsu—

worked to the advantage of John Kennedy. Not only was an agenda-setting function apparent during the 1960 debates, but its effect apparently benefited one candidate more than the other. Thus, if debates dominate the discussion of issues, their agenda-setting ability could conceivably help shape the outcome of the race.

Later studies, however, were more skeptical about the supposed power of debates to influence the national agenda. Sears and Chaffee, summarizing the 1976 debate research, concluded that the Carter–Ford confrontations did not have much effect on the prominence of various campaign issues.[49] The major issue that dominated the national agenda throughout 1976—inflation in wages and prices—continued to preoccupy voters after the debates, despite the fact that it received surprisingly little attention during the encounters. In addition, energy issues (specifically, concerns about gasoline shortages and dependence on foreign oil) did not gain salience with voters, even though Ford and Carter addressed these problems extensively.

According to Sears and Chaffee, only two findings contradicted the strong case against agenda-setting in 1976. Voters, it seems, were more likely to discuss domestic issues after viewing debates devoted to these topics, and more likely to talk about foreign affairs after the second Ford–Carter debate (which focused on international relations). The agenda-setting in this case, however, did not generally extend to specific issues within the domestic and foreign policy domains.

Secondly, Gerald Ford's unfortunate comments about Eastern Europe were well reported by the media, extensively discussed by voters, and definitely dominated the national agenda for at least one week in October. The authors, however, point out that the Eastern Europe controversy was "simply an incident, not an issue that arose because it was emphasized in the debate."[50] Moreover, they add, for all the attention given Ford's gaffe, the question of the independence of the Soviet Union's European satellites did not rise as a significant issue during the 1976 election.

Other Effects of Debates on Public Opinion

While most researchers have been concerned with the effects of debates on the course of election campaigns, some scholars have considered questions that transcend any single race for the presidency. Specifically, they are interested in the effects of these events on variables such as system support, political efficacy, and national prestige. Such questions suggest the possibility that presidential debates may have benefits for the

United States beyond those generally claimed by supporters. Although few studies have considered these issues, some evidence is available. The most important of these findings are presented below:

Debates may enhance support for the political system by legitimizing both nominees. One unique feature of debates among other forms of political communication is the size of their audience. General election debates generate audiences comparable only to major sporting events such as the Superbowl or the World Series. Moreover, this cannot be explained simply by the fact that they are carried simultaneously by all major television networks. The quadrennial political conventions, after all, also draw such coverage, but recent ratings "sweeps" report that viewers abandon the conventions in droves, in favor of independent television stations and alternative cable programming.[51] By contrast, Americans actually seek out presidential debates and watch them with great interest. In so doing, they expose themselves to the arguments and appeals of both the Democratic and Republican nominees.

For many candidate supporters, this may be their first and only exposure to the opposition contender. Even those viewers who tune in to debates in order to cheer on their favorite candidate must spend at least half the time listening to his or her rival. Consistency theory, of course, suggests that we denigrate the efforts of those with whom we disagree and, to be sure, highly partisan viewers are unlikely to give the opponent an entirely fair hearing. Nevertheless, it has been reported that the images of *both* candidates may actually improve in the wake of a presidential debate.

This raises two interesting questions. First, is it possible that the debate, by allowing both candidates to present their best face to the voters, increases citizens' support for the new president, regardless of who is ultimately elected? Or at the very least, might debates (which are typically marked by calm discussion and an abundance of patriotic rhetoric) give viewers a more positive feeling toward their political system and government institutions?

As early as the 1960 Kennedy–Nixon debates, a few scholars attempted to deal with these questions. Katz and Feldman reported, with some surprise, that voters "learned something [even] about the candidate they opposed."[52] If nothing else, viewers learned "that [the opponent] was human, that he could become nervous, tired, etc."[53] As a result, they noted, the debates helped to lower the proportion of voters who named "dislike [of] the other candidate" as a reason for their own choice. The authors concluded by lamenting the preoccupation of most studies with the competitive aspects of the debates at the expense of learning more about the "latent consequences of the institution."[54]

In 1976, a number of scholars (although still relatively few) investigated the issues discussed by Katz and Feldman sixteen years before. Sears and Chaffee, in their review of the debate-generated literature, noted that the Carter–Ford confrontations apparently resulted in "moderately" better evaluations of national institutions on the part of viewers.[55] Further, the studies of 1976 replicated the earlier findings that the debate improved voters' impressions of both nominees. Indeed, one study extended this point to include the vice presidential candidates as well.[56] At first glance, the 1960 and 1976 studies suggest that debates may play an important role in creating greater support for the incoming chief executive than would otherwise be enjoyed.

Sears and Chaffee, however, caution that these findings are far from conclusive. They point out that the gains for the debating politicians were dominated by those viewers who supported each candidate in the first place.[57] Aggregate results showing improving candidate images, therefore, may not always represent a softening of strong partisans' views toward the candidate they originally opposed. Moreover, the findings reported during studies of the 1976 campaign were rarely strong. Sears and Chaffee concluded that "neither with respect to the broad institutions of government nor with specific support for the new administration is the evidence very complete or compelling."[58]

Debates may strengthen adolescents' bonding with the political system. One fascinating study of the 1976 debates considers the events as an agent of political socialization.[59] Robert P. Hawkins and his colleagues measured the reactions of over 500 junior high and high school students near Madison, Wisconsin. They found that the experience of viewing the debates bonded adolescents to their preferred candidate and his party, and strengthened their support for the political system. The effects of the debate, the authors concluded, extended beyond merely incidental learning about the candidates and their issue positions. Interestingly, however, only limited evidence is found suggesting that exposure to the debates enhanced adolescents' level of political efficacy. One might have thought that debate-induced increases in knowledge and partisanship might have given these students a greater sense of self-confidence in their own role as a future voter. Unfortunately, this was not the case.

Debates may improve the image of America and American institutions abroad. Given the position of the United States in the world community, American politics is often highly interesting even to citizens and elites in foreign countries. It should come as no surprise, therefore, that American presidential debates have been broadcast in over one hundred countries on every populated continent.[60] While the effects of debates on the opinions of foreigners may be interesting, few studies have actually been undertaken away from American soil. And even those studies (many conducted in Canada) have dealt primarily with the "horse race" questions and are of little use here. Indeed, Sears and Chaffee were only able to find one study (in the Netherlands) that addressed the appropriate questions.[61] While methodologically flawed, this study was "at least consistent with the proposition that exposure to debates can engender confidence in new potential [American] national leaders and an understanding of the general thrust of American political decisions."[62]

As interesting as the studies above may be, they only begin to help us determine whether debates have salutary effects on Americans' support for their own political system and its leaders, as well as foreigners' understanding and appreciation of the U.S. electoral system. Unfortunately, few researchers have addressed these questions, and the results of their work have been promising but inconclusive. Clearly, this is an area in the study of presidential debates that requires (and deserves) further consideration.

COGNITIVE EFFECTS: THE QUESTION OF INFORMATION GAIN

The rational voter is an informed voter. He or she is an information-seeker who analyzes the issue positions of the candidates and chooses the nominee whose philosophy and policies are most in line with his or her own. At best, this is not an easy task. Candidates lie, obfuscate, call each other nasty names, and sometimes ignore substantive matters altogether.[63] In a world of sound bites, attack ads, and "horse race" journalism, the information costs of rational voting are often daunting. Ideally, a forum would exist in which presidential contenders would be forced to address the issues side by side, allowing for comparisons of their perspectives on foreign, domestic, and economic policy.

Early—and optimistic—proponents of presidential debates saw these encounters as just such a forum. "For the first time," gushed an NBC executive in 1960, "the two major candidates for the presidency of the United States are meeting face to face in a systematic effort to exchange views on the great issues of the day."[64] Debates, then, would be important purveyors of issues, reducing information costs and increasing the "rationality" of the electorate. No longer would the average citizen need to scour newspapers and campaign literature in order to prepare his or her vote. The supporters of presidential debates must have been gratified to learn that millions of Americans were actually tuning in to these contests.

Social scientists, however, have been unwilling simply to assume that debates increased the information levels of voters. Candidates and viewers, after all, do not necessarily have to conform to the hopes and expectations of debate proponents. Nominees might still speak in generalities and talk around the issues; voters might concentrate more on candidates' personalities than on their issue pronouncements. Thus, a number of studies have been conducted around the question of whether or not presidential debates actually increase the information levels of viewers. Interestingly, the results have been mixed.

The measurement of information gain, like most other questions of measurement, is often more complicated than it would first appear. It is generally acknowledged that the best design for such research is a pre-test/post-test study, comparing gains in information levels between those who watched the debate and those who did not. Not all studies, however, have employed this method.[65] Some researchers use the panel design without the control group. Others consider information gain over the course of the entire series of debates, running the risk that positive findings might be due, at least in part, to campaign information unrelated to the candidate encounters.

Diversity can also be found in the different operational definitions of information gain used by various researchers. Some, for example, have defined it in terms of voters' perceptions of the nominees' stands on the issues. Thus, a debate has contributed to viewers' information levels if they see greater differences between the candidates on the issues after the debate than they did before. Here, no effort is made to check the accuracy of voters' perceptions.

Other scholars have dealt with this problem by creating an index of various campaign issues and asking subjects to identify the candidates' stands. In this case, information gain is recorded when viewers are more accurate in their post-debate issue placements than they were in their pre-debate assessments. Or, similarly, information gain may be said to occur if viewers can correctly describe the nominees' views on *more* issues in the post-test questionnaire than on the pre-test instrument. A further check can be made here by separating issues between those that were discussed extensively during the debate and those that were largely ignored. In this way, we are better able to determine that any information gain found was actually "caused" by watching the encounter.

Finally, some researchers have operationalized debate-induced learning as subjects' ability to recall the major arguments and positions of the candidates. Typically, this is done through open-ended survey items. The apparent assumption here is that if information is truly learned, no "priming" is needed in order for the respondent to remember debate content. Nevertheless, it is possible that such a design might underrepresent the actual information gain that does occur. Such survey items are, after all, "difficult to answer and still more difficult to analyze."[66] They may put a premium as much on a subject's ability to articulate as on his or her actual retention of knowledge.

Regardless of the question of measurement, information gain has been found fairly consistently in the debate literature. In the face of so many nonfindings in the search for debate-induced opinion change, the discovery of issue learning may have seemed especially impressive to some scholars. One researcher, studying the 1960 debates, announced that these events "threaten to upset one of our more deeply rooted political habits—the habit of not listening to the candidates."[67] Information gain has been found in the studies of the 1960, 1976, and 1988 debates.[68] At least in the short run, it appears that debate watchers do know more about the candidates and issues after viewing any given debate. That alone, say many observers, justifies their continuation.

To be sure, not all studies have found impressive learning effects. Doris A. Graber and Young Yun Kim, for example, described information gain from the 1976 debates as "modest."[69] They concluded that a number of factors contributed to minimizing learning from these confrontations. They argued that much of the information presented during debates is redundant, having been aired extensively in television advertisements and news broadcasts. Further, viewers may be inclined to ignore the nominees' issue-oriented discussions, dismissing them as mere rhetoric. Finally, the complexity of the messages and the sketchiness of post-debate media commentary might discourage voters from paying closer attention to the debaters' arguments. Even if debate-induced learning is generally greater than that found by Graber and Kim, their speculations help us to understand the limits of information gain and suggest why few studies have reported enormous changes.

Within the general findings regarding debates and information gain, a number of interesting observations and possibilities stand out. Some of the most important ones are discussed below:

Although debates highlight differences between the candidates on the issues, they may be better at spotlighting differences in images and personalities. While lauding debates as producing "a better informed electorate than would have [otherwise] existed," Miller and MacKuen note that much of that information is nonsubstantive.[70] "The information obtained . . . ," they reported, "was largely focused on candidate competence, performance, and personality attributes rather than on issues."[71] While some issue learning did occur, it was weaker and less significant.

One might certainly argue that rational, informed voting can be based on such nonsubstantive considerations (all Americans desire a competent, honest, strong leader). Nevertheless, these findings suggest that the relatively weak information gain reported in some studies might result from the priorities of viewers. Many may seek information about personality factors from debates, rather than knowledge about issue positions. Appropriate or not, this tendency could have serious consequences for electoral accountability.

A primacy effect may be influencing debate-induced learning. Sears and Chaffee reported that the strongest evidence of information gain from the Carter–Ford debates in 1976 occurred during the candidates' first meeting in Philadelphia.[72] After the second debate, voters' recollections were dominated by Ford's statements about Eastern Europe, but little other learning was recorded. The later vice presidential debate between Walter Mondale and Robert Dole was similarly unenlightening.

While this evidence is far from conclusive, there is some reason to expect a primacy effect with regard to information gain. Voters who are fairly unfamiliar with the candidates probably receive their greatest input of new information from the initial debate between the nominees. Each successive debate, in which many of the campaign's familiar themes are restated, should have less net impact. Nevertheless, more investigation in this area is required.

Media commentary may have little effect on issue learning. Surprisingly, the importance of the media in shaping post-debate public opinion does not carry over into the area of information gain. Attention to post-debate analysis apparently does not enhance the learning process. This may be due to the relative lack of substantive focus in media analysis of each debate.[73] Journalists, of course, concentrate on the "horse race" aspects of the event, and their discussions and film clips more often than not involve heated exchanges, gaffes, and candidate humor. Thus, viewers seeking clarification of the nominees' issue positions receive little new guidance from television, and perhaps not much more from newspapers and magazines.

Gladys Lang and Kurt Lang suggested that this lack of media attention to the issues may have resulted in "dissipation" of learning on one issue—the environment—after the first 1976 debate. "Those who cared about the environment," the Langs reported, "may have been scrutinizing the debate for clues about [each] candidate's stand on this issue, but the lack of emphasis in the post-debate commentary helped condemn it to oblivion."[74] One interesting exception here was the role of the media in promoting some issue learning after the 1976 vice presidential debate.[75] As noted above, however, the overall information gain from that event was quite small.

Selective perception is not an important factor in viewers' recall of candidates' arguments. Cognitive consistency theory might lead us to expect that debate watchers would be better able to remember the statements of their preferred candidate, and more likely to ignore or "block out" the appeals of the opposition. Such a pattern, however, does not emerge from the research on presidential debates. In his study of the 1960 Kennedy–Nixon encounters, Richard F. Carter found that partisans of the two candidates were able to recall the arguments of *both* the Democratic and the Republican nominees.[76] For those who see debates as a boon to rational voting, this is a very important finding. It suggests that the millions of Americans who regularly watch these events are not only exposed to the arguments of both sides, but actually hear and remember those arguments. The supposed drive toward cognitive consistency, therefore, does not prevent debates from serving what many consider to be their primary function.

While some issue learning apparently occurs, it may be short-lived. As noted previously, the Langs reported some dissipation in post-debate information gain in 1976. Recent research by one of the authors, this time concerning the second 1988 debate between George Bush and Michael Dukakis, was even more pessimistic.[77] In a three-wave panel study, it was found that debate watchers gained substantially on an "information index" (identifying the nominees' stands on the issues) from before to immediately after the encounter. Non-watchers showed no similar improvement.

However, in a second post-test survey, conducted two weeks after the debate, the study found that the early gains were largely extinguished (although they remained statistically significant). Worse still, after controlling for political interest, there was no difference in two-week-old information gain between those who watched the debate and those who did not. "The extinction effects found here," therefore, "must cast doubt on the longevity of information gain reported elsewhere."[78] If information gain is truly short-lived, it must also raise questions about the ability of presidential debates to inform and rationalize the electorate in any meaningful way. These findings, then, may challenge the primary justification for holding such encounters.

It is possible that only the "knowledge-rich get richer." George F. Bishop and his colleagues presented one finding in their study of the 1976 debates that must give pause to many debate proponents.[79] According to their study, the greatest debate-induced increase in information on the issues occurred among those subjects who were already most knowledgeable about the candidates and the campaign. Less knowledgeable voters, on the other hand, gained "little, if anything," from the debates.[80] The authors concluded that debates are quite limited in their ability to increase voter rationality, especially among the less educated and involved. They contended that the complexity of the issues discussed during these events thwarts many watchers in their efforts to learn about the nominees and their platforms. Bishop et al. concluded by questioning whether presidential debates are worth continuing, especially since they contribute to an arguably undesirable "political-informational division of labor" among the electorate.[81] Those who support debates, the authors argued, "must accept the responsibility for a growing information gap between the political haves and have-nots in the emerging postindustrial society."[82]

Debates and Political Learning

Many observers have argued that, at least in terms of information gain, debates have fulfilled their promise of creating a better (i.e., more informed and interested) electorate. Sidney Kraus, one of America's leading authorities on presidential debating, notes that "over half of the voting age public rely on televised debates for decision making. Having them makes voters winners."[83] Even if we suspect that many voters are giving "civic-minded"—rather than truthful—answers to questions about debate uses, the fact remains that these events do generate a massive audience for political discussion. No other form of campaign media—conventions, interviews, newscasts, or advertisements— is seen by as many people at one time as a single ninety-minute presidential debate. Since numerous studies have shown at least moderate debate-driven information gain, it would seem, at first glance, that these millions of viewers are well served by the candidate confrontations.

Kathleen Jamieson and David S. Birdsell consider debates in terms of the "challenge of creating an informed electorate."[84] The potential benefits of debates, they argue, are numerous and important. First, debates expand on the arguments and "sound bites" available from television news and campaign advertisements. Presumably, they help place these conflicting claims and snippets of speeches into a broader context. Second, presidential debates provide information that helps to generate the kinds of voters preferred by most democratic theories. Put simply, voters who know and understand more are generally considered "better" voters. Third, by demanding responses from candidates on specific issues and policies, they enhance accountability for candidates' claims (recall how Jimmy Carter was often lambasted in 1980 over his 1976 references to the "misery index"—which, it turned out, had risen to new heights during his own tenure). Fourth, the performance of the nominees themselves—their reactions, styles, and overall behavior—help us to predict and explain the kinds of presidents they may become. Finally, according to Jamieson and Birdsell, debates provide for all Americans, regardless of personal ideology or bias, contrasting views of the real and ideal political worlds.

Clearly, the promise of presidential debates is substantial, and there is indeed some limited evidence that they have, to some extent, performed their desired function. Still, lest we become too sanguine about the usefulness and importance of these events, it is necessary to bear in mind that much of the information gain discussed above was either slight or limited. In addition, much of it was nonsubstantive or arguably trivial (for example, the "learning" of Gerald Ford's views on the independence of the Warsaw Pact nations). Perhaps most importantly, there are a number of troubling aspects to many of the major findings on issue learning.

For one thing, there is no proof that the information gain reported above is very robust. In fact, it is possible, especially given the nature of contemporary media coverage, that nonsubstantive debating incidents persist in viewers' minds long after issue-oriented statements and exchanges have been forgotten. Worse still, strong evidence exists that debates are best at serving the constituency that needs them least (the most knowledgeable voters), while the complexity of issue-oriented pronouncements leaves many knowledge-hungry viewers left to whet their appetites on the minutiae of dramatic moments, physical appearance, and catchy phrases and slogans (e.g., "There you go again"). Finally, as mentioned before, issue learning does not guarantee rational voting: viewers may simply revise their own opinions in line with those of their favorite candidate, rather thank using their new knowledge to choose the best nominee.[85] Indeed, one might question, as Bishop and his colleagues did, whether the effects of debates are more beneficial than harmful.

In any event, the findings discussed in this section, like many of those presented earlier, are based on a disturbingly small amount of research. At the very least, future scholars should explore the longevity of information gain, the "division of labor" thesis, the role of the media, and the importance of issue learning to voters' actual decisionmaking calculus. Only when these and similar questions are answered can we determine whether or not voters are actually the "winners" of televised presidential debates.

BEHAVIORAL EFFECTS: PRESIDENTIAL DEBATES AND THE VOTE CHOICE

A cursory glance at the studies of presidential debates since 1960 is sufficient to demonstrate at least one point conclusively: journalists are not the only people preoccupied with the "horse race" questions of candidate preference and vote choice. A majority of scholarly research has concerned itself, at least in part, with the impact of debates on actual electoral outcomes.[86] There is, of course, nothing surprising about this. Campaigns are, in the final analysis, about winning and losing, and presidential debates occur only when candidates calculate that participating in them will improve their electoral prospects (or, perhaps, that nonparticipation might hurt them). Indeed, scholarly interest in opinion change and information gain is largely motivated by a concern over how these factors influence vote choice. Attitude change may be a precursor to changes in voting behavior; information gain is expected to help rational voters make better decisions at the polls.

To be sure, vote choice represents a unique expression of political attitudes. It is not measured in degrees or shades of opinion. A vote is truly a choice among alternatives. For a debate to influence voting behavior, it must cause some people to move from the ranks of the undecided to become full-fledged candidate supporters. It must cause others to renounce a choice already made (at least tentatively) and throw in with the opposition. If political attitudes in general are not easily changed, it seems that candidate preferences (which often grow out of such long-term commitments as party identification) might be especially difficult to alter on the basis of a ninety-minute debate.

It is hardly surprising, therefore, that political scientists have concluded that debates do not shake the foundations of candidate support, as many may have expected before 1960. Rather, what is striking is that there is some limited evidence that debates do, at times, influence voters, and that these effects might be decisive in a close race. The truth, of course, often gets stretched in the telling, and the characterization of the Kennedy–Nixon debates as critical has been exaggerated over the years (as have accounts of subsequent encounters). Nevertheless, under some circumstances debates apparently *do* influence the "horse race." The following are some conditions under which debate-induced vote change has been said to occur:

Debates may have a particular influence over the choices of previously undecided voters. Among those studies indicating even moderate vote change, such change generally occurs among previously uncommitted viewers. This would certainly be in keeping with the dominant theories of attitude change. While candidates' supporters may view each debate through biased lenses (because of strong party and/or candidate loyalties), undecided voters, unencumbered by prior preferences, may use debates as an aid to their decisionmaking.[87]

Interestingly, this "crystallization" of choice among the undecided may also be consistent with underlying party identification. Kurt and Gladys Lang, for example, reported that the post-debate movement in favor of John Kennedy in 1960 came primarily from previously uncommitted Democratic identifiers.[88] Such voters were no doubt inclined to support the Democratic nominee in the first place, and the debates may have served to alleviate whatever uncertainties they may have and about the young, relatively unknown Massachusetts senator.

Debates may have an influence when candidate support is "soft." Because voting decisions are an "either-or" proposition, we don't always know what an intended vote choice measures. Among those professing a candidate preference on both fervently and weakly committed supporters. It makes sense that the more "soft" supporters there are in the electorate, the more likely that voting intentions will be changed during the course of the campaign. In 1976, for example, some studies attributed unusually high post-debate fluctuations in candidate preferences to the generally low regard voters had for both Gerald Ford and Jimmy Carter.[89] This suggests that in an election with stronger preferences (say, 1984), such changes would be much less likely, regardless of debate outcomes. While these findings are consistent with various theoretical approaches in social psychology (and common sense), it should be noted that in one study conducted in 1988 (another year in which many voters disapproved of both nominees), professed vote choices did *not* change significantly as a result of the second debate (considered by many to be a one-sided victory for George Bush over Michael Dukakis).[90]

Debates may have an influence if voters learn something new. John Geer argues that one of the reasons debate effects have been fairly limited is that they typically provide only a rehash of the candidates' major themes.[91] Such themes have already reached voters in the form of news clips (the ubiquitous "sound bites") and paid advertisements. According to this argument, the "normal" debate, where candidates parrot carefully prepared phrases and address well-covered issues, will make little difference to most voters. On occasion, however, unusual or unexpected information will be provided by a debate (as when Ford shocked voters with his Eastern Europe comments in 1976 or when Ronald Reagan raised doubts about his age and competence in 1984). These, Geer suggests, are the sorts of events we should be studying if we wish to observe meaningful debate effects.

Debates may have an influence when the media anoint an overwhelming "winner." We might recall from chapter 2 that Ford's comments on Eastern Europe during the second 1976 debate were largely ignored by their original viewing audience, and only dominated public perceptions after days of media scrutiny. In their study of the first Carter–Ford encounter, Lang and Lang found substantial differences between the post-debate reactions of those who had viewed media analysis of the event and those who had not.[92] While the latter group concluded that Jimmy Carter had won the debate, the "media-contaminated" group accepted the verdict of the press that President Ford had triumphed.

These mediated effects showed up most strongly among previously undecided voters. In this group, Ford had a post-debate lead of 10 percentage points among media watchers; Carter, on the other hand, led by 24 points among those who had not been exposed to the journalists' collective wisdom.[93] Similar effects were apparent in the case of previously aligned voters, but the differences were much smaller. Media commentary, the Langs concluded, had given victory and a larger vote share (at least temporarily) to Gerald Ford.

Debates may have a special influence during primary elections. Unfortunately, little data exist to test this proposition. Nevertheless, the discussion above indicates that debates have their greatest impact on voting behavior among two groups of viewers: those who have not yet made a firm commitment to one of the candidates and those who are not influenced by party affiliations.

Primary season debates fit both of these criteria. Since they usually occur well before most voters have thought about the election, their audiences are largely "undecided." In addition, since all participants are members of the same party, viewers' party identification provides no attitudinal "anchor" to limit opinion change. In fact, our study of a single primary debate in 1988 found some evidence that candidate preferences were strongly altered by viewing the event.[94] We must caution, however, that audiences for primary debates are generally quite small, so the effects of such debates may not ultimately amount to much.

Debates may affect the candidate preferences of knowledge-poor voters. Uses and gratifications theory might suggest that politically knowledgeable voters do not "need" debates as much as their less knowledgeable counterparts. To the well-informed citizen, a debate may provide an opportunity to cheer on a favorite candidate or experience the excitement and suspense of viewing a live, unrehearsed confrontation. Such a voter is likely to have decided between the candidates prior to the debate and would probably learn nothing new from the event. In addition, a knowledgeable voter is better able to put candidate gaffes and poor makeup jobs in perspective and, thus, is less likely to be affected by them.

For the knowledge-poor voter, on the other hand, the debate may represent one of his or her few chances for direct exposure to the candidates and their issue positions. This type of voter, lacking in education and political interest, may be much more reliant on this single media event for forming his or her judgments. What might be shopworn rhetoric to the knowledge-rich debate watcher could be an important piece of political information to the less knowledgeable voter. In 1980, for example, the major effect of the Carter–Reagan debate on knowledgeable voters was reinforcement. For less knowledgeable voters, however, substantial changes in candidate preferences were found, providing a measurable boost to Ronald Reagan in his final-week surge toward a landslide election.[95]

It should be emphasized that even among the studies that did record fluctuations in viewers' candidate preferences, the changes were far from overwhelming. Such effects would probably only influence the outcome of a very closely contested election (which might be similarly "decided" by any number of other minor opinion swings unrelated to debates). In addition, we should note that other studies, covering the same elections, were unable to detect *any* noticeable debate-induced vote change.[96] Still, the evidence above suggests that the potential effects of debates may be somewhat greater than is normally described by social scientists.

Other issues must also be considered, however, lest we be too anxious to buck the conventional wisdom. First, it is questionable just how persistent the effects of debates actually are. Debate-induced changes in candidate preferences are not nearly so important if they wash away well before election day. One study, for example, casts doubt on the longevity of Gerald Ford's vote loss due to his comments on Eastern Europe. "Voters," Frederick Steeper noted, "were easily deflected from Ford by a surge of 'bad news' about him, but . . . many snapped back to him when the initial trauma of the candidate's statements faded in their minds."[97]

Another problem with ascribing changes in vote choice to debate watching involves attributions of causality. A number of early studies found that the winning candidate gained votes after his debating victory, but little effort was made to verify that this newfound support actually resulted from the debate (rather than some contemporaneous news event or opinion trend). As careful researchers, the Langs pointed out that growing support for John Kennedy during the 1960 campaign may not have been due entirely to the debates. These voters, they warned, may have been "responding to inclinations that had clearly been present earlier and might have been activated even without the debates."[98] When more rigorous experimental methods are employed by researchers, debate-induced shifts in candidate support are much less common (although, as noted above, some have been found).

Experimental methods, however, may face their own problems. While they do provide researchers with greater internal validity (i.e., the ability to demonstrate causality), they may be poorly suited to the study of presidential debates. In such research, an experimental group generally watches a debate, while a control group does not. Debate effects are then defined as the differences in post-debate attitudes between these two groups.

Such studies may underestimate the power of presidential debates. If the effects of debates are largely triggered by media analysis and interpretation, it is possible to be influenced by such an event without actually having watched it. Perhaps a true control group in this case would be a sample of voters who had neither viewed the debate nor been exposed to post-debate commentary. Unfortunately, such a study would be very difficult to conduct and would be subject to criticism over a lack of external validity (since the exposure situations would be artificial and unrepresentative of actual behavior).

Finally, a number of studies have relied on viewers' self-reports as to how important a given debate was in affecting their vote choices.[99]

Using this method, researchers have attributed an unusually large influence to debates, one that has not been borne out in more rigorous studies. One problem with such research is that it assumes that voters are capable of correctly identifying the factors affecting their own attitudes. Research in social psychology casts substantial doubt on this assumption.[100] Fortunately, such studies are increasingly uncommon in modern debate research.

CONCLUSION: PRESIDENTIAL DEBATES AND PUBLIC OPINION

The 1960 and 1976 debates led to a flurry of scholarly activity unlike anything seen before in the study of a single campaign event. Clearly, many of these researchers were motivated by the novelty of the debates, but many were also excited by the opportunity to observe a true electoral turning point. It was with some surprise, perhaps, that students of political debating concluded that the overall effects of these confrontations were minimal. They did not "make" John Kennedy and Jimmy Carter, nor did they destroy Richard Nixon and Gerald Ford. They may have helped to make the difference in two close elections, but the same could be said for any number of other short-term issues or incidents. To many scholars, the "great debates" were a great bust.

After 1976, the study of debates, particularly in political science, was all but abandoned. Book-length volumes dealing with earlier debates were replaced by an occasional article (often in a "minor" journal), but little else. The dominant paradigm in debate research centered on cognitive consistency theory. One study concluded that "only when the powerful impacts of prior beliefs and preferences are considered can one fully understand why presidential debates have not had the marked influence on election outcomes that many early observers anticipated."[101] Debates had gone from all-important determinants of electoral success to relatively unimportant diversions of little consequence to the campaign. It was as though we now knew all there was to know about the effects of these events: they changed very few votes, had limited effects on candidate images, changed few minds on the issues, and generally sustained or reinforced viewers' previous biases.

This chapter has suggested the possibility that debates may be a good deal more consequential than is currently supposed. To be sure, many factors do serve to limit debate-induced attitude change, whether a general drive toward cognitive consistency or the existence of attitudinal anchors such as party identification. Further, where debate effects are found, they are often in the form of reinforcement. Nevertheless, many viewers are *not* blinded by their pre-debate preferences. A surprising number of debate watchers are willing to concede a superior performance on the part of a candidate they oppose. Moreover, post-debate changes in candidate images are not always tied to earlier preferences. Indeed, many surveys suggest that *both* candidates may benefit from participation in these encounters. Finally, a few studies, contrary to expectations, have been unable to find any debate-induced reinforcement effects at all.

Reinforcement, of course, may be important in and of itself. As noted above, such findings have often been treated as substantively useless, merely a preservation of pre-debate attitudes. *True* reinforcement, however, may be far more meaningful. It would be unwise to trivialize previous findings that debates reinforce preferences. Reinforcement *is* politically significant. It can turn tentative preferences into actual votes. In its absence, uncertainties about candidates may well multiply, causing erosion in the support of frontrunners and defection from the ranks of underdogs. Were reinforcement the only measurable effect of debates on viewers, this alone would make them electorally consequential.[102]

Be that as it may, consistency theory is not adequate to explain many of the other effects discussed above. For one thing, debates *do* appear to have a measurable influence on candidate preferences under some conditions. In the case of primary season debates, for instance, that effect may actually be quite large. But even during general election debates some attitude change has been observed. Among the factors said to influence candidate preferences are the amount of new information provided by the debate, the nature of post-debate media analysis, the strength of pre-debate preferences, and the relative knowledge levels of viewers.

Other theoretical perspectives may be necessary for understanding these findings. For example, in some cases (such as primary debates), voters may actually behave as the rational, attentive information gatherers described in some of the early political communication literature. In addition, the functional theory of attitude change may help us to explain why some debates have effects on certain viewers while others do not. Attitudes that serve a knowledge function may be changed if new information is forthcoming that challenges voters' earlier perceptions of the nominees. The propensity of some Americans to "join the bandwagon" in favor of a winning debater (especially one so anointed by the media) may be explained, in part, by a desire to fit in with prevailing public opinion (suggesting an "instrumental" attitude change).

Uses and gratifications theory might also help us to explain many of the findings reported above. While highly partisan and politically knowledgeable voters may be drawn to debates by a desire for reinforcement and supporting arguments, less knowledgeable or committed voters may be more interested in guidance and information. Perhaps most importantly, many voters may switch on televised debates simply to enjoy the drama and excitement of the confrontation. If this is the case, it may help to explain why some debates elicit limited responses from viewers. Much of this discussion must remain speculative until we find a way to accurately determine debate watchers' motivations.

Avenues for Further Research

1. *How persistent are debate effects?* This is, of course, a crucial question, but one that has been substantially ignored by researchers. Post-debate attitude change, whether involving candidates or issues, is only meaningful to the extent that it is lasting. Only one presidential debate (the Reagan–Carter confrontation in 1980) has been held within a week of election day. Thus, for a debate actually to exert an influence on the outcome of an election, debate-induced opinion change must persist for at least two or three weeks. Steeper speculated that the profound effects of Gerald Ford's notorious Eastern Europe gaffe in 1976 may have been short-lived and, perhaps, inconsequential (although he added that they might have been important in breaking Ford's early autumn momentum).[103] It may be possible, then, that some of the observed attitude change reported by social scientists is "elastic," and snaps back shortly after the debate is over.[104]

Future researchers should emphasize panel designs, studying the reactions of debate watchers for a longer period of time than the typical "snapshot" study. Such an approach could certainly help us determine whether debate effects extinguish over time. In addition, longitudinal research may allow us to discover possible "sleeper effects," in which some time passes between exposure to the debate and the onset of opinion change. During both 1980 and 1988, for example, journalists commented that the true effects of debates occurred only after several days of media commentary, interpersonal conversation, and individual reflection.[105] More researchers should take this possibility into account.

2. *Does the scheduling of debates make any difference?* Does it matter

whether debates are held early in the campaign (when public opinion may not yet have solidified) or shortly before election day (when undecided voters may be looking for some final guidance)? Our study of primary season debates suggests that their influence may stem from the fact that they are conducted before most voters have decided which candidate to support.[106] If this is true, an August or early September general election debate might have a greater effect on viewers than the typical October encounter. On the other hand, the supposed importance of the Reagan–Carter debate in 1980 was due, in part, to its proximity to election day.[107] If that is the case, later debates may have the greatest effect.

Similarly, scholars might reconsider an issue raised as early as 1960. In a series of debates, is there a primacy effect, in which the first debate (regardless of when it is scheduled) has the greatest impact on voters? Is there a law of diminishing returns in which later debates (say, the third of fourth in a series) have a smaller marginal influence over viewers' opinions? We can only deal with these questions by continuing to study future debates with the same attention given the first televised confrontations in 1960 and 1976.

3. *Under what conditions do primary season debates influence public opinion?* While primary season debates have received virtually no attention from social scientists, our research has shown that they have the potential to make a significant difference in voters' candidate preferences.[108] Still, it is impossible to generalize from a single study from just one election year. Future research could help determine whether the findings from this single event in 1988 are characteristic of primary debates in general.

A number of questions remain to be addressed. For example, do the effects of primary season debates vary with the number of participants? Does the placement of a debate within the primary season affect its influence (do April debates have the same effects as January debates)? Does it make a difference whether the race for the nomination is close or whether a clear frontrunner has emerged? And finally, do the news media—which do not cover these events as extensively as they do their general election counterparts—have a major influence over voters' evaluations of primary season debates? Because of the prevalence of weak and uninformed candidate loyalties, the primary season may be the best place to look for strong debate effects. Such hopes, however, must be tempered by the knowledge that these debates typically generate small audiences. Nevertheless, an audience largely composed of likely voters and probable opinion leaders may be significant even if tiny.

4. *Do the lessons drawn from presidential debate research apply to debates at other levels?* Since the "success" of the Kennedy–Nixon debates in 1960, televised debates have been attempted at the sub-presidential level as well. Candidates for governor, senator, and even mayor (in some large cities) have agreed to square off publicly before a television audience. Often these events are carried by public television stations and are not seen by many voters, but sometimes they do receive higher ratings and extensive media coverage. It might be interesting to determine whether these encounters have the same effects on viewers as debates between candidates for president. Unlike presidential contenders, nominees for governor or U.S. senator often do not enjoy strong name recognition and may be largely unknown to most voters. It is possible, therefore, that a debate at this level might provide citizens with a rare opportunity to hear the candidates discuss the issues (and each other). Here, as in the case of primary season debates, we may expect such events to have a sizable influence on those voters who watch them. In addition, given the frequency with which such events are held, sub-presidential debates give us the chance to add to our knowledge of debate effects without having to wait four years between research opportunities.

5. *Which candidate strategies are most successful in maximizing voter support?* As noted in chapter 3, a small research tradition has emerged in the study of presidential debates that concentrates on the content of the candidates' statements.[109] Through content analysis of these events, it may be possible to identify and label various debating strategies. Such strategies might include personal attack (in which debaters skewer the record or integrity of an opponent); self-presentation (in which candidates concentrate on highlighting their own record and qualifications; specific group appeals (in which nominees gear their arguments toward individual subsets of the population (say, blacks, women, union members, "yuppies," etc.); and partisan appeals (where candidates emphasize their own links to the values and traditions of a specific political party). Indeed, a number of strategies may apply uniquely to primary season debates (see chapter 3 for further discussion of strategies).

By linking candidates' statements to voters' responses, we may be able to answer a number of important questions regarding presidential debates. For example, are substantive, issue-oriented discussions effective, or are voters more persuaded by personality-based appeals (emphasizing experience, leadership, competence, etc.)? Do negative attacks on one's opponent plant doubts about him or her in voters' minds, or are viewers merely annoyed and alienated by them? Can appeals to specific groups (i.e., women, minorities, trade unionists) generate support for one's candidacy without "turning off" other voters? Answers to these questions might move us much closer to understanding how and why candidates are judged winners and losers in presidential debates.

6. *Why do the media have such a profound effect on viewers' debate evaluations?* Media "instant analysis" of political events became very controversial in the 1970s, especially in the wake of journalists' coverage of the Watergate scandal.[110] Indeed, after numerous reports of the media's power following the second 1976 Carter–Ford debate (which included Ford's gaffe), television reporters have become increasingly circumspect in their post-debate analyses, often showing reluctance even to name a consensus "winner." Nevertheless, television newscasters (as well as print journalists) do publicize polling results (allowing the public to name the "winner") and repeatedly show the most important (read: most dramatic) moments in the debate. Evidence suggests that even if the media have altered their approach to debate coverage, they still help to shape (and reshape) voters' recollections.

While scholars have been quick to document this phenomenon, few have considered what features of media coverage are most consequential. Once again, content analysis of television reporting of presidential debates would allow us to isolate specific types of coverage (for example, issue-oriented discussion, "horse race" concerns, emphasis on "heated exchanges," etc.). Through the use of experimental designs, it might be possible to isolate the most effective (or influential) features in shaping viewers' perceptions of any given debate. Moreover, an experimental design might help us to understand the effects of post-debate media coverage on the views of those citizens who choose *not* to watch the event when first broadcast.

Presidential debates are, as we have suggested previously, part of a larger pattern of events and circumstances that make up a political campaign. Until now, most researchers have been satisfied to study in depth a small part of that pattern (usually taking up only one or two research questions within the context of a single debate). These studies have, of course, rendered valuable and enduring information about the power and possibilities of debating. The suggestions above, however, are our attempt to recommend a look at the broader pattern. By considering the persistence of debate effects, variations in the role of the media, candidate strategies, and pre-convention debates, social scientists may be able to learn more about the *cumulative* effects of presidential debates, which are so often posited—and so rarely verified—by journalists and politicians.

NOTES

1. Daniel Nimmo, *Political Communication and Public Opinion in America* (Santa Monica, CA: Goodyear Publishing Company, 1978).
2. Carl I. Hovland, I. L. Janis, and H. H. Kelley, *Communication and Persuasion* (New Haven: Yale University Press, 1953); selected information on these and other theories of attitude change is taken from Carol Barner-Barry and Robert Rosenwein, *Psychological Perspectives on Politics* (Englewood Cliffs, NJ: Prentice Hall, 1985).
3. Barner-Barry and Rosenwein, *Psychological Perspectives*, pp. 157–58.
4. *Newsweek*, November 21, 1988, p. 123.
5. David L. Watson, Gail deBortali-Tregerthan, and Joyce Frank, *Social Psychology: Science and Application* (Glenview, IL: Scott, Foresman and Company, 1984), pp. 177–78.
6. David J. Lanoue and Peter R. Schrott, "The Effects of Primary Season Debates on Public Opinion," *Political Behavior* 11 (1989): 289–306.
7. Leon A. Festinger, *A Theory of Cognitive Dissonance* (Stanford, CA: Stanford University Press, 1957).
8. Barner-Barry and Rosenwein, *Psychological Perspectives*, pp. 152–53.
9. Charles A. Kiesler, Barry E. Collins, and Norman Miller, *Attitude Change: A Critical Analysis of Theoretical Approaches* (New York: John Wiley and Sons, 1969), ch. 6.
10. Ibid., 241.
11. Ibid., 244.
12. Barner-Barry and Rosenwein, *Psychological Perspectives*, pp. 153–54; Daniel Katz, "The Functional Approach to the Study of Attitudes," in Morris Janowitz and Paul M. Hirsch, eds., *Reader in Public Opinion and Mass Communication*, 3d ed. (New York: Free Press, 1981), pp. 38–49.
13. Katz, "The Functional Approach," p. 44.
14. Barner-Barry and Rosenwein, *Psychological Perspectives*, p. 154.
15. Kay Deaux and Lawrence S. Wrightsman, *Social Psychology in the '80s*, 4th ed. (Monterey, CA: Brooks/Cole, 1984), pp. 301–2.
16. See, for example, Jay G. Blumler and Elihu Katz, *The Uses of Mass Communication: Current Perspectives on Gratifications Research* (Beverly Hills, CA: Sage, 1974).
17. Nimmo, *Political Communication*.
18. David O. Sears and Steven H. Chaffee, "Uses and Effects of the 1976 Debates: An Overview of Empirical Studies," in Sidney Kraus, ed., *The Great Debates: Carter vs. Ford, 1976* (Bloomington: Indiana University Press, 1979), p. 257.
19. David J. Lanoue and Peter R. Schrott, "Voters' Reactions to Televised Presidential Debates: Measurement of the Source and Magnitude of Opinion Change," *Political Psychology* 10 (1989): 275–85.

20. See, for example, Sears and Chaffee, "Uses and Effects of the 1976 Debates," p. 243.

21. Lanoue and Schrott, "The Effects of Primary Season Debates."

22. Frederick T. Steeper, "Public Response to Gerald Ford's Statements on Eastern Europe in the Second Debate," in George F. Bishop, Robert G. Meadow, and Marilyn Jackson-Beeck, eds., *The Presidential Debates: Media, Electoral, and Policy Perspectives* (New York: Praeger, 1978); Gladys Engel Lang and Kurt Lang, "Immediate and Mediated Responses: First Debate," in Kraus, *The Great Debates* (1979); and David J. Lanoue, "The 'Turning Point': Viewers' Reactions to the Second 1988 Presidential Debate," *American Politics Quarterly* 19 (1991): 80–95.

23. See, for example, Lanoue and Schrott, "Voters' Reactions"; and Lanoue and Schrott, "The Effects of Primary Season Debates."

24. Kurt Lang and Gladys Engel Lang, "Reactions of Viewers," in Sidney Kraus, ed., *The Great Debates: Background, Perspective, Effects* (Bloomington: Indiana University Press, 1962); Herbert W. Simons and Kenneth Leibowitz, "Shifts in Candidate Images," in Kraus, *The Great Debates* (1979); Lanoue and Schrott, "Voters' Reactions."

25. Percy H. Tannenbaum, Bradley S. Greenberg, and Fred R. Silverman, "Candidate Images," in Kraus, *The Great Debates* (1962).

26. Saul Ben-Zeev and Irving S. White, "Effects and Implications," in Kraus, *The Great Debates* (1962).

27. Jarol B. Manheim, *The Politics Within* (Englewood Cliffs, NJ: Prentice-Hall, 1975), p. 26.

28. Paul R. Hagner and Leroy N. Rieselbach, "The Impact of the 1976 Presidential Debates: Conversion or Reinforcement?" in Bishop, Meadow, and Jackson-Beeck, *The Presidential Debates*, p. 160.

29. Lanoue, "Turning Point," p. 91.

30. John E. Bowes and Herbert Strentz, "Candidate Images: Stereotyping and the 1976 Debates," in Brent D. Ruben, ed., *Communications Yearbook 2* (New Brunswick, NJ: Transaction Books, 1978), pp. 391–406.

31. See, for example, Lanoue and Schrott, "Voters' Reactions . . . "

32. J. Richard Eiser, *Social Psychology: Attitudes, Cognition, and Social Behaviour* (New York: Cambridge University Press, 1986), pp. 14–19.

33. Alan Abramowitz, "The Impact of a Presidential Debate on Voter Rationality," *American Journal of Political Science* 22 (1978): 680–90.

34. See, for example, Lanoue, "Turning Point."

35. Mark H. Davis, "Voting Intentions and the 1980 Carter–Reagan Debate," *Journal of Applied Social Psychology* 12 (1982): 482.

36. Geer, "The Effects of Presidential Debates."

37. Ben-Zeev and White, "Effects and Implications."

38. Ibid., 336–37.

39. Ibid., 337.

40. Sears and Chaffee, "Uses and Effects of the 1976 Debates," p. 245.
41. Ibid.
42. Bowes and Strentz, "Candidate Images," p. 402.
43. Jacob Jacoby, Tracy R. Trautman, and Tommy E. Whittler, "Viewer Miscomprehension of the 1980 Presidential Debate: A Research Note," *Political Psychology* 7 (1986): 297–308.
44. Abramowitz, "The Impact of a Presidential Debate."
45. Lanoue and Schrott, "Voters' Reactions."
46. Lanoue and Schrott, "The Effects of Primary Season Debates," p. 297.
47. Maxwell E. McCombs and Donald L. Shaw, "The Agenda-Setting Function of the Press," in Doris A. Graber, ed., *Media Power in Politics* (Washington, D.C.: Congressional Quarterly Press, 1984), p. 69.
48. Elihu Katz and Jacob J. Feldman, "The Debates in the Light of Research: A Survey of Surveys," in Kraus, *The Great Debates* (1962), p. 203.
49. Sears and Chaffee, "Uses and Effects of the 1976 Debates."
50. Ibid., 234.
51. See, for example, *Los Angeles Times*, August 19, 1988, p. 5.
52. Katz and Feldman, "The Debates in the Light of Research," p. 219.
53. Ibid.
54. Ibid.
55. Sears and Chaffee, "Uses and Effects of the 1976 Debates," p. 248.
56. Ibid., 249.
57. Ibid.
58. Ibid.
59. Robert P. Hawkins, Suzanne Pingree, Kim A. Smith, and Warren E. Bechtolt, Jr., "Adolescents' Responses to Issues and Images," in Kraus, *The Great Debates* (1979).
60. Sears and Chaffee, "Uses and Effects of the 1976 Debates," p., 249.
61. Ibid.
62. Ibid., 250.
63. For a discussion of the incentives of parties and candidates to avoid specific discussion of issues, see Anthony Downs, *An Economic Theory of Democracy* (Boston: Harper and Row, 1957).
64. Robert W. Sarnoff, "An NBC View," in Kraus, *The Great Debates* (1962), p. 56.
65. Sears and Chaffee, "Uses and Effects of the 1976 Debates," p. 234.
66. David Nachmias and Chava Nachmias, *Research Methods in the Social Sciences*, 3d ed. (New York: St. Martin's Press, 1987), p. 257.
67. Samuel Lubell, "Personalities vs. Issues," in Kraus, *The Great Debates* (1962).
68. See, for example, Katz and Feldman, "The Debates in the Light of Research"; Sears and Chaffee, "Uses and Effects of the 1976 Debates"; Lanoue, "Turning Point."

69. Doris A. Graber and Young Yun Kim, "Why John Q. Voter Did Not Learn Much from the 1976 Presidential Debates," in Ruben, *Communications Yearbook 2*, p. 407.

70. Arthur H. Miller and Michael MacKuen, "Informing the Electorate: A National Study," in Kraus, *The Great Debates* (1979), pp. 269–97.

71. Ibid., 291.

72. Sears and Chaffee, "Uses and Effects of the 1976 Debates," p. 234.

73. Ibid., 235.

74. Gladys Engel Lang and Kurt Lang, "The Formation of Public Opinion: Direct and Mediated Effects of the First Debate," in Bishop, Meadow, and Jackson-Beeck, *The Presidential Debates*, p. 75.

75. Sears and Chaffee, "Uses and Effects of the 1976 Debates," pp. 235–36.

76. Richard F. Carter, "Some Effects of the Debates," in Kraus, *The Great Debates* (1962), pp. 253—70.

77. Lanoue, "Turning Point."

78. Ibid., 15.

79. George G. Bishop, Robert W. Oldendick, and Alfred J. Tuchfarber, "The Presidential Debates as a Device for Increasing the 'Rationality' of Electoral Behavior," in Bishop, Meadow, and Jackson-Beeck, *The Presidential Debates*, pp. 179–96.

80. Ibid., 193.

81. Ibid., 196.

82. Ibid.

83. Sidney Kraus, *Televised Presidential Debates and Public Policy* (Hillsdale, NJ: Lawrence Erlbaum and Associates, 1988), p. 128.

84. Kathleen Hall Jamieson and David S. Birdsell, *Presidential Debates: The Challenge of Creating an Informed Electorate* (New York: Oxford University Press, 1988).

85. Abramowitz, "The Impact of a Presidential Debate."

86. In 1960, for example, more than half of the empirical studies collected by Katz and Feldman were concerned, at least in part, with viewers' assessments of who won the debates. See Katz and Feldman, "The Debates in the Light of Research."

87. Lang and Lang, "Reactions of Viewers," in Kraus, *The Great Debates* (1962).

88. Ibid., 315.

89. Lang and Lang, "The Formation of Public Opinion," p. 79.

90. Lanoue, "Turning Point."

91. John G. Geer, "The Effects of Presidential Debates on the Electorate's Preference for Candidates," *American Politics Quarterly* 16 (1988): 486–501.

92. Lang and Lang, "Immediate and Mediated Responses."

93. Ibid., 309.

94. Lanoue and Schrott, "The Effects of Primary Season Debates."

95. David J. Lanoue, "One That Made a Difference: Cognitive Consistency, Political Knowledge, and the 1980 Presidential Debate" (Paper presented at the 1990 meeting of the Midwest Political Science Association, Chicago).

96. See Katz and Feldman, "The Debates in the Light of Research"; and Sears and Chaffee, "Uses and Effects of the 1976 Debates."

97. Steeper, "Public Response to Gerald Ford's Statements," p. 101.

98. Lang and Lang, "Reactions of Viewers," p. 317.

99. See, for example, Russell Middleton, "National TV Debates and Presidential Voting Decisions," *Public Opinion Quarterly* 26 (1962): 426–29.

100. Manheim, *The Politics Within*.

101. Lee Sigelman and Carol K. Sigelman, "Judgments of the Carter–Reagan Debate: The Eyes of the Beholders," *Public Opinion Quarterly* 48 (1984): 627.

102. Lanoue, "One That Made a Difference," p. 3.

103. Steeper, "Public Response to Gerald Ford's Statements," p. 101.

104. Deaux and Wrightsman, *Social Psychology in the '80s*, pp. 301–2.

105. *Newsweek*, November 17, 1980, p. 28; November 21, 1988, p. 140.

106. Lanoue and Schrott, "The Effects of Primary Season Debates."

107. Lanoue, "One That Made a Difference."

108. Lanoue and Schrott, "The Effects of Primary Season Debates."

109. See, for example, Robert G. Meadow and Marilyn Jackson-Beeck, "A Comparative Perspective on Presidential Debates: Issue Evolution in 1960 and 1976," in Bishop, Meadow, and Jackson-Beeck, *The Presidential Debates*; Kendall L. Baker and Helmut Norpoth, "Candidates on Television: The 1972 Electoral Debates in West Germany," *Public Opinion Quarterly* 45 (1981): 329–45; Lanoue and Schrott, "Voters' Reactions to Televised Presidential Debates."

110. See David L. Paletz and Richard J. Vinegar, "Presidents on Television: The Effects of Instant Analysis," *Public Opinion Quarterly* 41 (1978): 488–97.

5

PUTTING IT ALL TOGETHER: DEBATES, POLITICIANS, AND VOTERS

The previous chapters have considered the history of presidential debates, the content of debates and strategies of the candidates, and the effects of these events on voters. We will now attempt to tie these issues together and discuss the power and prospects of presidential debates. It is, of course, easier to describe and analyze political communication than it is to evaluate its effectiveness and importance. Still, it is possible to speculate on the past and future of debates by considering how well they fulfill each of their purported functions. This, in turn, will lead us to certain normative conclusions which we will take up below.

WHY ARE THERE DEBATES?

The Public Interest

Voters, as a rule, rate presidential debates quite favorably. They see them as a significant source of information about the candidates and their issue positions. As we have seen, the evidence does, to a limited extent, bear out this belief. Voters, however, also view debates as often decisive to their own choices of how to vote. The evidence on that point, of course, is quite a bit more mixed. In any event, general election debates are unique in their ability to generate massive audiences for political discussion. In a world of cable television and endless entertainment options, this is, in itself, remarkable. Clearly, the American people are voting with their channel selectors in favor of these events.

There is, to be sure, no evidence to suggest that the high ratings for presidential debates indicate a national hunger for political information. Primary season debates receive negligible ratings, as do weekend news commentary shows. Indeed, later debates in a series (e.g., the fourth debate of 1976) almost invariably receive poorer ratings than their predecessors.[1] George Bush's proclamation during his second encounter with Michael Dukakis that "there will be no more debates" in 1988 may well have struck a responsive chord with many Americans. Clearly, there can be too much of a "good thing." It is unlikely that James Karayn's proposal for a series of five debates and two major candidate addresses would generate much public enthusiasm (or receive very high television ratings).[2] The public appetite for politics (and, therefore, presidential debates) is limited.

Nevertheless, it is possible that voters have come to expect that their candidates will debate and that the politicians have taken notice. The Kennedy–Nixon debates in 1960 represented a novelty. Frontrunners during the three subsequent elections were not apparently harmed by their refusal to agree to similar encounters. In 1976 and 1980, close elections persuaded both sides to participate (although, in the latter case, the agreement came only at the last moment). Since 1980, however, debates have occurred even in elections that were not apparently close. If Americans now consider debates to be an integral part of the campaign season, candidates—especially frontrunners—may have to weigh the costs of nonparticipation against the risks of debating. It is therefore possible that debates are an institution that will persist without recourse to legal and technical strategies that would require them.

Candidate Perspectives

Campaign managers are about as close as American politics gets to the Downsian "rational actor," concerned primarily with winning elections, and crafting strategies and proposals in order to achieve that end.[3] To the considerable extent that these operators determine the actions and statements of the nominees, the candidates' choices will be similarly rational. As a consequence, we can expect presidential debates to occur only when both major candidates perceive some likely benefit in participating. We would not be the first scholars to note that debates are most likely when an election appears close or when the frontrunner is relatively unknown and wishes to assuage public doubts about him or herself (for example, Jimmy Carter in 1976). Likewise, it is scarcely a revelation to suggest that underdogs are generally desperate to debate and are willing to make great concessions to draw the opposition in.

What is more interesting, however, is the question of what it means to "win" within the context of different candidate strategies. Generally, we think of winning in terms of large numbers of voters shifting from one side to the other (or shifting from undecided status) as a result of a debate. To be sure, this has been the goal of underdog candidacies since debates began. Nevertheless, two equally valid—and probably more common—strategies are to try to reinforce the tentative preferences of potential supporters and to appeal to the long-standing loyalties of wavering partisans.

The first strategy was employed by Jimmy Carter in 1976 and Ronald Reagan in 1980, both with apparent success. The second strategy was used by John Kennedy in 1960 and research shows that, indeed, he was able to bring undecided Democrats into the fold through his confident, competent performance.[4] Clearly, then, it is possible to win a debate even when social scientists are unable to perceive an "effect." It is, of course, also possible to lose: Richard Nixon (in 1960), Jimmy Carter (in 1980), and Michael Dukakis (in 1988) enjoyed considerably less success with these tactics.

Very few candidates actually attempt to achieve the "home run," the one- or two-debate "knockout" that makes a contender out of a near-certain also-ran. More, of course, would like to try (Goldwater and McGovern come to mind), but it is a rare frontrunner who permits such a challenge. There is, moreover, little evidence that "home runs" occur, or that if they do, they are irreversible. Walter Mondale's defeat of Ronald Reagan in their first 1984 debate (a rare frontrunner-underdog encounter) had little net effect;[5] neither did the one-sided vice presidential debate between Lloyd Bentsen and Dan Quayle in 1988.[6] As noted previously, scholars are even mixed as to how ultimately meaningful the fabled first Kennedy–Nixon debate was in 1960, as well as the "Eastern Europe" debate between Ford and Carter in 1976.[7]

This is, of course, not to say that debates are incapable of converting voters. Examples of such conversion do exist and are detailed above. Instead, we argue that a number of perceptual filters exist that militate against the "home run." Perhaps, to stretch the baseball analogy further,

Figure 5.1
A Model of Debate Effects

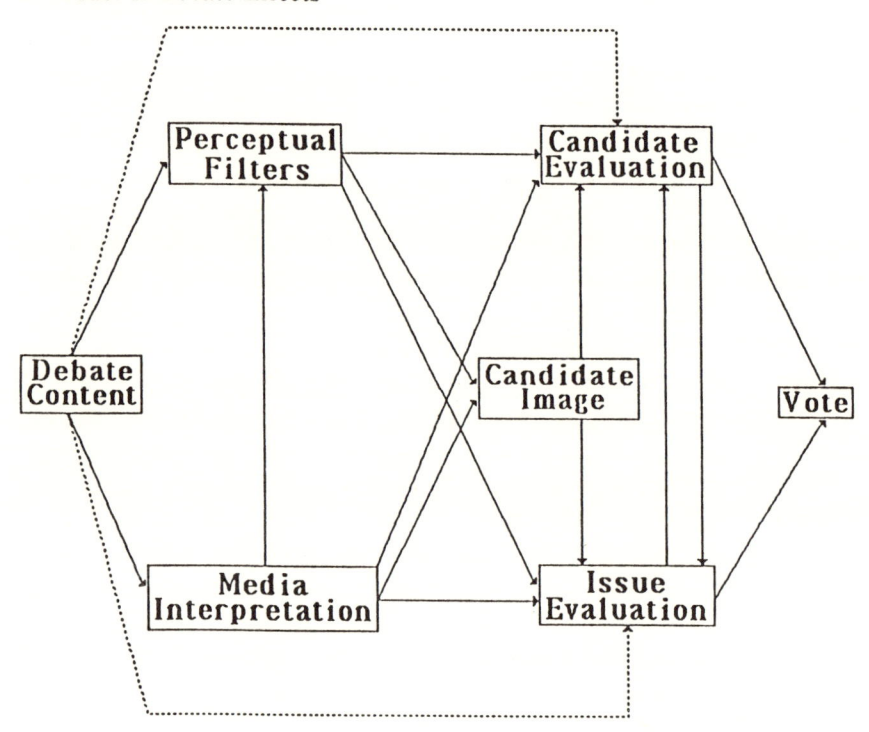

[Diagram: Boxes labeled "Debate Content", "Perceptual Filters", "Media Interpretation", "Candidate Evaluation", "Candidate Image", "Issue Evaluation", and "Vote", connected by arrows showing relationships among them.]

a successful debater must settle for "singles" and "doubles." But, surely, such hits may also contribute significantly to winning ball games.

A MODEL OF DEBATE EFFECTS

It is clear by now that the processes by which debates help to shape public opinion (and thus electoral outcomes) are more complicated than previously assumed. Debates are no more likely to produce instant "hypodermic" effects on the viewing public than any other type of media presentation.[8] The effects of debates, we would argue, may be substantial, but they are generally indirect. Debates exert their greatest influence on candidate images (and, to a lesser extent, issue evaluations). Still, if candidate images are, aside from partisanship, the single strongest predictor of presidential voting behavior, an event that alters these images must be considered electorally consequential. The following discussion ties together the various threads of research reported above, and attempts to model the actual effects of presidential debates. The model is presented in Figure 5.1, and each of its components will be treated individually.

Debate watching actually suggests two separate, but critical, issues. The first, of course, is whether or not a person actually chooses to tune in to a given debate. Even with fairly strong viewership, it remains the case that debate watchers are a group self-selected in terms of education, political interest, strength of partisanship, and so forth. We noted in our discussion of primary elections that those voters most apt to watch a debate are also those least likely (due to their presumably strong pre-debate views) to be affected by it. Nevertheless, general election debates *do* draw in less politically minded viewers as well, and these voters may find the encounters particularly useful in evaluating the nominees.

More importantly, it may not even be necessary to watch debates in order to be affected by them. Because of the attention such events receive from the mass media, it is possible to become familiar with the "high points" (i.e., dramatic moments, gaffes, etc.) of a debate without actually having watched it (surely, nonwatchers learned quickly of Lloyd Bentsen's "You're no Jack Kennedy" put-down of Dan Quayle in 1988). A particularly positive or negative media assessment of a candidate's debate performance, therefore, might influence the candidate evaluations of less attentive voters. To be sure, such nonviewers would probably not benefit from debate-induced information gain (post-debate media reports are, after all, generally nonsubstantive). Still, only the most oblivious Americans (probably nonvoters) could get through the "debate season" entirely unaware of who had won and lost and what, generally, had transpired.

Arguably, a more important variable than actual viewership is the nature of the debate itself. As we have seen above, all debates are not alike. Not all debates will have a measurable effect on public opinion. Indeed, it is the unpredictability of the form that makes it so attractive to the media and to voters (and so terrifying to politicians and their handlers). It is clear, for instance, that only rarely are debates considered, in terms of public opinion, to be one-sided affairs. Although commentators and viewers may strain to find a clear winner in every confrontation, one does not always emerge. And if the candidates are unable to distinguish themselves in terms of performance, it seems unlikely that the voters will respond in any perceptible way. Thus, it goes without saying that not all debates in a series will have an identical impact on viewers. Few would disagree that the first Kennedy–Nixon debate in 1960 (or, perhaps, the second Carter–Ford confrontation in 1976) was more consequential than the rest.

Moreover, dramatic moments seem to have the greatest potential to move viewers and alter their opinions. Not only do dramatic debating moments affect the way voters look at the candidates, they may also have an impact on the longevity of these judgments. Evaluations that change as a result of a "memorable" debate may be far more persistent than those that do not. As discussed below, the media may serve to intensify this effect. It should be apparent, in any event, that presidential debates do differ, and we can thus expect different reactions to each.

Likewise, we can expect different reactions from different viewers. Just as each debate is unique, each voter processes it in his or her own way. These reactions will depend on the voter's various personal characteristics—partisan loyalty, prior political knowledge, "ego involvement" in the campaign, and reliance on the news media, as well as the usual cast of ethnic and socioeconomic attributes. For voters with limited political information and few preconceived biases, the debate may actually have a direct—that is, unmediated—effect on candidate and issue evaluation. Similarly, a particularly good or bad candidate performance may provide such a stark contrast in voters' minds as to bypass the usual mediating filters. In 1984, for example, Republican as well as Democratic viewers were able to perceive Ronald Reagan's shaky first debate performance even before it was dissected by the media illuminati, and his opponent's image improved even among the president's supporters.[9] For this reason, we have specified arrows indicating the possibility of a *direct* relationship between debate watching and issue and candidate evaluation.

Generally, however, the effects of debate watching on political evaluations (and thus vote choice) are not direct. Rather, they are mediated by each viewer's perceptual filters and the power of the mass media. We will begin by discussing the *role of the media*. We have already demonstrated the influence of the media in shaping voters' debate evaluations. Without the persistence of journalists, Gerald Ford's Eastern Europe gaffe would have gone unnoticed by the vast majority of those who had watched the second 1976 debate.[10] In addition, there is ample evidence suggesting that television reports, in particular, affect recollections of debates over time, especially on the question of who won and lost each encounter.[11]

One might argue that the media have become more circumspect in recent years, sensitive to criticism about the power of "instant analysis" to harm politicians and alienate viewers.[12] Clearly, the unfettered exchange of post-event opinion that characterized television news commentary in the 1970s has given way to a more careful approach. During the 1988 debates, for example, network analysts seemed particularly wary of declaring one or the other candidate as the winner, even after Bentsen's superior showing against Quayle. Balance, both in the statements of commentators and in the interviews of candidate spokespersons (the so-called "spin doctors"), is now the hallmark of television's approach to covering these events. It might, therefore, seem likely that the influence of the media on viewers' debate perceptions is not nearly so great today as it was during the "bad old days" of instant analysis.

Recent evidence, however, suggests that this is not entirely the case. Although analysts may be more reluctant than before to render instantaneous judgments, this has not lessened journalists' commitment to "horse race" coverage of presidential campaigns. Shortly after each confrontation, reporters begin an active assessment of how the debate helped and hurt each candidate. The new tool in this effort seems to be the reporting of post-debate public opinion polls as an "objective" indicator of winning and losing. While no network has repeated ABC's unfortunate "900-number poll" of 1980, there are more than enough organizations engaging in immediate post-debate "scientific" polling. And, of course, these numbers tend to take on a life of their own. One of the authors found, for example, that after the second Bush–Dukakis debate in 1988, the proportion of viewers naming George Bush as the winner of the encounter grew over time, presumably in response to media reports of his victory.[13]

Moreover, even with the media's apparent self-conscious commitment to balance, journalists still determine what moments during debates will be elevated above all others. Scholars are mixed as to whether or not debates serve an "agenda-setting" function with respect to the issues surrounding the presidential campaign.[14] There is little controversy, however, over the media's ability to set the agenda with regard to post-debate analysis and discussion. It was, as noted above, the media that made Ford's gaffe the "story" of the 1976 debates (although Ford's own subsequent statements clearly did not help matters). Likewise, television undoubtedly had a role in making "You're no Jack Kennedy" a household phrase in the fall of 1988.

By emphasizing certain debating moments, journalists may well help to "prime" viewers' evaluations of the events.[15] This may hold as much for issue-oriented discussions as it does for heated exchanges (George Bush's careless comments about the possibility of prosecuting women who have abortions caused a minor ruckus in 1988, which blew over only after deft "spinning" by his handlers).[16] In short, so long as the media dominate our post-debate thoughts and recollections, they have the capacity—regardless of their intentions—to enhance the influence of a debate on candidate and issue evaluations (and thus, perhaps, on vote choice).

Television, newspapers, and news magazines, then, represent an important intervening point between the experience of viewing a debate and the act of interpreting it. The media generally serve to sharpen the contrast between the candidates and to provide a reference point for evaluating the most important features of their confrontations. In this way, journalists' reports can have a direct effect on the way that voters see the nominees and the major issues of the campaign. A debate may only be beneficial (or harmful) to a candidate *after* viewers have been exposed to post-debate analysis.

The vast literature on political communication, however, informs us that media effects are not always (or perhaps not even often) direct. Instead, they, too, are usually mediated by the *perceptual filters* common to all people. Early assumptions of extreme media effects (based on anecdotal evidence, particularly the perceived success of the propaganda campaign in Nazi Germany) turned out to be greatly exaggerated.[17] Scholars from the 1940s through the 1960s generated an impressive body of evidence suggesting that media effects could only be understood in terms of the preconceived biases, opinions, and personal associations of each individual. The same may be said for presidential debates and their media analysis. Like other political information, we expect that these stimuli will be filtered through each voter's prevailing system of attitudes. The strength and coherence of these attitudes will, in turn, influence the extent to which a single presidential campaign encounter can shape public opinion.

According to the authors of the seminal (and still influential) book, *The American Voter*, party identification is the most important of these filters.[18] Party loyalty, as conceptualized by this model, is a deep-seated, internalized fealty to a certain political party, learned at the parents' knee and strengthened through a lifetime of commitment. As such, it is central to an individual's political worldview. Cognitive consistency theory (see chapter 4) would suggest that such biases are likely to lead to selective perception and retention of information.[19] That is, viewers will see what they want to see, and recall only the most favorable data.

The research discussed above indicates that this premise has some validity. Those claiming party loyalties do tend to see "their" candidate in a much better light than viewers claiming the opposite (or no) identification. We would assume that media commentary is similarly filtered by feelings of party affiliation. While this might seem to be (and often is) a force working against debate effects, it does not have to be. We might recall that research from the 1960 debates indicates that Democratic identifiers felt much better about John F. Kennedy after the encounters.[20] This is especially important because it includes voters who had previously been undecided between the candidates. Apparently, the nationally televised Democratic-Republican matchup activated these voters' sense of loyalty, and led them to sympathize with (and thus support) their fellow Democrat. It is possible that the same effect benefited Jimmy Carter in his series of debates with Gerald Ford in 1976. In short, perceptual filters do not necessarily render debates meaningless.

Of course, party identification, as conceptualized by the "Michigan Model" during the 1950s, has taken quite a beating in subsequent decades.[21] Challenges have been both methodological and conceptual. Perhaps most damaging has been the fact that loyalties have been broken down over the past thirty years, with increasing numbers of Americans refusing to declare any party allegiance. Some now suggest that the concept was never really valid to begin with, or that it is an artifact of the non-ideological politics of the Eisenhower era.[22] It is possible, therefore, that this important perceptual filter, which has dominated analyses of politics since the 1950s, is less important today.

Party identification, however, is far from the only perceptual filter available to voters. Even without such loyalties, voters often develop strong preferences for certain candidates and issue positions. Further, they strengthen those ties through interaction with like-minded associates and opinion leaders (the so-called "two-step flow" of information)[23] and by defending their views against opposing arguments. Such discussion enlarges a person's stake in his or her views, increasing the level of ego involvement. By the time of presidential debate, many such preconceptions and preferences will have become well entrenched. Thus, selective perception and retention can result in these cases as well.

These pre-debate preferences, like those implied in the concept of party identification, are generally a force for stability in opinion. Nevertheless, for many voters these views may be less than fully formed. As Downs notes, "quasi-informed" individuals, while holding tentative preferences, are still subject to persuasion.[24] Thus, it may be possible for debates to convert those who had planned to vote for the opposition.

More likely, however, even a preliminary candidate preference will mediate viewers' reactions to debates and result in reinforcement of prior predilections. This should be especially true for voters who view the debate (or discuss it afterward) with people who have made the same tentative (or more firm) decision. It is in this way that reinforcement becomes more than just a trivial, if interesting, finding. If a voter is subject to the effects of persuasion, his or her vote remains in doubt. If enough citizens fall into this category, the outcome of the election remains in doubt. It is certainly possible that the reinforcing effects of some presidential debates have helped to solidify a candidate's lead and ensure ultimate victory.

Many, for example, argue that the 1980 election provided one such case. Ronald Reagan, holding a lead in the polls throughout most of the campaign, still faced voter misgivings about his concern for the disadvantaged and his propensity to use force as a first resort (the so-called "mad bomber" issue). The Reagan camp saw its job as reassuring the American people that its candidate was concerned about peace and sensitive to the plight of the poor. To the extent that Reagan was able to get that message across, and tell tentative supporters what they wanted to hear, he may have cleared the last hurdle facing his election. In this way, reinforcement of prior preferences, far from being a statistical curiosity, may have been critical to the outcome of the election.

There is one more type of perceptual filter that may be useful in the study of presidential debates. Political psychologists have become increasingly interested in understanding public opinion in terms of a concept known as the *schema*. According to these researchers, a schema is a device for organizing the endless flow of information into manageable "chunks." To these scholars, each citizen is a "cognitive miser" who seeks to limit the amount of time and energy necessary to understand politics.[25] According to Milton G. Lodge and Ruth Hamill, schemas serve a number of functions, including "providing categories for labeling people . . . [and] events," determining "what information will be attended to, encoded, and retrieved from memory," and providing "a basis for making more confident decisions and predictions."[26]

Using schema theory as their guide, Arthur H. Miller, Martin P. Wattenberg, and Oksana Malanchuk have attempted to explain voters' use of personality factors in evaluating and deciding between presidential candidates.[27] They take issue with the proposition that voter concerns with leadership, competence, and integrity represent "superficial and idiosyncratic assessments."[28] Rather, they suggest, voters measure nominees against a well thought out standard of expected presidential personality, in effect a schema of presidential behavior. Personality-centered evaluations, they conclude, "actually concentrate on instrumental concerns about the manner in which a candidate would conduct governmental affairs."[29] In short, in a complicated and uncertain world, and given only questionable promises and vague rhetoric on which to rely, the rational voter looks to the campaign for cues about each candidate's character, and uses these cues to help determine what kind of president to expect.

It is not difficult to see the relevance of this research to the study of presidential debates. Those who watch televised debates may have a similar agenda—measuring the candidates against expectations of "presidentialness." Journalists seem intuitively to understand this phenomenon, often speaking of how successful debating candidates have been at sounding "presidential" and reassuring voters of their fitness to hold the nation's highest office. To the extent that this refers to the debaters' abilities to project competence, to think well under pressure, and to enlighten and inspire, such analyses dovetail nicely with the schematic approach discussed above.

In 1980, for example, media commentators spoke at length about Ronald Reagan's success in sounding measured and "presidential."[30] By implication, the incumbent, Jimmy Carter, did not measure up equally. If these analyses of public reactions are accurate, they might go a long way toward explaining the supposed link between the 1980 debate and Reagan's last-minute surge to victory (and perhaps, as well, why these effects are not as apparent in the debating literature).

If significant debate effects are most likely to occur when these events activate voters' schemas, then, clearly, one major research objective should be discovery and analysis of these attitudinal constructs. Unfortunately, for the moment, such research is virtually nonexistent. Thus, we may only speculate about some of the findings from debate research, and how they may be consistent with a schematic approach. Such an analysis may help to tie together research reporting voters' reactions to candidates' statements, their images, and even their appearances. If voters have a schema for the way a president should act, for example, they may likewise have a schema for the way a president should look. The debate-related problems faced by Richard Nixon in 1960 (and perhaps also by Michael Dukakis in 1988)[31] may have come as a result of such factors, which were (especially in the latter case) entirely out of the candidates' control.

In addition to presidential schemas, many viewers probably also maintain active partisan schemas. A number of scholars have written persuasively about the well-formed and interconnected attitudes and expectations voters hold about the major American political parties.[32] In that sense, partisan schemas may also be a force for stability in voters' reactions to presidential debates. Lodge and Hamill note that voters are more likely to "hear" and remember statements from candidates that are consistent with prevailing political schemas.[33] As a consequence, there may be a tendency on the part of debate watchers to pay closest attention when Democratic debaters sound like "Democrats," and when Republicans sound like "Republicans." A viewer in 1988, for example, may have paid greater attention to Dukakis' critique of military spending (a stereotypical Democratic concern) than to his statements about successful crime fighting as governor of Massachusetts (a more typically Republican issue). Thus, it may be difficult for a candidate to break out of the "party mold" (as Dukakis attempted to do), even if voters have misgivings about many of the party's positions.

On the other hand, it may also be possible that a performance (or statement) that is strongly and surprisingly contrary to voters' partisan expectations will generate special attention. This may be particularly true when the media point out the discrepancy. When Gerald Ford spoke of the "independence" of the Eastern European nations, it was reported not only as an error in fact, but also as a particularly unusual statement coming from a conservative Republican. Once reported and attended to, this gaffe may have been more shocking—and therefore more salient—because it contrasted so starkly with voters' expectations about the foreign policy positions and statements of Republican presidents.

In addition to partisan schemas, voters may also hold more specific candidate-centered schemas about well-known political figures.[34] Not all who participate in such debates are equally well known, of course. John Kennedy and Jimmy Carter were not as familiar to the American public at the time of their first debates as were their opponents, Vice President Nixon and President Ford. Nevertheless, if citizens have developed certain attitudes and expectations about their political leaders (beyond partisan or more general "presidential" considerations), these schemas, too, should guide their debate evaluations. Once again, voters should be more likely to remember and elevate statements that are consistent with these expectations.

We are left here to speculate on some possible examples of these candidate-centered schemas affecting viewers' judgments of presidential debates. We can offer no evidence (other than anecdotal) in support of these assertions. Nevertheless, it is possible to identify two cases in which viewers' evaluations of supposedly "critical" debates were apparently affected, at least in part, by information that seemed to confirm preexisting negative candidate perceptions.

Ford's comments on Eastern Europe, and his subsequent mishandling of the media fallout, may not have been so damaging had they emanated from another candidate. Unfortunately, Gerald Ford had been tagged during the 1970s with an image as a "bumbler." Much was made of this athletic president's tumbles down ski slopes and near-falls from airplane steps. One interviewer went so far as to question the president's intelligence to his face (Ford answered this question with a recitation of his performance at the University of Michigan and Yale Law School).[35] Thus, the damage done to Ford due to the Eastern Europe comments may have been greater because it reinforced viewers' preconceptions about Gerald Ford's shortcomings.

By the same token, part of Richard Nixon's problem in 1960 may have been the way that the first debate reinforced fears and concerns that people had about him. A number of analyses of Nixon's personal appearance during his first debate with Kennedy mentioned, in addition to his poor makeup job and light suit, the fact that he looked nervous, even "shifty-eyed."[36] There is no question that Nixon had an image problem in 1960, dating back to his earlier red-baiting days, and especially to 1952 when, as Dwight Eisenhower's vice presidential nominee, he had to defend himself against charges of influence peddling (part of that defense being his now famous "Checkers" speech). Once again, it may have been Nixon's misfortune that his first debate appearance activated in voters' minds some of their old worries. Perhaps from another candidate, such behavior, while not beneficial, would not have been so harmful.

It is worth repeating that almost all of the examples discussed above are speculative. Debate researchers have not typically been alert to the possible usefulness of schema theory to understand why certain debates and certain incidents seem to be more critical than others (this, of course, includes the authors of this book). As we noted in chapter 4, John Geer has argued that debates are of greatest consequences to a campaign when they present new or unusual information.[37] Perhaps this may best refer to information that dramatically contradicts pre-debate schemas (Geer, for example, mentions Ronald Reagan's woeful first-debate performance in

1984, as a clear case of viewer expectations—of a confident performance by the "Great Communicator"—being violated).

On the other hand, Geer suggests that reinforcement should be the expected consequence of debates when candidates' arguments are largely consistent with their major campaign themes. Here, too, schema theory may get to the root of the question. If candidates are talking (and acting) in accordance with viewers' expectations, then we should expect little or no opinion change to result from the debate, although reinforcement may well take place. What is clear, in any event, is the need for students of presidential debating to consider schema theory as a way of bringing together all the disparate strands of research that current exist, and to understand schemas as perhaps one of the most important perceptual filters mediating debate evaluations.

The final factor in our model, separating the initial act of debate watching from the ultimate vote choice, is viewers' evaluations of issues and candidates. It is unreasonable to expect a debate, per se, to have a direct effect on voters' final decisions. Presumably, most voters recognize that a debate is simply a single, if dramatic, event within the context of a much longer campaign. Indeed, one of the major themes of this chapter is that presidential debates do not occur in a political vacuum. To the extent that such events matter, it is because they have prompted voters to review or alter their evaluations of the candidates' issue positions and/or their assessments of the candidates' personal strengths and weaknesses. The information provided by the debate, then, helps to shape those factors that ultimately contribute to the voter's choice.

We will begin with a discussion of the role of *issue evaluations*. Public choice theory, of course, assumes that the candidates' relative policy positions play a major role in citizens' election day decisions.[38] At its simplest level, rational voting occurs when voters consider the platforms of the competing parties, as well as their past performances in government, and select the party that will most likely increase their own utility. Although public choice theorists since Downs have begun to give candidate-specific factors greater attention in their efforts to describe voters' calculations,[39] issues continue to hold a central place in this model.

From the Downsian perspective, we would assume that debate watchers are particularly attentive to the policy proposals of the candidates and their answers to issue-oriented questions. While debates, like most election-time political communication, suffer from politicians' rational tendency toward vagueness,[40] it is clear that, in many cases, they do help to illuminate substantive distinctions between the participants. Moreover, even if we often complain about the level of discourse during these events, we must put them in perspective: as noted in chapter 3, content analyses have demonstrated that, for all their shortcomings, more information is provided by presidential debates than by most other common purveyors of persuasive messages, including candidate speeches and political advertisements.

At least to some extent, then, debates do seem to provide the opportunity to enhance voters' ability to choose rationally. Unfortunately, few scholars have investigated this question, and the results of the few studies that have been done are mixed. Though information gain does occur (that is, voters *do* learn more about the debaters' views), it is less evident that viewers actually *use* this information. No study has been able to make this link conclusively. Our own work (on the first 1984 debate) provides suggestive evidence that, even as he was performing poorly, Ronald Reagan was able to score some points against Walter Mondale with his appeals on taxation and spending issues.[41] It is questionable, however, just how electorally important these effects were and whether or not they persisted in the ensuing days, as media coverage focused public attention on Reagan's surprisingly inept performance and the so-called "age factor."

As we noted in chapter 4, Abramowitz's study of debates and voter rationality does not provide encouragement for the disciples of Anthony Downs.[42] Rather than evaluating the candidates on the basis of their issue pronouncements, Abramowitz suggests that viewers' desires for cognitive consistency lead them to move their own policy preferences closer to those of their favorite candidate. These voters, in short, do not actually evaluate what the candidates say; instead, they adopt issue positions consistent with their preferred nominee. At first glance, this, too, suggests that debates are of minimal consequence.

These findings, however, do suggest reinforcement and, as we have argued above, no true finding of reinforcing effects is actually meaningless. If the act of viewing presidential debates leads voters to be more satisfied with "their" candidate's stands on the issues (regardless of the process by which this transformation occurs), then it may lead to more positive evaluations of the favored nominee and, therefore, a greater ultimate likelihood of supporting him or her. Thus, there does appear to be some evidence that debate-induced bonding effects (between viewers' and nominees' positions on the issues) may help to influence voters' decisionmaking calculus. Nevertheless, this is clearly a field in need of further research.

Although we have often used the terms interchangeably (and will continue to do so below), *candidate images and candidate evaluations* are not exactly identical. An image is made up of the characteristics and attributes voters' assign to the competing politicians. An evaluation, on the other hand, represents a citizen's cumulative judgment about a candidate. Causally, we expect specific images to influence more general evaluations that, in turn, help to determine the ultimate vote choice. Nevertheless, while each represents a separate concept (and is included individually in our model of debate effects), there has been a great deal of overlap in the debate research on images and evaluations. For that reason, we will consider both together in the following discussion.

The question of images and evaluations is, as noted above, one that has received a great deal of attention in the literature on presidential debates. This is especially important since many political scientists have arrived at the conclusion that such factors are, in our increasingly dealigned political world, the most important proximate influences in determining vote choice.[43] And, while the images of *both* debaters may improve after a debate (perhaps due to public appreciation of the courage needed to face such an unscripted event),[44] voters are clearly capable of making distinctions between relative candidate performances. Some evidence, presented previously, even suggests that many viewers are able to overcome partisan biases and recognize a superior performance on the part of their least preferred candidate (or relative failure on the part of their favorite).[45] To the extent that these assessments (in either a positive or negative way) are persistent, they may have a meaningful influence on the outcome of an election.

It is important to recall, once again, that each debate is but a single event in the overall presidential race. Candidate images (and, to a greater extent, evaluations) are a function of many, many other political cues as well. Thus, debate effects are unlikely to have an immediate, overwhelming impact on candidates' standings in the polls (though some noticeable post-debate changes have been recorded in the three- to ten-point range, an unquestionably meaningful movement).[46] Candidates, in most cases, have ample opportunity to recover from debate-related image problems (as Reagan did on the "old age" question and Ford could have done—but failed to do—after the Eastern Europe incident). Thus, as suggested by one scholar in his analysis of John Kennedy's 1960 debating and election victories, debate-induced image changes will be of greatest consequence when they are consistent with other emerging campaign information.[47] They may also, as in the case of Ronald Reagan in 1980, be useful in allaying sympathetic voters' concerns about alleged personality flaws (or, as in the case of Kennedy, worries about relative youth and questionable competence).

THE ELUSIVE QUESTION OF MOMENTUM

Debates are single, discrete events in a dynamic and evolving campaign. Any effect they have on public opinion must, therefore, be considered in the context of the changing election-year situation. This raises one particularly interesting question that social scientists may have some difficulty answering: Do debates influence the momentum of the campaign? Can they help to maintain or enhance a candidate's surge in the polls? Or, perhaps more important, can a faltering performance by a candidate in front of a nationwide audience temporarily—or permanently—stem the tide of growing support for his or her candidacy?

First, of course, we must consider whether or not momentum in politics actually exists. It is, to be sure, easy to observe a string of consecutive improvements in public opinion polls and conclude that the "Big Mo"—to use George Bush's less-than-felicitous phrase from 1980—is at work. It is also possible, however, that each improvement in a politician's public standing may result from a specific campaign event, and that success, in and of itself, does not necessarily breed further success. Indeed, even in empirical analysis of sporting events, whose colorful metaphors so often grace campaign commentaries, researchers have begun to doubt the validity of momentum (in the case of "hot" and "cold" players and teams).[48]

Some, however, continue to insist that political momentum is a real phenomenon. The "spiral of silence" theory, developed by Elisabeth Noelle-Neumann, speaks to the possibility that momentum can take hold during a political campaign.[49] Noelle-Neumann suggests that as people perceive "their" side of a debate (or in this case, "their" candidate) gaining greater public acceptance, they will feel freer to express their own support openly. If, however, they see their own position on the decline (i.e., becoming increasingly unpopular), they will be more reticent about making their views known. As one side becomes more vocal and the other more passive, the spiral continues, working increasingly to the benefit of the more "popular" viewpoint. Eventually, this effect may influence voting behavior, as well, as citizens rally around the "consensus" position and abandon the less popular one (or, in the case of elections, fail to vote at all).

There is also empirical support, specifically pertaining to American elections, for the concept of momentum. In his research on primary election campaigns, Bartels demonstrates that perceptions of success, especially as reported by the news media, do indeed trigger favorable movement in public opinion.[50] Voters are concerned with candidates' viability, and many actually gravitate toward winners in the manner of a "bandwagon" effect. For better or worse, then, the "Big Mo" apparently does exist in primary races (although it certainly has the capacity to change direction quickly, as Bush found out within weeks of coining the phrase).

Some observers, in fact, have argued that presidential debates *have* influenced candidate momentum and are, in that sense, arguably critical events in election campaigns. Patrick Caddell, who masterminded Jimmy Carter's polling effort in 1976, is convinced that the most important effect of the Carter–Ford debates was that they stalled the Ford campaign on three separate occasions when the polls suggested that the Republican incumbent was closing in on the Democrat's lead.[51] Lacking other political news, it is likely that the same stories will continue to dominate the media agenda, even if they are as trivial as Jimmy Carter's ill-advised and awkward interview in *Playboy* magazine. The intervention of a presidential debate, however, stops most other political news in its tracks. The attention received by the debate story (before, during, and after the event) supersedes all other stories. As a result, the "spiral" of negative or positive press is temporarily halted.

Steeper, as noted in chapter 2, specifically suggests that the second Carter–Ford debate (which included Ford's comments on Eastern Europe) may have been particularly important in halting Ford's positive momentum (or, perhaps, ending Carter's tailspin).[52] He notes that Ford was "never able to start [this momentum] again" before his eventual defeat at the polls in November.[53] In addition, there are other possible candidates for this momentum-halting effect: Richard Nixon's recovery in the second 1960 debate and, perhaps, Walter Mondale's showing in his first debate in 1984. Likewise, one might suggest some nominees for the title of "momentum-enhancing" debate, in which the winning candidate contributes to his own growing popularity: Kennedy's first debate in 1960, Ford's strong performance in the first 1976 encounter, and Ronald Reagan's solid effort against Jimmy Carter in 1980.

Such effects, unfortunately, are not easily established empirically. To be sure, we can observe minor (or perhaps, as in 1980, major) changes in post-debate public opinion polls, which might suggest a debate-induced surge or decline in candidate support. We can only speculate, however, how these figures would have been different if no debate had taken place. Would the momentum of the pre-debate campaign have persisted? If so, then the debate may have been consequential even if no obvious changes occurred in the polls (or even if social scientists could discern no "debate effects"). The solution to this yet unanswered question will require greater creativity on the part of debate reseachers.

CONCLUSION: PRESIDENTIAL DEBATES AND THE VOTE CHOICE

Finally, the debate, filtered through personal biases and media analyses and interpreted in terms of images and issues, has its effect on the vote. We have attempted to argue, on the one hand, that this effect is far more limited than that usually assumed by candidates, journalists, and much of the public. This argument is, of course, consistent with the conventional wisdom among social scientists. No candidacy was ever made by a presidential debate, and none was ever undone by one. But the same could generally be said of any other incident in a campaign, no matter how supposedly critical it was. The fact remains, as it was first outlined by Lazarsfeld, Berelson, and Gaudet in the 1940s, that most voters have come to a final decision well before the traditional Labor Day campaign kickoff and thus, well before the first presidential debate is held between the parties' nominees for president.[54]

Nevertheless, campaigns *do* matter. As Herbert B. Asher points out, few elections are decided by wide popular vote margins, and even beneath electoral college blowouts, we often find a number of states whose outcomes have been decided by relatively few voters.[55] Moreover, wide swings in public opinion polls are often seen during election seasons (consider, for example, the ups and downs of the 1988 race), further testifying to the significance of the campaign. And if campaigns are important, then it likely follows that debates may be important, too.

Note that our argument for debate effects is not a minimal one. We do not assert that debate effects may make a difference, but only in the context of a near-even race, and only then as one of thousands of "decisive" factors. We argue, instead, that debates have the capacity to be uniquely meaningful. No other event draws similar attention from its audience or from the news media. Certainly, no other campaign event generates the same careful—and often paranoid—preparation on the part of the contenders. If it seems so paradoxical that presidential campaign staffs and media elites could get so involved in an event declared trivial by social scientists, we would contend that the problem is not with the professionals, but with their academic observers.

Important debate effects, as we have outlined above, do occur. Perhaps they do not occur directly or in all segments of the population at once. As a result, many debate studies may have been unable to isolate these effects. Certainly, they do not occur after all such events: primary season debates seem particularly influential (at least potentially), and not all general election debates are equally decisive. It is also possible that a large portion of debate effects dissipates over time as candidates recover or campaign issues change. It is likely that the greatest effects of debates may not be in the conversion of committed voters, but in the reinforcement of wavering candidate supporters. But these effects, too, are important.

Given these facts, candidates are well advised to take debates as seriously as they do. Media representatives are correct to pay close attention to their results (although one could certainly disagree with the tone and priorities of their coverage). Finally, social scientists would be well advised to broaden their outlook on presidential debates and consider new ways of studying and analyzing them. There is, we would argue, a great deal more to be learned.

WHITHER THE DEBATE FORMAT?

As we noted previously, the format of American presidential debates has not been especially popular with journalists and scholars. As early as the very first televised debates in 1960, critics were assailing the "press conference" format. One of the best argued of these attacks was presented by J. Jeffery Auer in 1962.[56] A debate, said Auer, must be a confrontation between "matched contestants," given equal time to persuade an audience on a given proposition.[57] By that widely recognized definition of debate, he argued, the Kennedy–Nixon encounters could only be labeled "counterfeit."[58]

First, Auer noted, the "Great Debates" of 1960 did not allow for candidate confrontation. He recalled, evoking the memory of America's most famous pre-television debates, "that it was Lincoln who put the questions to Douglas at Freeport, not an itinerant journalist."[59] In addition, he complained that the three-minute time period for answers was equal for each candidate, but clearly inadequate, creating "the illusion that public questions of great moment can be answered" in three minutes.[60] And, of course, Auer pointed out the obvious, that American presidential debates do not involve a given proposition, but an "oral examination" on many (often unrelated) questions.[61] While lamenting the format and criticizing the emphasis on images over issues, the author ended on a hopeful note. He suggested that the "obvious inadequacies" of the Kennedy–Nixon format might lead to a "real" debate in future years.[62]

As we know, Auer's wish, thirty years later, remains unfulfilled. When debates returned in 1976, and in the years since, the "press conference" format has persisted. As Sidney Kraus correctly observes, candidates are extremely reluctant to face one another directly and submit to a nationally televised grilling by the opposition.[63] It is true that, on occasion, debating candidates do address one another personally (two examples would be Bentsen and Quayle's exchange over the Kennedy legacy and Mondale's rebuke of Reagan's reuse of the phrase, "There you go again"). Nevertheless, most comments made by debaters are in response to journalists' questions, and any nominee who is temporarily "on the ropes" on one topic need merely wait for the next panelist to change the subject.

Just as the format has not changed since 1960, neither has the criticism died down. After the 1976 debate, Lloyd Bitzer and Theodore Rueter, in their book, also decried the debates as "counterfeit."[64] They, however, conceded that the problems with debates emanate from three sources, only one being the "press conference" format. One problem, they said, is that candidates rationally seek to exploit debates for short-term purposes and, as a consequence, eschew detailed substantive discussions of policy. In addition, the medium of television itself may simply be kinder to some politicians than to others. In any event, candidates' debating success depends, to some extent, on their ability to adapt themselves and their appeals to the demands of TV broadcasting. They are required to "charm, instruct, and persuade" a massive and diverse audience.[65] Clearly, any candidate who is more practiced and comfortable with television (and this was written *before* Ronald Reagan's success in 1980) will be at a distinct advantage.

Like their predecessors, Bitzer and Rueter also assailed the modern presidential debate format. Because of the variety of issues discussed (even in so-called "domestic" or "foreign" policy debates), candidates are given little time for reflection as the conversation swings wildly from one topic to the next. Moreover, as Auer first noted, the time available for responses and rebuttals is relatively short, and does not allow candidates to supply well-formed, clearly stated positions (although Bitzer and Rueter would no doubt agree that a longer period of time would not guarantee that candidates would actually provide greater enlightenment). The authors further argued that the candidates are hampered in their appeals because the debate agenda is set by the panelists—if the journalists want to talk about abortion, or civil rights, or taxation, the debaters have no choice but to address those issues.[66]

Kraus comments further on the effects of journalists' presence on debate panels.[67] The invitation to participate on such a panel is, Kraus notes, "a mark of recognition, if not achievement."[68] But journalists also have their own goals, which may not be entirely consistent with the overall goal of informing the public about the issue positions of (and differences between) the nominees. Some critics of debates, in fact, have suggested that panel members often want to "discover something sensational about the debaters, . . . check out [their own] suspicions about one thing or the other, . . . trap the debaters, or . . . ask hostile questions."[69] Indeed, there can be no doubt that the questioners, perhaps increasingly, have come to view debates as an opportunity to probe and challenge the nominees on their weakest points. Thus, Peter Jennings asks Michael Dukakis if he is a passionate leader or "the smartest clerk in the world"; Bernard Shaw predicates consecutive questions to Dukakis and George Bush with the rape and murder of the former's wife and the sudden death of the latter (forcing Dukakis to reiterate his unpopular opposition to capital punishment and Bush to address Dan Quayle's fitness to succeed to the presidency).

A number of observers have suggested solutions to the presumed weaknesses of presidential debates. Among the most popular include limiting (or eliminating) the role of panelists in the proceedings;[70] allowing the debaters to address one another directly;[71] allowing candidates access to notes and other materials to help them recall and deliver their key points;[72] and reverting to a modified Lincoln–Douglas format, in which a single issue is placed on the agenda and discussion is limited to that item.[73] All these suggestions, of course, presuppose that problems exist with presidential debates and that these shortcomings may be partially rectified by altering the debate format.

It may be useful, therefore, to reflect on the major criticisms of American presidential debates in order to determine the extent to which a change in format would bring about the desired end. Clearly, one of the leading complaints, the nonsubstantive style of media coverage and its effects on viewers' evaluations, will not be solved by reworking the format of these encounters. As we have noted in detail in previous chapters, the actual content of these debates is far more substantive than is subsequently reported in the press. It is, therefore, not the demands of the format that generate the "undesirable" coverage, but the perceived demands of journalists to interest (and thus keep) their audience. If anything, direct candidate confrontation would probably only result in more heated exchanges, of the sort that television producers love to turn into "sound bites."

Another major criticism is that debaters address issues with rehearsed chunks of used campaign rhetoric and vague platitudes. Once again, however, there is no reason to believe that a change of format would alter candidate strategies. Anthony Downs, among others, highlights the rationality of candidate vagueness as a means to reach out to as many voters (and offend as few voters) as possible.[74] True, a candidate confrontation may lead to a greater exchange of charges and countercharges, but it is unlikely that much new and useful information (as envisioned by democratic theory) would be acquired by voters as a result.

It is, of course, possible that by limiting debates to a single topic, candidates might be forced, over a sixty- or ninety-minute period, actually to address it in some detail. Still, this assumes that such a topic of singular nationwide interest would exist in every election. It is hard to think of a single issue in 1988, for example, that would have kept viewers glued to their seats (solutions to the budget deficit? national health insurance?). But even in an election year with one outstanding issue, it is hard to imagine, given the risks of addressing such an important matter, that the debaters would shed their usual cloak of reticence and paranoia. It is difficult, for instance, to envision either Hubert Humphrey or Richard Nixon providing specific solutions to the Vietnam crisis in 1968 no matter how much time they were given. It is possible, then, that even this sort of debate would, in the end, be useless and relatively boring to viewers.

In terms of these two major criticisms of presidential debates, that the candidates are uninformative and the post-debate coverage is trivial, it is unlikely that changing the format would have much of an effect. These problems stem much more from the incentives of politicians and journalists than they do from the structure of the events themselves.

This is, of course, not to say that there is no room for improvement. A number of less sweeping proposed reforms might indeed be helpful. Kraus' suggestion that candidates be given access to notes and limited visual aids may help the debaters make clearer, more intelligent presentations on the issues.[75] While some may emphasize the desirability of forcing candidates to think on their feet, there is already no question about the extent of each participant's preparation for these events. Allowing notes would only recognize a condition that already exists. Debates are opportunities for presidential candidates to give their best arguments as to why they should be elected. It should logically follow, then, that the debate format should allow them to be at their best.

In addition, proposals to allow more time for responses, follow-up questions, and rebuttals may be valid as well. Debaters should have enough time to make their case, and panelists should get a chance to probe more deeply on each specific issue. Nevertheless, we should remember that good debates must, to some extent, also be good theater. Those of us whose job and hobby are observing and analyzing politics often forget that most voters are not similarly engaged. Any format change that overly limits the topics under discussion, or gives candidates too much time for speechmaking, may well bore, and thus lose, much of the audience.

Another suggestion that has been made is to open the role of panelist to those who are not journalists. Academics, business and labor leaders, and even "ordinary" citizens should have the opportunity to question the candidates.[76] In this way, the argument goes, debates will not be held hostage to journalists' egos and biases, and the style of questioning might be more enlightening and less confrontational. It is, of course, difficult to determine how successful this change would be. Journalists are not the only people with well-developed egos and biases. Moreover, journalists, unlike most Americans, have spent their careers studying candidates and public issues and, unlike even political scientists, are practiced in the art of framing and delivering questions to crafty politicians. There is no guarantee that opening up the role of panelist would improve presidential debating.

Greater candidate interaction has been a goal of many of those who would tinker with the debate format.[77] Allowing debaters to challenge one another directly, they say, would add to the excitement and "spontaneity" of these events. There is, to be sure, little doubt about that. It is less clear, however, whether such confrontations would actually improve American presidential debates in a normative sense. Spontaneous interaction between debaters would undoubtedly produce more dramatic and intense competition, perhaps even generating "telling" moments and candidate gaffes. It would also be a very popular format change.

But it is just this kind of interaction that is most likely to appear on post-debate news shows, and is most often criticized as meaningless by academic observers. There is no reason to believe a confrontational format would elevate the substantive content of the encounters (primary season debates, which sometimes allow direct candidate confrontation, are not especially more enlightening than their general election counterparts). In addition, it is highly unlikely that presidential nominees can be convinced to submit themselves to such an uncertain, and potentially devastating, arrangement.

"In their present format," writes political scientist Nelson Polsby, "presidential debates are uninteresting, uninformative, and unedifying."[78] Perhaps Polsby's analysis of debates is valid, but we would argue that the format is not the primary problem. It is hard to imagine another format that would coax substance out of cautious politicians and "hard" analysis out of ratings-conscious television networks. If foreign debates often seem more substantial to some observers than American debates, it may be more because of the stronger ideological differences between the competing parties than because of the differences between formats. If by "interesting" we mean "entertaining," format adjustments may certainly produce the desired effect. But if we are most concerned with the use of debates by rational voters for gaining substantive insights into candidates' platforms and policy positions, the solution may require more radical surgery on the body politic than that envisioned by the would-be format tinkerers.

PRESIDENTIAL DEBATES IN THE 1990s

Going into the final decade of the twentieth century, it appears that presidential debates have become a regular feature of American political campaigns. Perhaps no candidate has done more to ensure the continuation of these events than Ronald Reagan. Not only did Reagan become the first frontrunner to agree to meet with a distant underdog (in 1984), he also demonstrated that a candidate could recover from a disastrous debate performance and still win the presidency. Nevertheless, the lesson of 1960 remains compelling. Many of those who participated in the Kennedy–Nixon debates must have assumed that they, too, had started an irreversible process. And yet, debates were not held again until sixteen years later.

Proposals to require debates have been argued by scholars and journalists ever since the long 1960-76 hiatus.[79] The most popular of these would link debate participation with receiving federal matching funds. This is, of course, a controversial suggestion, with some debate observers (for example, Myles Martel) arguing that it would represent an intrusion on the candidates' freedom to seek votes in whatever legal manner they deem most beneficial.[80] Such an action, he suggests, would have negative implications for democratic theory far beyond whatever benefits are derived from the debates themselves.

In addition, such proposals butt heads with political reality. Politicians will always be unwilling to allow "outsiders" to dictate the terms of their campaigns. Presumably, both parties have sufficient strength (in congress and elsewhere) to block any legal attempts to change the rules. Thus, candidates will continue, as they have done in the past, to base their decisions on rational cost-benefit analyses. As we noted earlier, it is now possible that public expectations have entered into these calculations. Debates, in short, will—and should—become institutionalized only when the public has decided they want them badly enough to "punish" nonparticipants.

In keeping with our discussion above, we do not expect serious changes in the current debating format. The "joint press conference" format did not develop by accident. It was created in order to keep the risks of debating low enough that candidates would not be scared off. There is little hope that scholars and journalists, however well-meaning, will be able to convince both nominees in a given election year to venture into the political unknown for the sake of "do-gooders' " perceptions of how to serve the public interest.

One change we hope will occur and persist well into the 1990s is that scholars and other educated observers will once again decide that presidential debates are worth studying. The purpose of this book has been to bring some perspective and organization to the study of presidential debates. We have argued that this can best be done by considering the analyses of empirical social scientists as well as nonacademic political experts (journalists, consultants, etc.).

We have tried to demonstrate that debates are nontrivial events in American politics. Just as media researchers in general moved away from the "minimal consequences" assessment of media effects after the 1960s, we would suggest that it is time to move away from the "minimal consequences" assessment of debate effects during the 1990s. To some extent, we hope we have raised as many questions in this book as we have answered.

NOTES

1. David O. Sears and Steven H. Chaffee, "Uses and Effects of the 1976 Debates: An Overview of Empirical Studies," in Kraus, *The Great Debates* (1979), p. 230.

2. Jim Karayn, "Presidential Debates: A Plan for the Future," in Kraus, *The Great Debates* (1979).

3. Anthony Downs, *An Economic Theory of Democracy* (New York: Harper and Row, 1957).

4. Kurt Lang and Gladys Engel Lang, "Reactions of Viewers," in Kraus, *The Great Debates* (1962), p. 315.

5. David J. Lanoue and Peter R. Schrott, "Voters' Reactions to Televised Presidential Debates: Measurement of the Source and Magnitude of Opinion Change," *Political Psychology* 10 (1989): 275–85.

6. *Newsweek*, November 21, 1988, pp. 138–39.

7. Elihu Katz and Jacob J. Feldman, "The Debates in the Light of Research: A Survey of Surveys," in Kraus, *The Great Debates* (1962); and Sears and Chaffee, "Uses and Effects of the 1976 Debates," p. 230.

8. Shanto Iyengar and Silvo Lenart, "Beyond Minimal Consequences: A Survey of Media Political Effects," in Samuel Long, ed., *Political Behavior Annual*, vol. 2 (Denver: Westview Press, 1989), pp. 21–38.

9. Lanoue and Schrott, "Voters' Reactions."

10. Frederick T. Steeper, "Public Response to Gerald Ford's Statements on Eastern Europe in the Second Debate," in George F. Bishop, Robert G. Meadow, and Marilyn Jackson-Beeck, eds., *The Presidential Debates: Media, Electoral, and Policy Perspectives* (New York: Praeger, 1978).

11. Gladys Engel Lang and Kurt Lang, "The Formation of Public Opinion: Direct and Mediated Effects of the First Debate," in Bishop, Meadow, and Jackson-Beeck, *The Presidential Debates*; Steeper, "Public Response."

12. David L. Paletz and Richard J. Vinegar, "Presidents on Television: The Effects of Instant Analysis," *Public Opinion Quarterly* 41 (1978): 488–97.

13. David J. Lanoue, "The 'Turning Point': Viewers' Reactions to the Second 1988 Presidential Debate," *American Politics Quarterly* 19 (1991):80–95.

14. See chapter 4 for a discussion on this topic.

15. For a description of media "priming," see Shanto Iyengar and Donald R. Kinder, *News That Matters* (Chicago: University of Chicago Press, 1987); and Iyengar and Lenart, "Beyond Minimal Consequences."

16. *Newsweek*, November 21, 1988, p. 124.

17. Iyengar and Lenart, "Beyond Minimal Consequences"; see also Joseph T. Klapper, *The Effects of Mass Communication* (New York: Free Press, 1960).

18. Angus Campbell, Philip E. Converse, Warren E. Miller, and Donald E. Stokes, *The American Voter* (New York: Wiley, 1960).

19. See, for example, Charles A. Kiesler, Barry E. Collins, and Norman Miller, *Attitude Change: A Critical Analysis of Theoretical Approaches* (New York: John Wiley and Sons, 1969), ch. 6.

20. Lang and Lang, "Reactions of Viewers," p. 315.

21. Richard G. Niemi and Herbert F. Weisberg, *Controversies in Voting Behavior*, 2d ed. (Washington, D.C.: Congressional Quarterly Press, 1984), pp. 393–405.

22. Norman H. Nie, Sidney Verba, and John R. Petrocik, *The Changing*

American Voter (Cambridge, MA: Harvard University Press, 1976).

23. Bernard R. Berelson, Paul F. Lazarsfeld, and William N. McPhee, *Voting* (Chicago: University of Chicago Press, 1954), p. 16.

24. Downs, *An Economic Theory*, p. 85.

25. Susan T. Fiske and Shelley E. Taylor, *Social Cognition* (New York: Random House, 1984), p. 12.

26. Milton G. Lodge and Ruth Hamill, "A Partisan Schema for Political Information Processing," *American Political Science Review* 80 (1986): 506.

27. Arthur H. Miller, Martin P. Wattenberg, and Oksana Malanchuk, "Schematic Assessments of Presidential Candidates," *American Political Science Review* 80 (1986): 521–40.

28. Ibid., 521.

29. Ibid., 536.

30. Myles Martel, *Political Campaign Debates: Images, Strategies, and Tactics* (New York: Longman, 1983), p. 27.

31. *Newsweek*, November 21, 1988, p. 139.

32. Lodge and Hamill, "A Partisan Schema"; Arthur H. Miller, "Partisan Cognition in Transition," in Richard R. Lau and David O. Sears, eds., *Political Cognition* (Hillsdale, NJ: Lawrence Erlbaum and Associates, 1986), pp. 203–31.

33. Lodge and Hamill, "A Partisan Schema," p. 505.

34. Allen J. Risley, "Political Learning during the Campaign: The Impact of Television Coverage of Campaign '84 on Knowledge about the Candidates" (Paper presented at the 1990 meeting of the Midwest Political Science Association, Chicago).

35. Ron Nessen, *It Sure Looks Different from the Inside* (Chicago: Playboy Press, 1978), pp. 164–65.

36. Kathleen Hall Jamieson and David S. Birdsell, *Presidential Debates: The Challenge of Creating an Informed Electorate* (New York: Oxford University Press, 1988), p. 183.

37. John G. Geer, "The Effects of Presidential Debates on the Electorate's Preference for Candidates," *American Politics Quarterly* 16 (1988): 486–501.

38. Downs, *An Economic Theory*.

39. See, for example, Samuel Popkin, John W. Gorman, Charles Phillips, and Jeffrey A. Smith, "Comment: What Have You Done for Me Lately? Toward an Investment Theory of Voting," *American Political Science Review* 70 (1976): 779–805.

40. Downs, *An Economic Theory*, p. 115.

41. Lanoue and Schrott, "Voters' Reactions."

42. Alan Abramowitz, "The Impact of a Presidential Debate on Voter Rationality," *American Journal of Political Science* 22 (1978): 680–90.

43. See, for example, Benjamin I. Page and Calvin C. Jones, "Reciprocal Effects of Policy Preferences, Party Loyalties, and the Vote," *American Political Science Review* 73 (1979): 1071–89.

44. Lang and Lang, "Reactions of Viewers"; Herbert W. Simons and Kenneth Leibowitz, "Shifts in Candidate Images," in Kraus, *The Great Debates* (1979); Lanoue and Schrott, "Voters' Reactions."

45. See, for example, Mark H. Davis, "Voting Intentions and the 1980 Carter–Reagan Debate," *Journal of Applied Social Psychology* 12 (1982): 481–92.

46. See, for example, John P. Robinson, "The Polls," in Kraus, *The Great Debates* (1979) on 1976; John F. Stacks, *Watershed: The Campaign for the Presidency 1980* (New York: Times Books, 1981), p. 245 on 1980; *New York Times*, October 11, 1984, p. B11 on 1984; and *Newsweek*, November 21, 1988, p. 140 on 1988.

47. Saul Ben-Zeev and Irving S. White, "Effects and Implications," in Kraus, *The Great Debates* (1962).

48. Bill James, *The Bill James Baseball Abstract 1988* (New York: Ballantine Books, 1988), p. 92.

49. Elisabeth Noelle-Neumann, *The Spiral of Silence* (Chicago: University of Chicago Press, 1984).

50. Larry M. Bartels, *Presidential Primaries and the Dynamics of Public Choice* (Princeton, NJ: Princeton University Press, 1988).

51. Herbert E. Alexander and Joel Margolis, "The Making of the Debates," in Bishop, Meadow, and Jackson-Beeck, *The Presidential Debates*, p. 30.

52. Steeper, "Public Reactions to Gerald Ford's Statements."

53. Ibid., 101.

54. Paul F. Lazarsfeld, Bernard R. Berelson, and Helen Gaudet, *The People's Choice* (New York: Columbia University Press, 1948).

55. Herbert B. Asher, *Presidential Elections and American Politics*, 4th ed. (Chicago: Dorsey Press, 1988), p. 300.

56. J. Jeffery Auer, "The Counterfeit Debates," in Kraus, *The Great Debates* (1962).

57. Ibid., 146.

58. Ibid., 142.

59. Ibid., 147.

60. Ibid.

61. *Newsweek*, November 21, 1988, p. 123.

62. Auer, "The Counterfeit Debates," p. 149.

63. Sidney Kraus, *Televised Presidential Debates and Public Policy* (Hillsdale, NJ: Lawrence Erlbaum and Associates, 1988), p. 147.

64. Lloyd Bitzer and Theodore Rueter, *Carter vs. Ford: The Counterfeit Debates of 1976* (Madison: University of Wisconsin Press, 1980).

65. Ibid., 7.

66. Ibid., 8.

67. Kraus, *Televised Presidential Debates*, p. 144.

68. Ibid.

69. Ibid.
70. Jamieson and Birdsell, *Presidential Debates*, p. 201.
71. Ibid., 195.
72. Kraus, *Televised Presidential Debates*, p. 153.
73. Jamieson and Birdsell, *Presidential Debates*, pp. 201–4.
74. Downs, *An Economic Theory*, p. 115.
75. Kraus, *Televised Presidential Debates*, p. 153.
76. Martel, *Political Campaign Debates*, p. 176.
77. Kraus, *Televised Presidential Debates*, p. 153.
78. Nelson W. Polsby, "Debatable Thoughts on Presidential Debates," in Austin Ranney, ed., *The Past and Future of Presidential Debates* (Washington, D.C.: American Enterprise Institute, 1979), p. 186.
79. Ranney, *The Past and Future*, p. 170.
80. Martel, *Political Campaign Debates*, p. 175.

BIBLIOGRAPHY

Abramowitz, Alan. "The Impact of a Presidential Debate on Voter Rationality." *American Journal of Political Science* 22 (1978): 680–90.

Abramson, Paul R., John H. Aldrich, and David W. Rohde. *Change and Continuity in the 1984 Election.* Washington, D.C.: Congressional Quarterly Press, 1986.

———. *Change and Continuity in the 1980 Elections.* Washington, D.C.: Congressional Quarterly Press, 1982.

Alexander, Herbert E., and Joel Margolis. "The Making of the Debates." In *The Presidential Debates*, edited by G. Bishop, R. Meadow, and M. Jackson-Beeck, pp. 18–32.

Arons, Leo, and Mark A. May. *Television and Human Behavior.* New York: Appleton-Century-Crofts, 1963.

Asher, Herbert B. *Presidential Elections and American Politics.* 4th ed. Chicago: Dorsey Press, 1988.

Auer, J. Jeffery. "The Counterfeit Debates." In *The Great Debates: Background, Perspective, Effects*, edited by Sidney Kraus, pp. 142–50.

Baker, Kendall L., and Helmut Norpoth. "Candidates on Television: The 1972 Electoral Debates in West Germany." *Public Opinion Quarterly* 45 (1981): 329–45.

Baker, Kendall L., Helmut Norpoth, and Klaus Schoenbach. "Die Fernsehdiskussionen der Spitzenkandidaten vor den Bundestagswahlen 1972 und 1976." *Publizistik* 26 (1981): 530–44.

Barner-Barry, Carol, and Robert Rosenwein. *Psychological Perspectives on Politics.* Englewood Cliffs, NJ: Prentice-Hall, 1985.

Bartels, Larry M. *Presidential Primaries and the Dynamics of Public Choice.* Princeton, NJ: Princeton University Press, 1988.

Ben-Zeev, Saul, and Irving S. White. "Effects and Implications." In *The Great Debates: Background, Perspective, Effects*, edited by Sidney Kraus, pp. 331–37.

Berelson, Bernard. *Content Analysis in Communication Research.* Glencoe, IL: Free Press, 1952.

Berelson, Bernard R., Paul F. Lazarsfeld, and William N. McPhee. *Voting*. Chicago: University of Chicago Press, 1954.

Bishop, George F., Robert G. Meadow, and Marilyn Jackson-Beeck, eds. *The Presidential Debates: Media, Electoral, and Policy Perspectives*. New York: Praeger, 1978.

Bishop, George F., Robert W. Oldendick, and Alfred J. Tuchfarber. "The Presidential Debates as a Device for Increasing the 'Rationality' of Electoral Behavior." In *The Presidential Debates*, edited by G. Bishop, R. Meadow, and M. Jackson-Beeck, pp. 179–96.

Bitzer, Lloyd, and Theodore Rueter. *Carter vs. Ford: The Counterfeit Debates of 1976*. Madison: University of Wisconsin Press, 1980.

Blumler, Jay G., and Elihu Katz. *The Uses of Mass Communication: Current Perspectives on Gratifications Research*. Beverly Hills, CA: Sage, 1974.

Bowes, John E., and Herbert Strentz. "Candidate Images: Stereotyping and the 1976 Debates." In *Communications Yearbook 2*, edited by Brent Ruben, pp. 391–406.

Broh, C. Anthony. "Horse-Race Journalism: Reporting the Polls in the 1976 Election." *Public Opinion Quarterly* 44 (1980): 514–29.

Campbell, Angus, Philip E. Converse, Warren E. Miller, and Donald E. Stokes. *The American Voter*. New York: Wiley, 1960.

Carter, Richard F. "Some Effects of the Debates." In *The Great Debates: Background, Perspective, Effects*, edited by Sidney Kraus, pp. 253–70.

Cerny, Karl H., ed. *Germany at the Polls*. Washington, D.C.: American Enterprise Institute, 1978.

Cheney, Richard B. "The 1976 Presidential Debates: A Republican's Perspective." In *The Past and Future of Presidential Debates*, edited by Austin Ranney, pp. 107–30.

David, Paul T., and David H. Everson, eds. *The Presidential Election and Transition, 1980–1981*. Carbondale: Southern Illinois University Press, 1983.

Davis, Dennis K. "Influence on Vote Decisions." In *The Great Debates: Carter vs. Ford, 1976*, edited by Sidney Kraus, pp. 331–47.

Davis, Mark H. "Voting Intentions and the 1980 Carter-Reagan Debate." *Journal of Applied Social Psychology* 12 (1982): 481–92.

Deaux, Kay, and Lawrence S. Wrightsman. *Social Psychology in the '80s*. 4th ed. Monterey, CA: Brooks/Cole, 1984.

De Sola Pool, Ithiel, ed. *Trends in Content Analysis*. Urbana: University of Illinois Press, 1959.

Downs, Anthony. *An Economic Theory of Democracy*. Boston: Harper and Row, 1957.

Drew, Elizabeth. *Campaign Journal: The Political Events of 1983–1984*. New York: Macmillan, 1985.

Drew, Elizabeth. *Portrait of an Election: The 1980 Presidential Campaign*. New York: Simon and Schuster, 1981.

Eiser, J. Richard. *Social Psychology: Attitudes, Cognition, and Social Behaviour*. New York: Cambridge University Press, 1986.

Ekman, Paul, Wallace V. Friesen, and Thomas G. Taussig. "VID-R and SCAN: Tools and Methods for the Automated Analysis of Visual Records." In *The Analysis of Communication Content*, edited by George Gerbner, et al. pp. 297–312.

Ellsworth, John W. "Rationality and Campaigning: A Content Analysis of the 1960 Presidential Campaign Debates." *Western Political Quarterly* 18 (1965): 794–802.

Festinger, Leon A. *A Theory of Cognitive Dissonance.* Stanford, CA: Stanford University Press, 1957.

Fiske, Susan T., and Shelley E. Taylor. *Social Cognition.* New York: Harper and Row, 1984.

Geer, John G. "The Effects of Presidential Debates on the Electorate's Preference for Candidates." *American Politics Quarterly* 16 (1988): 486–501.

Gerbner, George, Ole R. Holsti, Klaus Krippendorff, William J. Paisley, and Philip Stone, eds. *The Analysis of Communication Content: Developments in Scientific Theory and Computer Technology.* New York: John Wiley and Sons, 1969.

Germond, Jack W., and Jules Witcover. *Blue Smoke and Mirrors: How Reagan Won and Why Carter Lost the Election of 1980.* New York: Viking Press, 1981.

———. "Presidential Debates: An Overview." In *The Past and Future of Presidential Debates,* edited by Austin Ranney, pp. 191–205.

Graber, Doris A., ed. *Media Power in Politics.* Washington, D.C.: Congressional Quarterly Press, 1984.

Graber, Doris A., and Young Yun Kim. "Why John Q. Voter Did Not Learn Much from the 1976 Presidential Debates." In *Communications Yearbook 2,* edited by Brent Ruben, pp. 407–21.

Hagner, Paul R., and Leroy N. Rieselbach. "The Impact of the 1976 Presidential Debates: Conversion or Reinforcement?" In *The Presidential Debates,* edited by G. Bishop, R. Meadow, and M. Jackson-Beeck, pp. 157–78.

Harwood, Richard, ed. *The Pursuit of the Presidency 1980.* New York: G. P. Putnam's Sons, 1980.

Hawkins, Robert P., Suzanne Pingree, Kim A. Smith, and Warren E. Bechtolt, Jr. "Adolescents' Responses to Issues and Images." In *The Great Debates: Carter vs. Ford, 1976,* edited by Sidney Kraus, pp. 368–83.

Hershey, Marjorie Randon. "The Campaign and the Media." In *The Election of 1988: Reports and Interpretations,* edited by Gerald M. Pomper, pp. 73–102.

Hogan, J. Michael. "Media Nihilism and the Presidential Debates." *Argumentation and Advocacy* 25 (1989): 220–25.

Holly, Werner, Peter Kuehn, and Ulrich Pueschel. *Politische Fernsehdiskussionen.* Tübingen: Max Neimeyer Verlag, 1986.

Holsti, Ole R. *Content Analysis for the Social Sciences and Humanities.* Reading, MA: Addison-Wesley, 1969.

———. "Introduction." In *The Analysis of Communication Content,* edited by George Gerbner et al., pp. 109–21.

Hovland, Carl I., I. L. Janis, and H. H. Kelley. *Communication and Persuasion.* New Haven: Yale University Press, 1953.

Iyengar, Shanto, and Donald R. Kinder. *News That Matters.* Chicago: University of Chicago Press, 1987.

Iyengar, Shanto, and Silvo Lenart. "Beyond Minimal Consequences: A Survey of Media Political Effects." In *Political Behavior Annual,* edited by Samuel Long, pp. 21–38.

Jacoby, Jacob, Tracy R. Trautman, and Tommy E. Whittler. "Viewer Miscomprehension of the 1980 Presidential Debate: A Research Note." *Political Psychology* 7 (1986): 297–308.
James, Bill. *The Bill James Baseball Abstract 1988*. New York: Ballantine Books, 1988.
Jamieson, Kathleen Hall, and David S. Birdsell. *Presidential Debates: The Challenge of Creating an Informed Electorate*. New York: Oxford University Press, 1988.
Janowitz, Morris, and Paul M. Hirsch, eds. *Reader in Public Opinion and Mass Communication*. 3d ed. New York: Free Press, 1981.
Jordan, Hamilton. *Crisis: The Last Year of the Carter Presidency*. New York: G. P. Putnam's Sons, 1982.
Joslyn, Richard. *Mass Media and Elections*. Reading, MA: Addison-Wesley, 1984.
———. "The Content of Political Spot Ads." *Journalism Quarterly* 57 (1980): 92–98.
Kaase, Max, and Hans-Dieter Klingemann, eds. *Wahlen und politisches System: Analysen aus Anlass der Bundestagswahl*. Opladen, West Germany: Westdeutscher Verlag, 1987.
———. *Wahlen und politisches System*. Opladen, West Germany: Westdeutscher Verlag, 1983.
Karayn, Jim. "Presidential Debates: A Plan for the Future." In *The Great Debates: Carter vs. Ford, 1976*, edited by Sidney Kraus, pp. 209–19.
Katz, Daniel. "The Functional Approach to the Study of Attitudes." In *Reader in Public Opinion and Mass Communication* edited by M. Janowitz and P. Hirsch, pp. 38–49.
Katz, Elihu, and Jacob J. Feldman. "The Debates in the Light of Research: A Survey of Surveys." In *The Great Debates: Background, Perspective, Effects*, edited by Sidney Kraus, pp. 173–223.
Kessel, John H. *Presidential Campaign Politics*. 3d ed. Chicago: Dorsey Press, 1988.
Key, V. O., Jr. *The Responsible Electorate*. Cambridge, MA: Harvard University Press, 1966.
Kiesler, Charles A., Barry E. Collins, and Norman Miller. *Attitude Change: A Critical Analysis of Theoretical Approaches*. New York: John Wiley and Sons, 1969.
Klapper, Joseph T. *The Effects of Mass Communication*. New York: Free Press, 1960.
Klingemann, Hans-Dieter. "Standardcode zur Verschlüsselung der Einstellungen zu den politischen Parteien in der Bundesrepublik Deutschland." Mimeo, ZUMA, Mannheim, West Germany, 1976.
Kracauer, Siegfried. "The Challenge of Qualitative Content Analysis." *Public Opinion Quarterly* 16 (1952): 631–42.
Kraus, Sidney. *Televised Presidential Debates and Public Policy*. Hillsdale, NJ: Lawrence Erlbaum and Associates, 1988.
———, ed. *The Great Debates: Carter vs. Ford, 1976*. Bloomington: Indiana University Press, 1979.
———. *The Great Debates: Background, Perspective, Effects*. Bloomington: Indiana University Press, 1962.
Krippendorff, Klaus. *Information Theory: Structural Models for Qualitative Data*. Beverly Hills, CA: Sage, 1986.
———. *Content Analysis: An Introduction to Its Methodology*. Beverly Hills, CA: Sage, 1980.

———. "Models of Messages: Three Prototypes." In *The Analysis of Communication Content*, edited by George Gerbner et al., pp. 69–106.
Lang, Gladys Engel, and Kurt Lang. "Immediate and Mediated Responses: First Debate." In *The Great Debates: Carter vs. Ford, 1976*, edited by Sidney Kraus, pp. 298–313.
———. "The Formation of Public Opinion: Direct and Mediated Effects of the First Debate." In *The Presidential Debates*, edited by G. Bishop, R. Meadow, and M. Jackson-Beeck, pp. 298–313.
Lang, Kurt, and Gladys Engel Lang. "Reactions of Viewers." In *The Great Debates: Background, Perspective, Effects*, edited by Sidney Kraus, pp. 313–30.
Lanoue, David J. "The 'Turning Point': Viewers' Reactions to the Second 1988 Presidential Debate." *American Politics Quarterly* 19 (1991): 80–95.
———. "One That Made a Difference: Cognitive Consistency, Political Knowledge, and the 1980 Presidential Debate." Paper presented at the 1990 meeting of the Midwest Political Science Association, Chicago.
———. "Debates That Mattered: Viewers' Reactions to the 1984 Canadian Leadership Debates." *Canadian Journal of Political Science* (forthcoming 1991).
Lanoue, David J., and Peter R. Schrott. "Voters' Reactions to Televised Presidential Debates: Measurement of the Source and Magnitude of Opinion Change." *Political Psychology* 10 (1989): 275–85.
———. "The Effects of Primary Season Debates on Public Opinion." *Political Behavior* 11 (1989): 289–306.
———. "The Effects of Primary Season Debates." Paper presented at the 1988 meeting of the American Political Science Association, Washington, D.C.
Lasswell, Harold D. *Analyzing the Content of Mass Communication: A Brief Introduction*. Washington, D.C.: Library of Congress, 1942.
Lau, Richard R., and David O. Sears, eds. *Political Cognition*. Hillsdale, NJ: Lawrence Erlbaum and Associates, 1986.
Lazarsfeld, Paul F., Bernard R. Berelson, and Helen Gaudet. *The People's Choice*. New York: Columbia University Press, 1948.
Lodge, Milton G., and Ruth Hamill. "A Partisan Schema for Political Information Processing." *American Political Science Review* 80 (1986): 505–19.
Long, Samuel, ed. *Political Behavior Annual*. Vol. 2. Denver: Westview Press, 1989.
Lubell, Samuel. "Personalities vs. Issues." In *The Great Debates: Background, Perspective, Effects*, edited by Sidney Kraus, pp. 151–62.
McClure, Robert D. "Media Influence in Presidential Politics." In *The Presidential Election and Transition, 1980–1981*, edited by P. David and D. Everson, pp. 133–56.
McCombs, Maxwell E., and Donald L. Shaw. "The Agenda-Setting Function of the Press." In *Media Power in Politics*, edited by Doris Graber, pp. 63–72.
Manheim, Jarol B. *The Politics Within*. Englewood Cliffs, NJ: Prentice-Hall, 1975.
Martel, Myles. *Political Campaign Debates: Images, Strategies, and Tactics*. New York: Longman, 1983.
———. "Debate Preparations in the Reagan Camp: An Insider's View." *Speaker and Gavel* 18 (1981): 34–46.
Meadow, Robert G., and Marilyn Jackson-Beeck. "A Comparative Perspective on Presidential Debates: Issue Evolution in 1960 and 1976." In *The Presidential Debates*, edited by G. Bishop, R. Meadow, and M. Jackson-Beeck, pp. 33–59.

Middleton, Russell. "National TV Debates and Presidential Voting Decisions." *Public Opinion Quarterly* 26 (1962): 426–29.

Miller, Arthur H. "Partisan Cognition in Transition." In *Political Cognition*, edited by R. Lau and D. Sears, pp. 203–31.

Miller, Arthur H., and Michael MacKuen. "Informing the Electorate: A National Study." In *The Great Debates: Carter vs. Ford, 1976*, edited by Sidney Kraus, pp. 269–97.

Miller, Arthur H., Martin P. Wattenberg, and Oksana Malanchuk. "Schematic Assessments of Presidential Candidates." *American Political Science Review* 80 (1986): 521–40.

Minow, Newton N., and Clifford M. Sloan. *For Great Debates*. New York: Priority Press, 1987.

Nachmias, David, and Chava Nachmias. *Research Methods in the Social Sciences*. 3d ed. New York: St. Martin's Press, 1987.

Nessen, Ron. *It Sure Looks Different from the Inside*. Chicago: Playboy Press, 1978.

Nie, Norman H., Sidney Verba, and John R. Petrocik. *The Changing American Voter*. Cambridge, MA: Harvard University Press, 1976.

Niemi, Richard G., and Herbert F. Weisberg. *Controversies in Voting Behavior*. 2d ed. Washington, D.C.: Congressional Quarterly Press, 1984.

Nimmo, Daniel. *Political Communication and Public Opinion in America*. Santa Monica, CA: Goodyear Publishing Company, 1978.

Noelle-Neumann, Elisabeth. *The Spiral of Silence*. Chicago: University of Chicago Press, 1984.

Norpoth, Helmut, and Kendall L. Baker. "Politiker unter sich am Bildschirm: Die Konfrontation von Personen und Sachthemen in den Fernsehdiskussionen, 1972–1980." In *Wahlen und politisches System*, edited by M. Kaase and H.-D. Klingemann.

Osgood, Charles E. "The Representational Model and Relevant Research Methods." In *Trends in Content Analysis*, edited by Ithiel de Sola Pool, pp. 33–88.

Page, Benjamin I., and Calvin C. Jones. "Reciprocal Effects of Policy Preferences, Party Loyalties, and the Vote." *American Political Science Review* 73 (1979): 1071–89.

Paletz, David L., and Richard J. Vinegar. "Presidents on Television: The Effects of Instant Analysis." *Public Opinion Quarterly* 41 (1978): 488–97.

Patterson, Thomas E. *The Mass Media Election*. New York: Praeger, 1980.

Polsby, Nelson W. "Debatable Thoughts on Presidential Debates." In *The Past and Future of Presidential Debates*, edited by Austin Ranney, pp. 175–86.

Polsby, Nelson W., and Aaron Wildavsky. *Presidential Elections: Strategies of American Electoral Politics*. New York: Charles Scribner's Sons, 1984.

Pomper, Gerald M., ed. *The Election of 1988: Reports and Interpretations*. Chatham, NJ: Chatham House Publishers, 1989.

Popkin, Samuel, John W. Gorman, Charles Phillips, and Jeffrey A. Smith. "Comment: What Have You Done for Me Lately? Toward an Investment Theory of Voting." *American Political Science Review* 70 (1976): 779–805.

Ranney, Austin, *The Past and Future of Presidential Debates*. Washington, D.C.: American Enterprise Institute, 1979.

Reid, T. R. "Kennedy." In *The Pursuit of the Presidency 1980*, edited by Richard Harwood, pp. 65–82.
Riley, Patricia, and Thomas A. Hollihan. "The 1980 Presidential Debates: A Content Analysis of the Issues and Arguments." *Speaker and Gavel* 18 (1981): 47–59.
Risley, Allen J. "Political Learning during the Campaign: The Impact of Television Coverage of Campaign '84 on Knowledge about the Candidates." Paper presented at the 1990 meeting of the Midwest Political Science Association, Chicago.
Robinson, John P. "The Polls." In *The Great Debates: Carter vs. Ford, 1976*, edited by Sidney Kraus, pp. 262–68.
Ruben, Brent D., ed. *Communications Yearbook 2*. New Brunswick, NJ: Transaction Books, 1978.
Sarnoff, Robert W. "An NBC View." In *The Great Debates: Background, Perspective, Effects*, edited by Sidney Kraus, pp. 56–64.
Schoenbach, Klaus. "Wahlprogramme und Wählermeinung." *Politische Vierteljahresschrift* 19 (1977): 360–407.
Schoenbach, Klaus, and Rudolf Wildenmann. "Election Themes and the Prestige Newspapers." In *Germany at the Polls*, edited by Karl Cerny, pp. 169–93.
Schram, Martin. *Running for President 1976: The Carter Campaign*. New York: Stein and Day, 1977.
Schrott, Peter R. "Electoral Consequences of 'Winning' Televised Campaign Debates." *Public Opinion Quarterly* (forthcoming 1991).
———. "West German Televised Debates from 1972 to 1987." Paper presented at the annual meeting of the American Political Science Association, Atlanta, 1989.
———. "Wahlkampfdebatten im Fernsehen von 1972 bis 1987: Politikerstrategien und Wählerreaktion." In *Wahlen und politisches System: Analysen aus Anlass der Bundestagswahl*, edited by M. Kaase and H.-D. Klingemann.
———. *The West German Television Debates: Candidate Strategies and Voters' Reactions*. Ph.D. dissertation, State University of New York, Stony Brook, 1986.
———. "The Content and Consequences of the 1980 Televised Debates in West Germany and the United States." Manuscript, State University of New York, Stony Brook, 1984.
Scott, Robert L. "You Cannot Not Debate: The Debate over the 1980 Presidential Debates." *Speaker and Gavel* 18 (1981): 28–33.
Sears, David O., and Steven H. Chaffee. "Uses and Effects of the 1976 Debates: An Overview of Empirical Studies." In *The Great Debates: Carter vs. Ford, 1976*, edited by Sidney Kraus, pp. 223–61.
Shneidman, Edwin S. "The Logic of Politics." In *Television and Human Behavior*, edited by L. Arons and M. May, pp. 178–99.
Siepmann, Charles A. "Were They 'Great'?" In *The Great Debates: Background, Perspective, Effects*, edited by Sidney Kraus, pp. 132–41.
Sigelman, Lee, and Carol K. Sigelman. "Judgments of the Carter–Reagan Debate: The Eyes of the Beholders." *Public Opinion Quarterly* 48 (1984): 624–28.
Simons, Herbert W., and Kenneth Leibowitz. "Shifts in Candidate Images." In *The Great Debates: Carter vs. Ford, 1976*, edited by Sidney Kraus, pp. 398–404.
Smith, Paul A. *Electing a President: Information and Control*. New York: Praeger, 1982.

Stacks, John F. *Watershed: The Campaign for the Presidency 1980*. New York: Times Books, 1981.

Stanton, Frank. "A CBS View." In *The Great Debates: Background, Perspective, Effects*, edited by Sidney Kraus, pp. 65–72.

Steeper, Frederick T. "Public Response to Gerald Ford's Statements on Eastern Europe in the Second Debate." In *The Presidential Debates*, edited by G. Bishop, R. Meadow, and M. Jackson-Beeck, pp. 81–101.

Stone, Philip J. "Improved Quality of Content-Analysis Categories: Computerized-Disambiguation Rules for High Frequency English Words." In *The Analysis of Communication Content*, edited by G. Gerbner et al., pp. 199–221.

Stroud, Kandy. *How Jimmy Won: The Victory Campaign from Plains to the White House*. New York: Morrow, 1977.

Tannenbaum, Percy H., Bradley S. Greenberg, and Fred R. Silverman. "Candidate Images." In *The Great Debates: Background, Perspective, Effects*, edited by Sidney Kraus, pp. 271–88.

Watson, David L., Gail deBortali-Tregerthan, and Joyce Frank. *Social Psychology: Science and Application*. Glenview, IL: Scott, Foresman and Company, 1984.

Wayne, Steven J. *The Road to the White House*. New York: St. Martin's Press, 1980.

Weber, Robert Philip. *Basic Content Analysis*. Beverly Hills, CA: Sage, 1985.

Weiler, Michael. "The 1988 Electoral Debates and Debate Theory." *Argumentation and Advocacy* 25 (1989): 214–19.

Weiss, Hans-Jürgen. *Wahlkampf im Fernsehen: Untersuchung zur Rolle der grossen Fernsehdebatten im Bundestagswahlkampf 1972*. West Berlin: Volker Spiess Verlag, 1976.

White, D. M. "The Gate-Keeper: A Case Study in the Selection of News." *Journalism Quarterly* 27 (1950): 383–90.

White, Theodore H. *The Making of the President 1972*. New York: Atheneum, 1973.

———. *The Making of the President 1960*. New York: Atheneum, 1962.

Witcover, Jules. *Marathon: The Pursuit of the Presidency 1972–1976*. New York: Viking, 1977.

INDEX

ABC News poll, 29, 137. *See also* Polls, public opinion
Abramowitz, Alan, 99, 145
Abramson, Paul R., 30, 36
Agenda Setting. *See* Debates, presidential, agenda-setting and
Agnew, Spiro T., 17, 39
Aldrich, John H., 30, 36
Allerton Conference. *See* Content analysis, Allerton Conference on
American Voter, The, 138
Anderson, John, 24–26, 30–32
Annenberg School Conference. *See* Content analysis, Annenberg School Conference on
Asher, Herbert B., 149
Attitude change, theories of: cognitive dissonance theory, 89–90; consistency theories, 89–92, 97, 105, 111, 119–20, 138; functional theory, 91–92, 120–21; social judgment theory, 90–92; social learning theory, 88–89; uses and gratifications theory, 93–94, 117, 121. *See also* Schema theory
Auer, J. Jeffrey, 150–51

Babbitt, Bruce, 44
Baker, Jim, 30
Baker, Kendall L., 71–72
Bartels, Larry, 46, 148
Bentsen, Lloyd, 39–40, 48, 133, 135, 137, 151
Ben-Zeev, Saul, 96, 100
Berelson, Bernard, 59, 149
Birdsell, David S., 6, 44, 113
Bishop, George F., 112, 114
Bitzer, Lloyd, 21, 151
Bowes, John E., 101
Broder, David, 41
Bush, George, 3, 35, 38–42, 45–46, 48–49, 69, 111, 116, 132, 137, 147–48, 152

Caddell, Patrick, 30, 148
Candidate images, measurement of, 94–95. *See also* Debates, presidential, candidate images and
Carter, Amy, 28
Carter, Jimmy, 16–32, 35, 45, 65–66, 70–71, 75–76, 104, 106, 110, 115–17, 119, 121–22, 124, 133, 135, 139, 141–42, 148

Carter, Richard F., 111
Chaffee, Steven H., 22, 93, 100, 104, 106–7, 110
Cheney, Richard B., 22
China, 14, 19
Cognitive dissonance theory. *See* Attitude change, theories of
Cognitive filters. *See* Perceptual filters
Consistency theories. *See* Attitude change, theories of
Content analysis, 55–80, 123–24; Allerton Conference on, 59; Annenberg School Conference on, 60; computer applications in, 60–61; historical developments in, 59–62; purposes of, 55–58; quantitative vs. qualitative, 59–61; standardization of categories in, 76–80; West German debates, 56, 71–74
Cuba, 13–14

Davis, Mark H., 99
Debates, Canadian, 3
Debates, presidential: adolescents' reactions to, 106; agenda-setting and, 103–4, 137; audience for, 1, 12, 20, 25–26, 105, 131–32, 135; Bush–Dukakis, (1988), 38–43, 69, 109, 111–12, 115–16, 121, 132–33, 137–38, 141–42; candidate images and, 69–71, 94–97, 134, 136, 138, 144, 146–47; candidate strategies in, 56–57, 71, 123–24, 133; Carter–Ford (1976), 11, 16–24, 64–66, 68, 71, 76, 96, 99, 102, 104, 106, 109–13, 115–16, 119, 121, 124, 132–33, 135–37, 139, 142–43, 148, 151; content of, 55–58, 62–71, 74–80, 145; effects on campaign momentum, 147–49; effects on national prestige, 105–7; effects on political efficacy, 104, 106; effects on system support, 104–6; effects on voting behavior, 15–16, 21–22, 30–32, 37–38, 42, 94, 114–19, 133–34, 140, 146, 149–50; format of, 150–55; future research on, 121–24; information gain from, 93–94, 107–14, 145; issue positions and, 101–4, 136, 138, 144–45; Kennedy–Nixon (1960), 1, 11–16, 21, 63–66, 68, 70, 76, 89, 96–97, 100, 103–7, 109, 111, 115, 118–19, 123, 132–33, 135, 139, 141, 143, 146, 148, 150, 155; media coverage of, 8, 12–16, 18–20, 23, 26, 29, 33, 36–39, 47–48, 58, 67, 95–96, 109–11, 121, 124, 136–39, 142, 150, 152–54; purposes of, 131–34; Reagan–Anderson (1980), 24–26, 30–32; Reagan–Carter (1980), 24, 26–32, 55–56, 68, 71, 75–76, 117, 121–22, 132–33, 137, 140–41, 146–48, 151; Reagan–Mondale (1984), 3, 32–38, 68, 95–96, 102, 133, 136, 143–45, 148, 155; reinforcing effects of, 97–101, 120, 140, 150; role of panelists in, 23–24, 152, 154; voters' opinions of 131–32
Debates, primary election, 43–47, 89, 132, 135, 154; candidate strategies in, 44, 69, 75; effects on voting behavior, 46–47, 95, 102–3, 116–17, 122, 150; media coverage of, 122
Debates, vice presidential, 20–21, 35, 39–40, 43, 106, 110–11, 133, 137
Debates, West German, 3, 7, 56, 68–69, 71–75
Dewey, Thomas, 43–44
Dole, Robert, 20–21, 40, 46, 110
Douglas, Stephen, 150, 152
Downs, Anthony, 139, 144–45, 153
Dukakis, Michael, 38–42, 69, 111, 116, 132–33, 137, 141–42, 152

DuPont, Pierre, 46

Eastern Europe. *See* Ford, Gerald R., Eastern Europe "gaffe"
Eisenhower, Dwight D., 12–14, 139, 143
Ellsworth, John W., 63–64, 68

Fairness doctrine, 5, 58
Feldman, Jacob J., 103, 105–6
Ferraro, Geraldine, 32, 35
Festinger, Leon A., 89
Ford, Gerald R., 11, 16–24, 65–66, 70, 96, 104, 106, 110, 115–16, 119, 124, 133, 135–37, 139, 142, 143, 146, 148; Eastern Europe "gaffe" by, 19–23, 48–49, 70, 96, 104, 110, 113, 116, 118, 121, 124, 133, 136–37, 142–43, 146, 148
Frankel, Max, 19–20
Freud, Sigmund, 91
Functional theory. *See* Attitude change, theories of

Gaudet, Helen, 149
Geer, John G., 99–100, 116, 143–44
General Inquirer, 60. *See also* Content analysis, computer applications in
Gephardt, Richard, 44, 69
Gerbner, George, 60
Germany. *See* Debates, West German
Germond, Jack W., 26, 29
Goldwater, Barry, 17, 133
Gore, Albert, 75
Graber, Doris A., 109
Greider, William, 20

Hagner, Paul R., 98
Hamill, Ruth, 140, 142
Hart, Gary, 46, 75
Hawkins, Robert P., 106

Hershey, Marjorie, 69
Holsti, Ole R., 60
Hovland, Carl I., 88–89
Howe, Quincy, 16
Humphrey, Hubert, 17, 44, 153

Information gain, measurement of, 108–9. *See also* Debates, presidential, information gain from
Instant analysis, 124, 136
Iran, hostage crisis in, 24, 27

Jackson, Jesse, 75
Jackson-Beeck, Marilyn, 64–65, 67, 70, 76
Jacoby, Jacob, 102
Jamieson, Kathleen Hall, 6, 44, 113
Jennings, Peter, 152
Johnson, Lyndon B., 13, 16–17
Joslyn, Richard, 67–68, 71, 76

Karayn, James, 132
Katz, Daniel, 91
Katz, Elihu, 103, 105–6
Kennedy, Edward M., 24
Kennedy, John F., 1, 12–16, 18, 21, 31, 40, 44, 48, 63–66, 70, 76, 100, 103–5, 111, 115, 118–19, 123, 132–33, 135, 137, 139, 142–43, 146–48, 150–51, 155
Kessel, John, 25, 28
Kim, Young Yun, 109
Kissinger, Henry, 19
Klingemann, Hans-Dieter, 68–69
Kracauer, Sigfried, 59
Kraft, Joseph, 23–24, 26
Kraus, Sidney, 5, 48, 112, 151–53
Krippendorff, Klaus, 60–61

Lang, Gladys Engel, 15, 111, 115–16, 118
Lang, Kurt, 15, 111, 115–16, 118
Lasswell, Harold, 74

Lazarsfeld, Paul F., 149
League of Women Voters, 25–26, 38, 55, 87
Lewis, Anthony, 28, 33
Lewis, Flora, 28–29
Lincoln, Abraham, 150, 152
Lodge, Milton G., 140, 142

McClure, Robert D., 30
McGovern, George, 17, 44, 133
MacKuen, Michael, 66–67, 70, 76, 110
Malanchuk, Oksana, 140
Mao Zedong, 14
Marcos, Ferdinand, 37
Martel, Myles, 6, 27–28, 44–45, 55–56, 69, 73, 155
Mass media. *See* Debates, presidential, media coverage of
Matsu. *See* Quemoy and Matsu
Meadow, Robert G., 64–65, 67, 70, 76
Media coverage. *See* Debates, presidential, media coverage of
Miller, Arthur H., 66–67, 70, 76, 110, 140
Mondale, Walter, 3, 20–21, 32–38, 46, 49, 68, 95, 102, 110, 133, 145, 148, 151

Netherlands, 107
New York Times, The, 12, 15, 19–20, 25, 27, 33, 38–39, 65
Newsweek, 21, 26, 36, 39, 43
Nightline, 29
Nimmo, Daniel, 93
Nixon, Richard M., 1, 11–18, 21, 30, 39, 42, 49, 63–66, 70, 76, 89, 96, 100, 103, 105, 111, 115, 119, 123, 132–33, 135, 141–43, 148, 150–51, 153, 155
Noelle-Neumann, Elisabeth, 147
Norpoth, Helmut, 72

Osgood, Charles E., 80

Party identification, 16, 43, 91, 98–99, 114–15, 117, 120, 138–39
Perceptual filters, 138–44. *See also* Attitude change, theories of
Persuasion. *See* Attitude change, theories of
Philippines, 36
Polls, public opinion, 15, 20, 29–30, 34, 37–39, 100, 137, 146, 148–49. *See also* Debates, presidential, effects on voting behavior
Polsby, Nelson, W., 11, 155
Pool, Ithiel de Sola, 59
Presidential debates. *See* Debates, presidential
Primary election debates. *See* Debates, primary election

Quayle, Dan, 39–40, 43, 48, 133, 135, 137, 151–52
Quemoy and Matsu, 11, 14, 103

Rafshoon, Gerald, 21
Reagan, Ronald, 3, 6, 24–38, 45–46, 49, 55–56, 68–69, 75–76, 95, 102–3, 116–17, 121–22, 133, 136, 140–41, 143, 145–46, 148, 151, 155
Reston, James, 20
Rieselbach, Leroy N., 98
Rohde, David W., 30, 36
Rueter, Theodore, 21, 151

Safire, William, 31, 33, 36, 39
Salk, Jonas, 41
Schema theory, 140–44. *See also* Attitude change, theories of
Schrott, Peter R., 73
Sears, David O., 22, 93, 100, 104, 106–7, 110
Shaw, Bernard, 41, 152
Shneidman, Edwin S., 69–70

Social judgment theory. *See* Attitude change, theories of
Social learning theory. *See* Attitude change, theories of
Soviet Union, 19, 103–4
Spiral of silence theory, 147. *See also* Attitude change, theories of
Stacks, John F., 45
Stassen, Harold, 43–44
Staubach, Roger, 28
Steeper, Frederick T., 20, 118, 121, 148
Stevenson, Adlai, 12
Stone, Philip, 60
Strentz, Herbert, 101

Tannenbaum, Percy H., 16, 96
Television coverage. *See* Debates, presidential, media coverage of
Time, 13, 15, 19–20, 27, 34, 41–42
Trewitt, Henry, 36

Truman, Harry S., 14

U-2 spy plane incident, 13
Uses and gratifications theory. *See* Attitude change, theories of

Vice presidential debates. *See* Debates, vice presidential
Vietnam War, 18, 22, 153

Washington Post, 20
Wattenberg, Martin P., 140
Weber, Robert Philip, 61
Weiss, Hans-Jurgen, 72
West Germany. *See* Debates, West German
White, Irving S., 97, 100
White, Theodore H., 12, 45
Wicker, Tom, 19, 39
Wildavsky, Aaron, 11
Wirthlin, Richard, 30
Witcover, Jules, 26, 29
Woodruff, Judy, 40

About the Authors

DAVID J. LANOUE is Assistant Professor of Political Science at the University of California, Riverside. He is also the author of *From Camelot to the Teflon President: Economics and Presidential Popularity since 1960* (Greenwood Press, 1988). He has written articles for *Western Political Quarterly, Journal of Politics,* and *Political Behavior.*

PETER R. SCHROTT is a Research Associate at the Mannheim Center for Social Sciences, University of Mannheim, Germany. Specializing in political communication, methodology, and electoral behavior, Dr. Schrott has also authored articles in *Public Opinion Quarterly, Political Psychology,* and *Political Behavior.*